GARDENER'S Q&A
500 Gardening Questions

GARDENER'S Q&A
500 Gardening Questions

MURDOCH BOOKS

This edition published in the United Kingdom in 2012 by Murdoch Books UK Limited

Murdoch Books UK Limited
Erico House, 6th Floor
93-99 Upper Richmond Road
Putney, London SW15 2TG
Phone: +44 (0) 20 8785 5995
Fax: +44 (0) 20 8785 5985
www.murdochbooks.co.uk
info@murdochbooks.co.uk

Conceived, designed and produced by
Quid Publishing
Level 4, Sheridan House
114 Western Road
Hove BN3 1DD
England

10 9 8 7 6 5 4 3 2 1

Printed in China by 1010 Printing International Ltd

Contents

Foreword

Long before I became President of the National Gardening Association I was a gardener. My story is similar to many; I grew up around grandparents and parents who loved to garden, but I didn't take advantage of the gardening prowess that had been passed down through so many generations. Like many people, as I matured my priorities shifted and my desire to grow beautiful things came into full bloom. I bought a home and started to focus on landscaping and creating kerb appeal. I began to question my food sources and thought about how to grow my own produce. That's the moment I realised I needed expert gardening advice.

This book will take the mystery out of some of the most nagging questions you'll have about how to garden. If you're like me, the biggest fear that I faced was doing something wrong! When do I trim that bush? What's the difference between an annual and a perennial? How much water is too much water? Does this plant like shade or sun? What I eventually found was that there was nothing to fear. Seeds and plants contain all the DNA materials they need to thrive. It's part of their reproductive mandate. It turns out that plants, veggies, flowers, shrubs and grass all WANT to survive and flourish. All they need from willing gardeners is just a little help at the right time and in the right place and you'll get outstanding results.

So plants are on our side. That's a relief! Now who is going to help me? Fortunately, solid expert advice can be found right inside these pages. There are many people who claim to have the secret to successful gardening but not all advice is the right advice. That's why we are pleased to offer gardeners of all ages and experience this all-inclusive book from the experts of the National Gardening Association. For over 35 years, NGA's horticultural staff has been providing authoritative advice designed to provide you and your plant partners with a wonderful growing experience. *Gardener's Q&A* provides you with direct, easy answers to most of your gardening questions.

This is an easy-to-use, beautifully illustrated, go-to book that will give you the confidence you need to grow like an expert. So go ahead, plant that vegetable garden and harvest your own food, install and expand your landscape gardens, plant those shrubs and trees, make a secret garden with your children, experiment with perennials, create an outdoor oasis to escape the cares of the day, and make your world a naturally more beautiful place by bringing out the gardener in you!

– Mike Metallo
President, National Gardening Association

The Basics

Have you ever wondered why some people seem to spend hardly any time in the garden, but their plots are always bursting with beautiful flowers or plump produce? The chances are that these successful gardeners are all following the same few basic principles explained in this chapter. From simple ways to improve your soil, to knowing which is the right plant for the right place, the following questions and answers could help you to enhance your outdoor space, whether it's a few pots on your balcony or established lawns and borders.

Climate and Weather

Small changes in the weather can lead to big changes in our gardens. Plants respond sensitively and rapidly to fluctuations in light and moisture levels. Plan wisely and you can get the best from every season.

1. I want to transplant some shrubs at some point this winter. Should I prune them first?

You don't need to prune the plants prior to digging and transplanting, but you can do so if they are too large to comfortably handle. Pruning while they are dormant won't hurt them at all. In the spring, when the weather warms, they'll put out healthy new growth.

Weather Extremes

Gardeners love talking about the weather and it's hardly surprising. A late frost can wipe out a huge selection of plants overnight, while a long dry spell will turn lawns brown and can cook tender new foliage to a crisp. However, there's a lot we can do to ameliorate the effects of any extremes of temperature, and to help harness the natural abilities of plants to cope with all that the weather can throw at them. For example, if you plant bulbs at their correct depth (around three and a half times their height is a good rule of thumb) then they will be better able to withstand early or late frost, drought and even periods of being waterlogged.

2. Could you suggest some attractive plants that will grow in containers in shade for most of the day?

You can grow lots of different flowers in your containers. Here are a few suggestions: Hinckley's columbine (*Aquilegia chrysantha* var. *hinckleyana*), ox-eye daisy (*Chrysanthemum leucanthemum*), tickseed (*Coreopsis grandiflora*), montbretia (*Crocosmia pottsii*), cigar plant (*Cuphea micropetala*), trailing lantana (*Lantana montevidensis*), perennial phlox (*Phlox paniculata*), autumn sage (*Salvia greggii*) and marigolds.

3. My Japanese maple has a split trunk held together with ties and screws. Should I let the bark grow around them?

Leave the screws alone but remove the ties before the bark grows over them. If you leave them in place they will girdle the tree as it grows and this could eventually kill it. The screws should keep everything together long enough for the bark to callus over and mend the cracks. Trees are resilient and can recover from damage as long as it does not encircle the whole trunk.

4. I planted some bulbs in early autumn and the plants have started growing. What will happen when the cold weather hits?

If you get a mild spell before winter then bulbs such as daffodils may start to push up green shoots. Don't worry though – even if they get hit by frost, they should flower normally in spring.

Most spring bulbs have foliage that is very able to withstand cold so it remains in good shape beneath a covering of frost. If the foliage ends up with a bit of 'burning' or browned tips, the bulbs should still be fine as long as they were planted deeply enough. Try not to worry – there isn't much you can do about it anyway! Always make a point of planting bulbs at the full recommended depth and add a generous layer of mulch over the top to help insulate the soil and moderate any temperature swings. The flowers should appear right on time, regardless of the premature foliage.

5. When is it safe to cut away the dead parts of a plant that has been frozen, and how far should I prune?

For safety's sake, wait another two weeks after the last freezing weather, until you're sure that it's definitely warming up, before doing any pruning. Remove all obvious winter damage and then let the plants guide you. When new growth appears, you may have to do a little more pruning to make each plant look attractive. Cut to just above the new growth to remove any additional damage that wasn't apparent the first time you pruned.

7. Should I wait until the danger of frost has passed before directly planting vegetables, or is it better to start them off indoors?

To some extent, the answer to your question depends on how much of a 'gambler' you are. Quick-growing crops, such as lettuce, peas and spinach can be planted out in early summer, but to get a good crop of heat-loving plants, such as tomatoes, chillies, melons and aubergine, they should be given a head start indoors. Tomatoes seeded outdoors seem to nearly catch up to the transplants, often running just two weeks or so later.

In order to get a good crop of tomatoes, it's usually best to sow the seeds indoors and keep them in a warm, light place. Plant them once all danger of frost has passed.

6. Can I plant shrubs such as rhododendrons, azaleas and hydrangeas during mild spells over winter?

As long as the ground isn't frozen it's okay to plant or transplant shrubs. Usually, plants that have the winter to establish themselves go through less shock than plants that are put into new locations in the spring. When planting, make sure the hole is deep and wide enough to accommodate the roots after you fan them out in their natural growth pattern. Get help to hold the shrub in place, if necessary, so that you can pile soil underneath and around the roots so that the shrub is planted at the same depth it was before. Replace the soil above the roots and water well.

As long as the ground isn't frozen, winter is a good time to plant shrubs such as rhododendrons. This gives them a chance to become established before the weather warms up.

8. How much water do roses require in various kinds of weather?

Roses will get by with about 2.5 cm (1 in) of water per week during the growing season. It's best to create a basin around each shrub and apply water by flooding the basin. You might want to dig down into the soil the day after watering to make sure that you've applied enough water to thoroughly wet the entire root mass. If not, plan on flooding the basin two or three times instead of just once every time you water. The amount of water you need to apply will depend upon your soil type and air temperature, but 2.5 cm of water per week is a good rule of thumb.

9. How often and for how long should I water a newly laid lawn?

New turf needs about 2.5 cm (1 in) of water per week to get established. The goal is to apply 2.5 cm of water per week to grass to help it to root well. If using a sprinkler, you can get a reasonable idea of how much water they put out by placing several bowls in various places on your lawn. Run it for 15 minutes and then check how much is in each one. Whether using a sprinkler or watering by hand, aim to give your lawn 2.5 cm of water once a week in normal conditions, or twice a week in hot weather. Avoid overwatering because it will leads to weak growth.

10. Is it wise to put mulch around trees and shrubs to protect them from winter weather?

You can place an organic mulch beneath your trees and shrubs to help moderate fluctuations in the soil temperatures and keep the plants from heaving out of the soil during the normal freeze and thaw cycle in the winter months. Shredded leaves or compost are ideal, but be sure to keep the mulch material away from the main stems or trunks. Placing mulch against the wood can cause rot if the material gets wet and holds the moisture against the stems or trunks.

A good layer of organic matter, such as shredded leaves, can be used as a mulch to improve the soil. It can also be used to protect trees and shrubs from fluctuations in temperature. Avoid placing it too near trunks and stems.

11. Do I need to wait until the weather has warmed up to plant a bare-root hybrid tea rose?

Bare-root roses are still dormant and can be planted in early spring, providing your soil is not frozen – which makes digging almost impossible! If the soil is frozen, store your rose in the original package, in a cool place. When you're ready to plant, remove the packaging and soak the roots in a bucket of water for 24 hours. Then dig a hole large enough to accommodate the roots without cramping them and place a small mound of soil at the bottom of the hole. Drape the roots over the mound so they hang naturally, making sure the graft (bud) union on the main stem will be a few centimetres below ground when you've filled in the hole. Tamp the soil around the roots and water.

12. I've received dahlia tubers in the mail. When should I plant them and what should I do with them until then?

Dahlias can be stored in a cool, dry place indoors until after the danger of frost, then planted outside, where they are intended to grow. Alternatively, you can put them into growth early in pots, keeping them in very bright light and setting the pots outdoors on warm days to keep the plants in bright sunshine. Plant them in the garden when the danger of frost has passed, but take care not to expose the foliage to freezing temperatures in the meantime.

13. I have a tree that lost most of a large limb last year due to lightning. The tree is still alive. Should I apply a compound or remove the limb?

Dahlias are quite tender and the tubers need to be protected from frost. They can be stored over winter in a cool, dry place and planted out again in spring.

If the wood is splintered, the best approach would be to remove the limb. A raggedy wound won't completely heal and a falling limb at some later

> University studies show that wound dressings do not aid in healing, and in some cases can actually interfere with the healing process.

date might do substantial damage to property or injure someone. If only a portion of the limb is damaged, you may be able to cut away this part so the tree can close and heal the wound. You may want to enlist the services of a licensed arborist to evaluate the tree. They can also do the actual work, which can be hazardous if you are untrained or poorly-equipped. Whether you remove the entire limb or just the damaged part, don't use a wound dressing. University studies show that wound dressings do not aid in healing, and in some cases can actually interfere with the healing process. Trees have the ability to compartmentalise damaged tissue and then callus over the wound.

Rosemary is an undemanding plant that is wonderful in the kitchen. Prostrate forms are great for ground cover, while the taller-growing varieties can be used as a subtle backdrop to a colourful herb garden.

14. Which vegetables, herbs and flowers can I consider for their drought resistance?

Most vegetables need a fairly consistent supply of moisture to thrive. Try choosing varieties that mature in the shortest amount of time. Herbs that originated in the Mediterranean region are used to hot, dry weather with limited rainfall. You might consider rosemary, oregano, thyme, lavender, fennel, santolina and sage. Flowers that will perform with less water include *Artemisia*, salvias, coreopsis, cosmos, dusty miller, gaillardia, tithonia, verbena and yarrow. Adding lots of well-rotted organic matter to the soil will also help it to retain moisture, which will give all your plants a chance to get established.

15. Can you suggest an evergreen hedge to provide a screen for us and cover for birds?

Evergreens for informal hedges include barberry, holly, rhododendron and azalea species. These plants are available in many heights and so by carefully selecting your variety, you can eliminate a great deal of pruning. The berries and flowers on these plants are attractive bonuses to the functional aspect of an informal hedge. You may even want to plant taller shrubs at the back and lower shrubs in the front to double the sound barrier. A wider range of plants will attract a greater variety of birds.

Cloches

To protect single plants from cold and heavy rain you can use bell or lantern cloches. These are traditionally glass, although modern designs consist of a plastic dome pinned to the ground with metal pegs. If these aren't available, try improvising with upturned glass jars. You should try to give your plants plenty of room to grow. Leaves that press against the outer envelope may soon begin to rot. Cloches work by creating a warm, sheltered environment that encourages early plant growth – several weeks before conditions are good enough in the rest of the garden. You can either sow direct outdoors and cover immediately with the cloche, or you can raise plants in a greenhouse and cover them when you plant them out.

16. What decorative shrubs can I plant that will thrive in a windy coastal area?

Finding just the right plants for areas whipped by the gusting winds fresh off the ocean can be a real challenge. Wind can damage plants by causing water stress, which increases evaporation through the leaves. Furthermore, if leaves are young and tender, they can be shredded by wind, leaving a tattered mess instead of a nice, neat appearance. Decorative shrubs that bloom and still stand up to strong winds include bottlebrush (*Callistemon*), wild lilac (*Ceanothus*), sweet bay (*Laurus nobilis*) and tea tree (*Leptospermum*).

Ceanothus is an attractive shrub that is very drought tolerant. The pretty blue flowers attract a host of butterflies and bees.

17. The green tips of the leaves on my tulips and hyacinths have already started to come up. Can I move them, or will it damage the bulbs?

You can transplant them while they are growing or blooming if you do it carefully. Prepare the new planting area ahead of time and water the bulbs the day before you move them. Dig them up, keeping as much of the surrounding soil as possible intact, so that you have not only the bulb itself but also the root system around and beneath it. Replant immediately into the prepared soil and water in. If you have taken enough of the root ball, they won't even know they've been moved.

18. I want to help wildlife out over winter. Where's the best place to site a ladybird house?

Beneficial insects, such as ladybirds, and their young can eat hundreds of pests every week. Attract more of them to your plot by putting up shelters for them.

Groups of ladybirds take shelter in dry crevices, often on the sunny and warm western exposure of a rocky location, or even in the walls, windowsills or attics of houses and other buildings. They will also shelter in old logs and under ground cover materials, so primarily, choose a site protected from the elements. It might be helpful to keep an eye out once the weather starts to get cooler and see if there are any places where they are naturally congregating and place it there. These beneficial insects are busy eating pests during the summer, then they take shelter in the autumn, emerging on warmer days, before finally leaving in spring. For this reason you may not find anything living in your ladybird house until next autumn, no matter where you put it.

> Ladybirds will also take shelter in old logs and under ground cover materials, so choose a site protected from the elements.

19. When and how should I deal with a dry, brown lawn in summer?

There is very little you can do to make your lawn turn green quickly, because heat and drought will make it go into dormancy. Watering will help to turn it green again, but it will take several weeks to recover so it may be best to simply wait for cooler, rainier weather.

20. Which decorative bushes or shrubs don't need to be watered too often in hot weather?

Here are a few dual-purpose shrubs for you to consider. *Achillea* 'Apple Blossom' produces bright pink flower heads, it is drought-tolerant once established, and can act as a fire retardant. It is sometimes used for its herbal qualities. Strawberry tree (*Arbutus unedo* 'Compacta') can grow to be 11 m (35 ft) tall and needs little water once established. It has shredding, reddish brown bark and dark green oblong leaves. The flowers are white and the fruit is strawberry-like. Flowering quince (*Chaenomeles speciosa* 'Toyo Nishiki') is also worth trying. It's similar to the red flowering quince, except that it produces pink, white, red and pink and white bicoloured flowers in the early spring.

Catmint (*Nepeta faassenii*) is a drought-tolerant perennial that mounds up to 0.6 m (2 ft) in height. It has aromatic leaves and lavender blue flowers that appear in early summer. Another good herb is 'Huntington carpet' rosemary (*Rosmarinus officinalis* 'Prostratus'). This fast-spreading, evergreen ground cover can grow to be 4 cm tall and has small aromatic leaves. It produces deep blue flowers and once established it needs little or no watering and provides good garden colour.

21. Do beans stop producing flowers when the weather gets hot?

Beans do indeed stop producing blossoms when the weather gets hot, but that shouldn't stop you from sowing bean seeds in late summer for a later crop. By the time the plants are up and ready to produce, the weather will be cooler and you'll be able to harvest up until the first frosts.

Protecting Your Plants
Once the danger of frost has passed, you will need to protect your crops from different threats – mainly scorching, wind and pests. In many cases, you can use the same method of protection as you did earlier in the year; netting and mulch or shade covers will provide shade and keep insects out. Of course it's vital to keep plants well watered, and for this reason many gardeners switch to insect mesh or fine netting. Be sure the nets don't touch your plants, or butterflies and other winged insects can land on nets and lay their eggs through the holes! It's also wise to provide shade in your greenhouse – invest in blinds or netting, or coat the walls with weather-sensitive paint that becomes clear when wet so your plants will still get plenty of light on dull, rainy days.

22. Will flowers like petunias, geraniums, dahlias and marigolds be killed in a late frost?

Frost can be harmful to these plants. It's better to be safe than sorry, so to adopt an overcautious approach whenever colder weather is forecast. Plant tissue can freeze when the temperature drops below −1°C (30°F), but as a precaution it would be a good idea to cover your plants whenever nights are expected to dip below about 4°C (40°F). This provides extra protection for especially cold-sensitive plants and also helps prevent delays in flowering. Perennials are less likely to suffer damage, so they should be fine left uncovered.

It's all too easy to get carried away and plant tender blooms in a warm spring, but be prepared to offer them protection if colder nights are forecast.

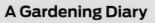 **A Gardening Diary**

The weather can fool even the most experienced gardeners. One way you can stay one step ahead of the weather is to keep a detailed diary. Record what you are growing, what the weather is like, including important dates, such as the first and last frost and any very dry spells, and where you have had successes and failures. This will help you to learn about what does well and what really isn't worth the effort in your area. It can also be a good way to get an overview and see if you should be concentrating your effort on long-term improvements, such as enriching the soil or setting up an irrigation system for example, instead of spending time on 'temporary' fixes such as watering every day in summer.

23. Why do the leaves of my young vegetable plants turn white in hot weather?

It sounds like sunburn, and fortunately most plants will recover, as long as the growing point was not damaged. Next year, try to acclimatise the plants gradually to the outdoors if a very hot spell is predicted. Place them in a sheltered spot for a few hours the first day, increasing the amount of sun and length of time they're out-doors over the course of a week or two.

24. How can I prevent unexpected frost damage to my strawberries?

Frost damages blooms and other plant tissues by causing ice crystals to form, which puncture the plant cell walls, causing the contents to leak out and the cells to collapse. The simplest way to protect strawberries on a frosty night is to cover them with the heavier weights of plant protection fabric. This reduces heat escaping from the soil and can provide a few extra degrees of protection, which is often enough. Allow the soil to warm, uncovered, during the day and then cover the plants late in the day so the air circulates.

Protect strawberry plants in early spring – any flowers that get frosted won't produce fruit. If you see a flower with a telltale black centre, simply nip it off and ensure your plants are given more cover.

25. What steps can I take now to prepare my garden for drought conditions?

The most beneficial action you can take to prepare for an extended period of dry weather is soil preparation. The plants in the best prepared soil will always have a much better chance of survival. Adding copious amounts of organic matter, such as chopped leaves, improves the soil structure, enabling it to hold more water for longer and also keeping it from becoming waterlogged. In the same vein, test your soil to see what it has and what it lacks and make improvements or add amendments based on the results. Finally, use an organic mulch to help keep the soil cool and moist and to help feed the soil as it breaks down.

26. Snow has covered my azaleas and rhododendrons since Christmas. Will they be dead when it finally melts?

As long as the ground isn't frozen, winter is a good time to plant shrubs such as rhododendrons. This gives them a chance to become established before the weather warms up.

Your plants are dormant so the snow is unlikely to do extensive damage. You'll know for certain in spring as you should see new growth on your plants when the weather warms. Rhododendron leaves have evolved to droop and curl when temperatures drop, then bounce back in the spring, so they are suited to cold weather.

27. How should I protect less hardy herbs over winter?

A thick layer (10–15 cm, or 4–6 in) of mulch once the temperature starts to drop should do the trick! It can be hay, straw, chopped up leaves or evergreen boughs. Keep it on until spring, when the new growth emerges.

28. What should I do with my container perennials once the cold weather comes?

Overwintering perennials in pots can be tricky. Some gardeners will cover the pots with a layer of heat-retaining fabric or place them in a cold frame. Another method is to sink them into the ground in order to insulate the plants' roots.

You will need to water less as the temperatures cool down, but the plants should never go bone dry.

Another is to mulch around them or otherwise insulate them. Keep them in a sheltered spot in the shade if possible – keeping them out of direct sunlight helps to keep them from freezing and thawing during temperature swings. Watering is a judgement call. You will need to water less as the temperatures cool down, but the plants should never go bone dry. On the other hand, if they are too wet they may rot, although this is not usually a problem if the pots are kept outdoors where air circulates freely. Finally, be aware that many terra-cotta pots are inclined to self-destruct if allowed to freeze.

29. Now that it's getting a little warmer, I was wondering when I can give the lawn its first mowing of the year?

You can begin cutting your grass as soon as it begins to grow. Try to mow often enough that you do not take off more than one-third of the total height at a time. In spring, this can mean mowing more often than once a week, if there is a lot of sunshine and rain and the grass is growing fast.

30. If I water my new lawn in very hot weather, will it scorch the grass?

It's important to choose drought-tolerant grass species that require less watering. Water in the very early morning rather than in the heat of the day. This way, your lawn won't burn and you won't be wasting precious water, which evaporates very quickly in full sun.

Promoting Early Germination

Seeds are programmed to germinate when the weather grows warm enough for the young plants to survive. If you can provide enough heat for them to germinate and grow you can start your growing season up to a month earlier. There are many ways to do this, from growing on the kitchen windowsill to building a fully heated greenhouse. Alternatively, try a simple cold frame (essentially a shallow wooden box with a glass lid). During cold weather you can use layers of corrugated cardboard or straw packed around the sides and underneath. The cold frame can be used for growing heat-loving plants, such as cucumbers and melons, over summer, and it's a great place to protect alpines over winter.

31. Do I need to restrain my bleeding hearts so that the wind doesn't break the stems?

It's a good idea to support bleeding hearts (*Dicentra*) even in areas that are not especially windy. The plants have rather tender stems that can fall over just because of their own weight. Place two stakes at opposite sides of the plant and gently tie the plants up in several areas along the stems, or place a tomato cage over the entire plant and pull the stems through the openings. As the plant grows, it will disguise the wire tomato cage, making it barely noticeable.

The delicate, arching stems of bleeding hearts can benefit from a little support, especially in windy areas, or the weight of the flowers can cause the stems to break.

Sage usually survives a cold winter, but it can look a little straggly. Wait until the plant is growing strongly before you trim it back into shape.

32. When should I prune purple sage so new growth will come?

It is better to leave sage (*Salvia officinalis*) plants alone until later in the spring when they are leafing out. Then you can trim away any bare portions that do not leaf out, and possibly give the plants a light trim to tidy them up. However, be careful to avoid cutting into the harder, woodier parts of the plant, however.

33. Can I plant seeds and onion sets in damp soil if the weather is warm?

If your soil is too muddy to dig, then you have to wait or you risk damaging its structure. For future reference, you could amend the soil with some sand and plenty of organic matter to try to improve it (do this when it is workable). You could also consider using raised beds, and relocating the kitchen garden to a better drained location.

If your soil is too muddy to dig then you have to wait or you risk damaging its structure . . . amend the soil with some sand and plenty of organic matter . . .

Soils and Fertilisers

It's easy to overlook the importance of your soil, but it's the most vital ingredient of a healthy plot. And if you get this part of your garden right, then everything else will simply fall into place.

34. Should we add some topsoil to the patchy areas of our lawn and then reseed?

Bagged topsoil can be of varying quality and, since it is often difficult to match the existing topsoil with new purchased soil, it is probably better to improve the soil you have. Generally, improving the soil means adding organic matter such as compost, rotted leaves or similar materials. Patching a lawn area requires several steps, incorporating any needed amendments into the existing soil and then reseeding. The specific amendments would be determined on the basis of soil tests. However, even before you patch those areas you might need to investigate and fix the drainage problem that caused the erosion in the first place. If you don't, the new soil and grass seed will erode, too. Drainage can be a very tricky thing, so if the problem is severe you should get professional advice. Sooner is better, because this type of problem tends to get worse over time.

Protecting the Soil

Most of us struggle with a less-than-ideal growing medium, and even those who are lucky enough to grow on deep, rich, loamy soil will need to get into a routine of replenishing what their crops take out each year. The joy of a pre-winter application of compost or manure every year is that the earthworms will give you several months of hard labour, free of charge, before you need to lift a fork and join them. Even the cold weather is an ally, breaking up the soil with repeated freezing and thawing. Don't forget that wind and rain can have a detrimental effect though – protecting the soil is as important as protecting young plants.

35. If I use a slow-release fertiliser when planting annuals, should I also apply a liquid fertiliser?

Slow-release fertilisers are designed to last about three months and will continually feed the roots of your plants during that time. An additional foliar feed, such as liquid seaweed, won't hurt your plants if you apply it every few weeks during the summer season. To guard against weak, sappy growth that attracts pests, it is better to feed your soil than the plants, so consider getting lots of organic material delivered and digging that into your beds instead.

36. Can you tell me what 'loamy' soil is and whether it suits lilacs?

Loamy soil is rich in organic matter, and it is able to retain moisture well without becoming waterlogged.

Technically speaking, loamy soil is a soil type composed of a friable mixture of clay, silt, sand and organic matter. Good loam should have at least five percent organic matter, which helps the soil to retain its moisture, and contributes to the never-ending process of decomposition and growth that occurs in soil. In other words, it's a good, workable, rich, well-drained garden soil. Lilacs are pretty flexible and will adapt to other soil types, but you're on the right track with your thinking. Work lots of aged manure into the soil around the planting area, not just in the planting hole, or else the roots may not want to grow beyond the hole! Lilacs prefer a near-neutral soil pH, and peat acidifies soil. If your plot is surrounded by buildings made with cement or mortar, a little peat is a good idea. During this first growing season, it's very important to water your lilac regularly. Mulch will help

> Work lots of aged manure into the soil around the planting area, not just in the planting hole, or the roots may not want to grow beyond the hole!

with moisture retention and will add nutrients as it decays. Most importantly, make sure the lilac gets plenty of sun, since that's what encourages these plants to bloom.

37. I filled my raised beds with topsoil and mushroom compost last year. Do I need to improve the soil again this year?

Topsoil and mushroom compost can vary widely in their composition, so it may be wise to run basic soil tests to find out for sure about the existing soil mix. This will also mean you can check the pH. As a general rule of thumb, it is a good idea to keep on 'feeding' your soil by regularly adding more organic matter, such as compost, rotted leaves or aged stable manure and bedding. Using a natural mulch will also feed the soil as it breaks down over time. The only other possible addition would be a bit of sand to assist with drainage, but this would depend on the ability of the existing mix in your beds to drain.

Adding lots of compost to your soil every year is one of the easiest ways to ensure you always achieve success with growing vibrant annuals such as zinnias.

38. Will I be able to grow vegetables in a coastal area with salty soil?

Lean soils need help to grow herbs and vegetables well. Incorporating compost or aged manure will help improve your vegetable patch and should help to produce healthy and happy plants. Spread a generous layer of organic matter over the top of the soil and dig or till it to approximately the depth of your spade. Then plant your veggies. You can mulch between the plants with another layer of compost and dig that in at the end of the gardening season. A few years of adding compost in this way will turn your soil into rich loam that will be the envy of all your neighbours!

39. The soil in my containers is bone dry underneath the surface. What can I do?

What you describe is not all that unusual. It's important to water containers thoroughly – until water freely drains from the bottoms of the pots – although air pockets can develop, meaning that the water will run out before the soil is completely saturated. There's an easy fix, though, and if you do this every two to three weeks during the growing season, the soil in the pots will remain moist. Simply submerge the pots in a larger container of water and leave them there until no more air bubbles come to the top. Then remove the pots and let them drain. It's easiest to use a larger container of water so that the pots are submerged past their rims. If you don't have a container large enough to accommodate the pot, you can simply set the container on a tray with a wide rim. Water the containers and then let them sit in the water that drains out into the tray. If you continue to add water, and let the containers sit for a while, the potting soil will absorb the water and eliminate the air pockets around the roots. Avoid leaving pots in water for more than a couple of hours, however, because this can cause the roots to rot.

One of the advantages of growing vegetables in raised beds is that you can improve the soil every year until it is rich and crumbly.

40. My vegetable garden is extremely rocky. Should I add more topsoil?

All vegetables do better in a deeply prepared soil, with ample quantities of organic matter worked into it, so that it is evenly moist yet well-drained and fairly rich. Rocky or stony soil in and of itself is not necessarily bad; the only way to tell about the soil you have is to run some basic soil tests and find out for sure. When the existing soil is inadequate, one option is to loosen the surface as best you can and then build raised beds on top of it. The beds do not have to have edges, although these can help keep things tidy; you can use wood to build your own or buy ready-made kits.

Soil Quality

The first step to improving your soil structure is to test it for its pH level and nutrient make-up. You can use a testing kit or even get professionals to do it for you. The good news is that most soils can be improved significantly. If you are starting with an area that has already been cultivated, single digging or the no-dig method may be the most appropriate ways to enhance it. New ground, or that which has become tired and compacted through overuse or heavy traffic, can sometimes require more drastic treatment, such as using a mechanical tiller or double digging. Soil is the most important commodity in the garden; look after it and you'll be rewarded with healthy and strong plants that are less prone to pests and diseases.

41. How can I improve alkaline soil?

The best thing you can do to improve your soil is to add organic matter such as compost. This is basically partially decomposed organic matter and it's the best possible soil amendment. It is readily available to buy and it's well worth making your own, too. When planting, mixing compost in with the backfill soil benefits the plant by creating food for microorganisms that will continue to decompose the organic material. Decomposition produces nutrients for the plant and also creates acid, which will offset your soil's alkalinity. Since most nursery plants come in potting soil, mixing compost with the native soil will create a transitional area for the plant's roots. You can also spread compost around the plant on the surface on a regular basis. It will help discourage the growth of weeds and will make it easier to remove any that do pop up. It will also facilitate decomposition on the surface, helping to enrich the soil. By digging in the old compost and adding fresh new compost each year, you will improve your soil over the years, ending up with wonderful garden loam and healthy plants.

42. Is horse manure good fertiliser?

Horse manure is an excellent source of nutrients and organic matter for your garden. Spread it out and let it age before mixing it into the soil. Weathering manure in this way allows the rain to leach out any concentrated urine that might be strong enough to injure new plants. Adding manure from animals that consume large quantities of grass is usually a great way of improving your soil, although there are sometimes problems with weeds in areas where manure has been spread. This is because the animals do not discriminate between weeds and grasses and any weed seeds consumed usually pass through the digestive tract without

> Decomposition produces nutrients for the plant and also creates acid, which will offset your soil's alkalinity.

being affected. Just mulch your beds heavily after planting to shade out the weed seeds and keep them from germinating. Or you can pull the weed seedlings by hand as soon as they appear to keep them from producing seed heads and spreading their seeds through the garden.

43. What is the best growing medium for large containers on a patio?

Plants growing in containers require more water and more food than plants in a garden bed. This is because the roots are not able to search out water and nutrients the way they can when planted directly in the earth. To overcome these restrictions, it's best to use a good quality potting soil rather than regular soil or even a mix of potting soil and garden soil. Commercially prepared potting soil is a mixture of organic matter, sand and perlite or vermiculite. The combination makes for a growing medium that is light and airy, and holds moisture yet drains well. You should consider using a prepared potting soil in your container (be sure the container has adequate drainage holes).

Fertilise throughout the growing season by applying a half-strength dilution of a liquid fertiliser every two weeks. This will keep a constant supply of nutrients available to your plants. Water when the top of the growing medium begins to dry out. When you water, apply slowly so that it wets the entire root mass.

44. How often do I have to change the soil in container pots?

Potting soil should be replaced every three or four years – the best way to do it is to unpot your plant, brush any loose potting soil off the roots, then add fresh potting soil to the container and replant. Plants normally outgrow their containers in three to four years, so it is easiest to simply plant them in the next sized container, in fresh potting soil. You can clean the old containers with a bleach and water solution – one part liquid chlorine bleach to nine parts water – then use them for other plants. Skimming just the top 3 cm (1 in) off the soil and replacing it is more of a cosmetic exercise and won't be as effective as replacing the potting soil where the roots are actively growing.

You can grow a selection of different vegetables in containers, and you can help boost your harvest by adding an organic food, such as liquid seaweed.

Plants such as rhododendrons and azaleas that naturally grow in pine forests like an acid, or ericaceous soil.

Soil pH can be lowered on a temporary and localised basis so you could incorporate a balancing product, available from garden centres.

45. Will Epsom salts help my container-planted azalea bush?

You can use a total of about two tablespoons of Epsom salts, diluted in plenty of water, in the container. It will help your azalea grow and bloom, but be careful not to over-apply; too much of a good thing is often worse than nothing at all.

46. How can we improve our clay soil for growing vegetables?

The addition of compost or aged manure will help improve the texture of your clay soil. The goal is good garden loam that is about four percent organic matter. It takes time to build but it will all be worthwhile when you're eating delicious homegrown produce!

47. What is the best way to lower the pH of an alkaline soil?

You may want to have a professional soil test taken because the simple tests that come in kits are sometimes misleading. The good news is that soil pH can be lowered on a temporary and localised basis, so you could incorporate a sulphur-based balancing product, available from garden centres. Follow package instructions for the amount to spread.

48. Why can't I grow root vegetables in my black, crumbly soil?

If your soil is rich, root vegetables should grow well. Perhaps you are planting at the wrong time of the year? These crops develop best in the cooler months. Try planting in early spring or in late summer for the tastiest produce and most bountiful harvests.

49. Do I need to remove grass from the surface before double digging?

Under certain conditions, grass can sprout and create a nasty weed problem. Double digging involves the removal of about a foot of topsoil in order to loosen, aerate and amend the subsoil beneath it. The topsoil is amended and replaced systematically in a trenching process that takes considerable time and effort. Because of the effort put into double digging, perennial weeds, including grass, are usually removed.

There are several alternative methods, including cultivating with a rototiller or removing the grass with a sodlifter. Each method has its appeal; the important point is to be sure the grass will not regrow. Killing the grass with a weed killer is another option, but many gardeners do not like using toxic chemicals on their soil – especially in places where they'll plant food. Simply removing the grass means that you are also removing all the nutrients in this top layer of soil, so if you do decide on this option, add the grass to your compost heap so that nothing is wasted.

With a project of this nature it's better to tackle a small area at a time and do it well, rather than to have a large area with only mixed results. It's too easy to become overwhelmed!

Choose the area you want to start on and cover the rest with black plastic or heavy layers of cardboard weighted to keep it in place. This will keep the light out and kill the grass. Several weeks later you can dig or rotovate, making repeated passes. On the final several passes, add compost or other organic matter to the soil. Then continue to amend the areas as you place each plant or sow seeds. Each season, add extra amendments in the form of mulch or compost. If possible, plant annuals rather than perennials for a year or two so you have the opportunity to completely rotovate again, adding more amendments.

Aerating the Soil

If your soil is in reasonable shape and is not compacted, it may require little more than light aeration. Single digging can help to loosen heavy soil, breaking up lumps and creating air pockets, which in turn improves drainage. Simply dig a trench to the depth of the head of your spade and throw the soil forward where it will sit behind your trench. Working systematically backwards from one end of the bed to the other, use the soil from each trench to fill the one dug previously and remove weed roots as you go. Nearly all soils at this stage would also benefit from adding organic material to boost nutrient levels. This is particularly important if you have very light and sandy soil. Single digging is a great way to open up previously cultivated soil prior to planting new flowers and shrubs, or creating a vegetable garden.

50. What type of soil do I need for asparagus?

It's smart to prepare the bed thoroughly before you purchase asparagus crowns. These are usually sold in bundles of a dozen or so and look dead at the time of purchase. A crown is a dormant asparagus plant, consisting of stringy roots that radiate outwards from a pointed growing tip. (The bundles are tied with the tip up and roots dangling downwards; you will plant them with the tip facing up.) Asparagus needs plenty of sun and very rich, well-drained soil with a pH near 6.5 and an ample amount of organic material worked in prior to planting. If your native soil is heavy, you might also add a bit of sand to ensure good drainage. This is important because the asparagus bed is a long-term planting which will last for many years, if prepared correctly at the outset. The plants should be spaced about 50 cm (18 in) apart in rows about 1.2 m (4 ft) apart. The mature plants are very large! Ideally, asparagus is planted in very early spring. First prepare the ground as deeply as is practical, because the roots can reach 1.5 m (5 ft) deep. Then dig a trench about a foot deep and wide enough to accommodate the crowns without crowding. Work in several centimetres of organic matter, such as compost or well-rotted manure, at the bottom of the

Asparagus is a perennial crop that you can harvest for many years. It pays to do your groundwork thoroughly first and be sure the soil is rich and freely draining.

trench, then plant the crowns. Cover them with around 8 cm of soil mixed with organic matter and water well. As the plants grow, continue adding layers of amended soil until the trench is filled in. Be sure to keep the asparagus bed well

Double Digging

This is hard work, but it will improve compacted soil in high-traffic areas. Start by making a narrow trench along one end of the bed, roughly the width and depth of the head of your spade, moving the soil into a wheelbarrow. When the first trench is complete, add a layer of compost or manure and use your fork to break up the bottom of the trench and work it into the soil. Turn the second 'row' of soil over into the first trench and break it up, removing weeds and stones as you go. Continue working backwards across the bed until you reach the end, where you will be left with a final trench to be filled with the soil in the wheelbarrow.

weeded and water regularly if needed during the summer. A mulch to keep down weeds is usually a good idea, too. Generally, it is a good idea to let the new plants grow and become established for the first year, therefore delaying any harvest until the next year. When you do begin to harvest, cut only those spears larger in diameter than a pencil.

51. Is seaweed a good mulch for the garden?

It can be a very useful mulch but it's a good idea to prepare it first. Make piles of fresh seaweed on a surface that allows water to drain but won't be affected by the salt, such as a gravel driveway. Rinse and turn the piles three to four times to wash out all excess salt. Spread the seaweed out and allow it to dry for two to three weeks. Then shred it or apply it directly as a generous mulch on your vegetable and flower beds. Seaweed is high in potassium and many minerals, and because it has little cellulose, it decomposes more quickly than hay or leaves. Rinsing will not remove significant amounts of its nutrients.

52. When should I start applying liquid fertiliser to sprouting seeds?

Seedlings can feed themselves up until their first set of true leaves appear, which will look distinctly different from the first two seed leaves. Once they do, you can feed them with a liquid food that's suitable for seedlings, but be sure it's diluted according to the instructions, because too much food can lead to weak, sappy growth. If in doubt, avoid fertiliser on young plants altogether.

53. I would like to grow some peonies. Do they have any special soil requirements?

Peonies will grow in almost any kind of soil, but because they're long-lived, the soil should be well prepared before they're planted. Work organic matter into the soil to two spades' depth before planting. The easiest way to do this is by spreading a generous layer of compost or aged manure over the garden plot and digging it in. Then plant your peonies at the recommended depth for that variety. Add support stakes near each tuber and fill in the hole. As winter approaches, when the foliage dies down, cut it off at soil level and remove it from the garden. Peonies will grow into 1.2-m (4-ft) clumps with flowers that are very heavy, especially when wet. Remove the spent flowers regularly to help keep the plant upright.

Before planting shrubs and perennial flowers that will be in your garden for many years, it is well worth enhancing your soil as much as possible.

54. I'd like to grow some blueberry plants in a pot. What do you advise?

Blueberries and cranberries like moist, acid soil. If your soil is alkaline, it is best to grow them in large pots instead.

It's advisable to put the plants in large containers and, as with all pots for plants, ensure that there are plenty of holes in the bottom for drainage. You can get special ericaceous (acid) potting mix for plants like blueberries and cranberries. Feed them regularly with a specialised fertiliser and ensure you water them regularly.

Compost improves soil structure . . . it improves drainage in clay soil, improves moisture retention in sandy soil and provides food for beneficial organisms, like earthworms.

55. Can I use sawdust as a mulch or will it withdraw nitrogen from the soil?

Raw wood, such as sawdust, can rob the soil of nitrogen when layered over the ground. This is because nitrogen is used by the sawdust during the decomposition process. It is safe, however, to use as a mulch because the amount of nitrogen it takes is so small. Other good mulches include chipped bark, leaf mould (made from last year's leaves) and homemade compost. Apply a generous layer but avoid the plant stems.

56. What is the best way to re-pot plants without damaging them?

If you carefully re-pot them one at a time and water each one well after the move, your plants should be just fine. Start by selecting containers that are the next size up from the current ones. You'll need a bucket or other large container to moisten the potting soil prior to use. Once the potting mix is moistened and drained (not soggy wet), put a little in the bottom of the container. You can set the current container into the larger one to make sure you have enough (but not too much) soil in the new container. Your goal is to ensure that plants are at the same soil depth as they are growing now.

Once you're satisfied that the depth of the soil in the bottom of the container is just right, you can unpot each plant by laying it on its side (you may need an assistant for this step of the project). Gently pull it out of the old pot. If the roots appear to be growing around and around, you may want to loosen them a bit. You should be able to massage damp roots to loosen them without breaking them, and to remove some of the old potting soil. If necessary, swish the roots in a bucket of water to help untangle them and remove some of the old potting soil. When you've loosened the roots a little, you can set the plant in the new container and fill around the roots with some of the new, moistened potting soil. Push it down gently until the container is filled and then water the plant well. This will help settle the soil in and around the roots. If necessary, add more potting soil to the top of the container to make the soil level the same as in the previous pot.

57. What's the best fertiliser for herb and vegetable seeds in containers?

Adding compost is one of the most effective ways of improving your potting soil: compost improves soil structure, making it more workable; it improves drainage in clay soil; it improves moisture retention in sandy soil; and it provides food for beneficial organisms, like earthworms. However, the nutrients in compost (nitrogen, phosphorous, potassium – the NPK listed on fertiliser containers) can vary considerably. Add a balanced organic food like liquid seaweed for best results.

The No-Dig Method

Many gardeners believe that digging isn't strictly necessary since it doesn't occur in nature. The no-dig method involves heavy applications of organic matter to the surface, which worms then spread throughout the layers of soil. Suitable materials for applying to the soil include compost, well-rotted manure, leaf mould, paper scraps and composted bark. If you find digging physically difficult, or you have very good soil that has been improved in the past, then the no-dig method may work well for you. It is best used in a raised-bed system, where the soil is not walked on. Established no-dig beds have been shown to retain moisture and nutrients better than soil that has been regularly turned over, and this method saves hours of hard work!

Shady sites with dry soil are sadly all too common, but luckily there are plenty of plants that thrive in this situation. Look for 'cottage garden' perennials like foxgloves, alliums and honesty.

Rototilling Soil

If you're taking over a new garden, or you have a lot of space to cultivate, it's well worth considering using a tiller or rotovator. The secret to successfully using these machines is to pick your time and place – don't leave it until the soil has dried out in the sunshine, and avoid cultivating stodgy, wet ground. Both environments will confound the most well-designed machine and make things harder for you too. The other firm rule is never to rototill soil with a high clay content – the spinning tines will scrape the soil into a slick 'pan' that is impermeable to water (causing drainage problems from then on) and hard for young roots to grow through. Tilling is ideal for new beds in sandy or loamy soils as it will smash the larger clods apart.

58. Could you suggest some perennials for a dry spot in partial shade?

If you're unable to correct the soil conditions, you'll want to choose plants that thrive in dry shade. Foxglove, lady's mantle, lily-of-the-valley, lungwort, bleeding hearts and coral bells are all good choices. Such traditional 'cottage garden' varieties were first bred long before we had irrigation systems and the time to pamper gardens with daily watering.

59. My new tomato plants are dying already. Could a lack of iron in the soil do this?

That is unlikely because iron deficiency shows up as yellow leaves with obvious green veins and is not a significant problem for tomatoes. Your plants are probably suffering from transplant shock. Try to provide them with temporary protection from the hot afternoon sun until they get established. Ineffective watering is another big problem with tomatoes – be sure that water is reaching through the entire root zone, not just moistening the very top layer of soil. Let the water soak slowly and deeply; don't sprinkle. The water should reach down to the whole depth of the root system. When transplanting, 'harden off' plants by setting outside for a few hours per day in a sheltered location, gradually increasing the time over a period of seven to ten days. This helps reduce transplant shock. Give your plants a few more days to acclimatise to their new surroundings and they will probably bounce back to the best of health.

60. What should I do about what looks like insect eggs in the soil of some plants that I bought?

It sounds like these might be slow-release fertiliser pellets. Many garden centres and nurseries use these gritty balls of plant food and new gardeners often wonder if they are cause for concern. Just leave them in place to do their thing – they'll break down slowly and release fertiliser.

Seedlings raised inside should be acclimatised to outdoor conditions before they are planted. This process is known as 'hardening off'.

61. I want to grow vegetables but my clay soil is difficult to cultivate. Should I dig in some topsoil?

Clay soil isn't all bad. It is often full of nutrients and can form the base for a decent growing medium – it just takes time and patience to achieve this. The best amendments are an annual application of a good layer of compost, rotten manure and other organic matter that will help to lighten and break up the clay. It may be easier for you to plant seedlings into the ground than seeds. You can buy them or start them yourself; you can also form raised beds on top of the clay with better soil and plant in those beds, or use containers for many vegetables.

62. Can you suggest some flowering shrubs or trees for alkaline soil?

Very alkaline soils can be challenging to many plants. Those that not only survive, but thrive, include Japanese cherry (including weeping cherry), Judas tree (*Cercis*), flowering crab apple and black pine. Shrubs include cistus, weigela, butterfly bush (*Buddleja*), mugo pine, hebe, burning bush (*Dictamnus*) and hardy plumbago (*Ceratostigma*). Grapes such as Buffalo, Niagara and Concord should provide lots of fruit, or you might check with a local nursery to see which other varieties perform well in your area. Choosing varieties that actually like their conditions makes life as a gardener a lot easier.

63. Lots of mushrooms are popping up in my topsoil. Is this bad?

The mushrooms are growing because the soil is rich in nutrients, but don't worry because they are harmless to your plants and soil. They are fairly common and nothing to be concerned about. It just means you have lots of organic matter that is fresh and moist. You can use a rake to move the soil around so that sunlight and air can reach it, therefore drying it out and preventing the mushrooms from growing.

Cherry trees are covered in decorative blossoms in spring and then you get the bonus of the fruits in late summer. They also thrive in alkaline soils.

64. Would you recommend chicken fertiliser for a vegetable garden?

Chicken manure is a particularly good fertiliser but it is very potent. It's so concentrated that large amounts applied directly to plants can burn them, much the same as if you use too much of an artificial product. Use it sparingly and work it into the soil in the spring, when you turn over your beds. Let the beds rest for a week or two before planting. If you'd like to fertilise with chicken manure throughout the growing season, you might try composting it first. Mix the pure manure with straw, sawdust or leaves, and let it sit for several months, turning occasionally and keeping it moist, but not wet. The resulting compost can be used for side-dressing growing plants like marrows and will not burn like fresh manure. It can give a real boost to hungry feeders and lead to bigger harvests.

65. The soil in my potted plants has become whitish around the edges. Is that okay?

The whitish material on the top of your potting soil is simply an accumulation of minerals from the water you use. As the moisture evaporates, it leaves a concentration of salts. You can scrape it off the potting soil if you don't like the appearance, but it won't harm your plants or the potting soil. However, don't forget that it is good gardening practice to replace the top layer of soil in your pots every year or so.

Members of the Cucurbitaceae family are all heavy feeders and will benefit from the application of well-rotted manure.

Winter Protection

In northern regions, during the winter months, there isn't much that can be done while the ground is covered in snow. In milder climates, the garden may be protected from the wind and rain. One simple way to do this is to cover it with a layer of cardboard or plastic, thoroughly held down with bricks or other weights. Another option is to plant a green manure, such as clover, alfafa or ryegrass. Whichever you choose, the covering will restrict the growth of weeds, warm the soil and also stop topsoil and nutrients being washed or blown away — this can be a particular problem with raised beds. Pull cardboard or plastic covers back occasionally to let the coldest weather break up the soil and kill any lurking pests.

Composting

Making compost is not just financially rewarding. While it's fun to turn waste into a valuable resource, the real pleasure comes from knowing what a boost it will give to all your plants.

66. Is it okay to put rhubarb leaves in the compost bin?

Although people should not eat the leaves due to their relatively high oxalic acid content, they do not pose a hazard to the compost. You can put a small quantity of rhubarb leaves at a time into compost with no problems. However, don't add them in such a quantity of fresh green material that the mix becomes too wet and high in nitrogen.

Making Compost

Compost is an essential ingredient for gardening. It is, of course, available to buy from garden centres, but it's far more cost-effective to make it from scratch. Producing your own compost performs two essential tasks. First, it provides a soil conditioner for all kinds of gardening jobs. Second (and of equal importance) it recycles garden and kitchen waste. Without composting, the average garden would produce bags and bags of organic waste that could go to a landfill. As a general rule, anything green and growing is suitable for composting, but it should be combined with plenty of drier, brown material, such as fallen leaves, shredded paper and twiggy prunings.

67. Do compost starters or activators really work?

These products may help, especially if the pile is new. However, if you build a pile with a good mix of green and brown stuff and keep it moist, things will progress well even without a starter product. Some gardeners add a shovel of rich garden soil or compost to help act as a starter by introducing microbes into the pile. You might want to try that instead of buying a starter product. If your pile lacks green stuff, then sprinkle a little nitrogen-rich fertiliser into the pile and water it in well.

68. Can the seeds be included when putting fruits and vegetables in the compost bin or should they be taken out?

Fruit and vegetable seeds are fine to include when you're composting. If your pile heats up sufficiently, the seeds will not be viable. As long as you turn your compost to keep it cooking, seeds should not cause a problem. If you do forget to turn the pile, the seeds may sprout next spring, but you can always pot them if you want them. If not, weed the seedlings out and leave them in the sun to dry out before putting them back on the heap.

69. What can I put in my compost bin and what is it best to avoid?

Most vegetable peelings and kitchen scraps, including coffee grounds and tea leaves, can be added to the compost bin. Avoid adding anything fatty, such as meat – this will attract pests.

Composting is a wonderful way to recycle organic matter (without overloading our landfills), and the finished compost will give back to your soil what your plants took earlier in the season to help sustain their growth. The cautions about what to compost and what to keep out of the pile are based on a couple of concerns. First of all, you don't want to introduce disease-causing pathogens into the organic matter that you'll be spreading around your plot. Therefore, experts warn not to include faeces from humans, pigs, dogs, cats or any other meat-eating creatures. If your pets are strictly vegetarian, then including their droppings shouldn't cause concern. Chicken manure will be very hot if added fresh, but if you mix it around in the pile,

> Composting is a wonderful way to recycle organic matter . . . and the finished compost will give back to your soil what your plants took earlier in the season . . .

it should be fine. (A pile that's too hot isn't as efficient as one that warms slowly and maintains the heat it's generating.) In terms of adding cooked veggies to the pile, you can do so, providing you don't include any fat with the veggies. Meat scraps, bread and butter or oil will attract rodents and other scavengers, as well as an abundance of flies and other pests. It's best to keep these things out, or at least keep their inclusion to an absolute minimum to avoid attracting the 'wrong element' to your compost pile; after all, you will need to turn it over regularly.

70. When is the best time of year to add compost to the garden?

You can topdress or spread a thin layer of compost over planting areas at any season apart from winter. Its effects are long term, so there is no critical 'best time' to do it. It is a good idea to apply compost on a regular basis, however – typically once or twice a year. You would probably also want to top it with mulch to keep it from washing away. To some extent, you may have to go by whether or not it is available at any given time, and what is most convenient for you.

Adding homemade compost to your beds every year will improve drainage on clay soils and enhance the moisture retention on sandy soils.

71. My compost bin is full of ants. Will they ruin the compost?

Don't be surprised if you find a wide array of insects in your compost pile. Rather than doing harm, they are actually helping to decompose the organic matter – whether they are microorganisms that you can't see with the naked eye, or larger things, such as grubs. The ants you find in your compost bin are excellent soil builders and, although unusual in a compost pile, they won't be harmful. It sounds as if your pile has 'cooled off' or else they wouldn't be there. If you turn the pile (which adds oxygen) and moisten everything, the decomposition process will heat up again and the ants will probably go elsewhere.

72. Is it possible to compost oak leaves or are they too acidic?

Oak leaves are actually very good for composting, despite their acidity. Since they are slow to break down, you should preferably shred the leaves first, either with a shredder or simply by running your lawnmower over the top of them a few times. In addition to this, be sure to layer the leaves with a nitrogen source, such as manure, to speed up the decomposition process. If you are adding a lot of the composted leaves to your plot, consider having a soil test done to determine your soil's acidity level. If found to be too acidic, the test results will give you recommendations on how to adjust your soil's pH level. Use the compost freely and take the time to test the soil every few years to ensure its pH level is just right.

73. Do worms and beetles help to speed up the composting process? What about other wildlife?

Worms are a valuable asset in the compost heap and the garden. Avoid adding large quantities of raw citrus peel and onions to the pile, because they can be toxic to worms.

A healthy compost pile should be teeming with creatures of all kinds, ranging in size from microscopic to as long as your hand. Worms and beetles are normal discoveries in a compost bin and, like most of the creatures you see, they won't hurt your garden or growing plants. Their preference is to feed on, and break down, organic debris. Many slugs, however, will feast on the plants you are growing, as well as decaying organic matter, so remove them if you see them. Turn the compost regularly to introduce some air and help excess moisture to evaporate. The pile will heat up when it has the right moisture content, and you can keep things cooking by moving the cooler material on the sides into the centre of the pile. Insects and worms will stay in the cooler parts to continue feeding on decaying organic matter. Your compost is ready to use when it's brown, crumbly and has unrecognisable bits of organic matter. It should smell like clean soil. If you can still identify roots or leaves, the compost needs more time. Apart from regular turning, speed up the decomposition process by leaving the pile open to the elements when it's hot and covering it up again at night or during rainy weather. A few layers of cardboard make an excellent 'lid' for compost piles.

74. I left the lid off my compost bin and now it's wet and smells bad. What should I do?

What you have now is anaerobic decomposition and it really does smell! The best way to remedy the situation is to introduce fresh air. Use a garden fork to turn the pile a couple of times a day until the excess water evaporates. Alternatively, you can rake the compost out of the bin or pile and spread it out on the ground or on plastic tarps for a day or two. The sunshine will dry it out and the smell will dissipate. You can then pile it back up to finish decomposing until it is usable compost. Adding lots of dry but airy material like scrunched-up corrugated cardboard will also help.

Starting a Heap

It is best to start the heap with easily degradable waste, such as vegetable peelings, because this will help establish the microorganisms it needs for decomposition. If starting from scratch, your first batch of compost will be ready in six months to a year. This depends upon your climate, the size of your composting bin or pile, and the type and quantity of waste used. Keep an eye on moisture levels: if the heap becomes too damp, the waste will putrefy rather than create usable compost. For this reason, it needs rain protection. Most commercial composters have a lid but, if you have made your own, cover the heap with waterproof material. Similarly, in warm weather, it can dry out, so you may want to add water to the pile.

75. Can I plant seeds in homemade compost?

To give seeds the best start in life, you'd generally use a finer mixture than you can make at home. It should be sterilised, too, to give the new seeds an opportunity to germinate and grow before they have to battle insects and diseases. You can, however, make potting soil out of your compost to use in planter boxes and containers. Just mix one part compost, one part sand and one part garden soil together in a wheelbarrow, then use it or store it for future use. Another excellent use for your compost is as a mulch over the top of a garden bed to help retain moisture and suppress weeds. Or you can spread a generous layer over the top of a garden bed and mix it into the soil to enrich the planting area. Worms will soon help out by carrying it underground and improving the soil.

76. I've heard you shouldn't put dog and cat waste in the compost pile. What should I do with it?

Composting pet waste may seem like a good idea, but the pathogens and parasites within the waste are not properly treated or removed under most compost conditions. It's better to dig a deepish hole in an out of the way place, shovel pet waste into it, then cover it with sawdust and a lid, such as a piece of plywood. Each time you add more waste, add more sawdust. The faeces will decompose and there will be no smell because of the sawdust and the lid. When you fill the hole (in a few years), cover it with soil and dig a new hole, so turning a problem into a material that will eventually neutralise and may even enrich the soil.

77. Can I use a mixture of freshly cut grass and chipped leaves as compost right away or do I need to leave it to break down?

It would be perfectly fine to use this in a thin layer. Be careful not to use too much, however, because the clippings are nitrogen-rich and 'hot' and will possibly burn plants if layered too deeply at a time. The combination of the leaves and grass will help keep it from packing down and becoming water repellent, the way plain clippings can.

You can make compost in black plastic bags by alternating layers of leaves and grass clippings.

78. Can you make compost in big black plastic bags outdoors?

It is possible to make compost in these bags. You need to add the materials to be composted and moisten them to the dampness of a well-wrung-out sponge. Make sure there is a good proportion of green stuff to brown stuff (or nitrogen to carbon), just as you would in your compost bin. Roll the bags around occasionally to mix the ingredients, and bear in mind that composting stops in cold weather so begin your composting project in the spring.

79. What's the best way to build and maintain a compost bin?

The simplest option is to make a pile without rigid sides, but most people prefer to build an enclosure out of wood or use a plastic bin. If you make your own, bear in mind that it's useful to allow air to enter the bin, so ensure that there are gaps in the wood. When you fill it, you'll need both green and brown material – green for nitrogen and brown for carbon. Grass clippings, dead annuals, vegetable peelings and anything else that's green will supply nitrogen, as will manure. For the brown layers, dried leaves are excellent; failing a supply of them, you could use newspaper or cardboard for the carbon portion of your compost pile. Tear it into strips and crunch it up so that it contains air pockets, which will help it to decompose faster. Start by tossing green material into the bin, then add brown material, and top it off with a few shovelfuls of soil to add microorganisms, which will speed the decomposition process. Water it down well. Wait a few days to a week and turn everything to mix it together. Water again, if necessary, so that it is damp but not soggy. Remember to turn the contents of your compost pile every week to ten days, moving the warm centre to the sides and the cold sides to the middle so that everything breaks down completely. Compost takes anywhere from a few months to a full year to mature, depending upon the size of the organic materials you put into the bin and how often you turn it. You can screen the compost prior to use, tossing the larger pieces back into the pile and using the well-decomposed parts in your garden.

Getting lots of air into your compost is very important so bins with large gaps can be very effective.

80. Can I add wild mushrooms and toadstools to the compost heap?

As long as your compost pile is cooking, you can safely compost any organic material. The heat from the decomposition process will kill the fungi and, since you won't be directly eating the compost, the wild mushrooms should have no effect on you. Be sure to turn the pile frequently to ensure that pathogens, fungal spores and seeds will be cooked enough to kill them. If you have lots of fungi growing in your garden, why not take a course to learn how to identify them?

If you spot any wild mushrooms growing in your garden, you can add them to the compost heap because the heat it generates will help them to decay and add valuable nutrients to the mix.

81. Can I use 'community' compost on my vegetable garden or could it contain toxic chemicals from other people's gardens?

Some chemicals take a very long time to break down, so be cautious about using matter that could have been treated with herbicides. Many 'weed and feed' products can contain herbicides that are effective against broad-leaf weeds. These don't affect grass so they're not a problem when used on the lawn. Unfortunately, your vegetable garden is full of broad-leaf plants! The compost should be fine to use for ornamental plants, although it may better to use organic compost or well-rotted manure on a vegetable garden.

Turning Your Heap

If left totally undisturbed, the compost in your heap will decay slowly and unevenly. It will therefore benefit from a thorough turning every few weeks, if possible. Use a large garden fork to get the mixture moving and aim to combine the fresher waste with the decomposing items. There is no hard and fast rule as to how often this task should be completed, but it is worth bearing in mind that the more the heap is turned, the quicker you get your compost. Since heat is a by-product of decomposition, the centre of the compost heap can reach high temperatures. To maintain the heap during the colder months, insulate the bin with straw, bubble wrap or an old blanket.

82. I've seen mushroom compost for sale very reasonably. Is it safe to use on all plants?

Mushroom compost can supply nutrients and increase the water-holding capacity of the soil. But it can be too much of a good thing for seeds, seedlings and young plants because it contains high levels of soluble salts and other nutrients. It's also not suitable for members of the heather family, such as rhododendrons, blueberries, and azaleas. It's worth mixing mushroom compost with garden soil before using it on young plants. Alternatively, order a supply of mushroom compost in advance and let it sit uncovered, to 'cure', over the winter, before using it all over your garden in the spring.

Using Your Compost

You can be confident that your compost is ready to use when it appears earthy and has a fresh, loamy smell. There may be a few pieces of eggshell or twig still visible, but this won't affect the quality. You can use the compost in containers, mixed with soil and sand for drainage as a mulch around established plants or dug into the soil to add nutrients. However, it is not generally suitable for starting off seedlings. Plants are very vulnerable to fungal disease (known as damping off) in their early stages, and so seed trays and the compost you use should all be sterilised. Similarly, you should only use tap water on seedlings and save the water from rain barrels for older plants.

83. What are the benefits of compost tumblers?

The main advantage of these designs is the ease with which you can turn the compost. This is a real benefit to anyone with back trouble. Composting methods really should fit your needs and circumstances, as well as your personality. For example, you may prefer to have a couple of different methods to meet specific needs. You could fill a plastic bin with vegetable peelings and kitchen scraps layered with leaves and weeds to keep pests from digging into the food scraps, as well as having piles of rough yard waste. They will compost at different rates, which is fine if you are in no hurry. But if time is of the essence, a tumbler is great – you can make compost really quickly, as long as the constituents of the mix are correct. Tumblers can be bulky, so consider where you'll put one before you order it!

84. Is it better to dig compost in or can I just lay it on top of my beds?

You can use compost in many ways. One way is to dig it into the soil, another is to apply a light layer as a topdressing and leave it on the surface, and another way is to use partially finished compost as mulch. If you are planning a new planting area, it's a good idea to prepare the soil deeply and incorporate as much organic matter as you can. This could include compost, old rotted leaves and aged stable manure and bedding. A layer of 15 cm (6 in) would not be too much to add. Nature is your ally and worms and a host of other organisms will get to work instantly, helping to spread the nutrients under the ground.

85. I've been advised to add plenty of compost to my garden. Is it possible to overdo it?

It's possible that there can be too much of a good thing, but organic matter is so helpful to the soil that you can safely spread a deep layer over the top of the soil and work it in without worrying. After planting, you can add a thinner layer of organic matter as a mulch to insulate the soil and improve moisture retention. At the end of the season you can dig this mulch into the soil. Since compost breaks down over time, you can add a similar amount year after year to your garden – the soil will simply get better and better.

You can improve the fertility and the texture of the soil in your vegetable garden by adding a generous layer of compost every year, followed by a layer of mulch.

86. Can I use compost from my bin to grow plants in?

Depending on the ingredients that went into the compost, the NPK (nitrogen, phosphorous, potassium) levels can vary considerably and pH levels could be acidic or alkaline. If you had plenty of variety in the compost ingredients, you might get away with planting directly in it. But, although compost is a fantastic soil amendment, it's usually lacking in some nutrients or minerals that are found in soil, which could show up as deficiencies in your plants. So it's best to add compost to the top of your soil, rather than planting straight into it.

Organic mulch can be used to help retain moisture in the soil and prevent weeds from germinating.

87. Is there a difference between compost and mulch?

The terms are often used interchangeably. However, compost is decomposed organic matter that can be incorporated into the soil to improve its fertility, structure, drainage (in clay soils) and water-holding capacity (in sandy soils). Mulch usually refers to different types of organic matter that can be layered on top of the soil to moderate its temperature, reduce weed germination and retain moisture. Compost can be used as a mulch, as can bark chips, straw or dried leaves. Of course, all of these materials can also be used to make your own compost. Another way of looking at it is that compost is generally in a more decomposed state than mulch.

88. I'm new to gardening and haven't made my own compost yet. Where's the best place to buy some for my lawn?

Compost is basically decomposed organic matter; you'll see bags of it for sale at any garden centre. You can use any readily available organic material, just spread it in a thin layer and water it into your turf. Most shops have staff who can offer advice about the best options for your needs, so ask about subjects that matter to you, such as whether a product is environmentally friendly.

89. I keep finding grubs in my compost bin. What am I doing wrong and what can I do to fix it?

You are not doing anything wrong! You actually have a successful compost pile. These grubs are usually the larvae of beetles and they're just some of the many creatures that are doing the work of breaking down your organic matter. They usually appear when the compost is fairly decomposed and 'rich'. There are numerous types of grubs and they come in various sizes depending on the type of beetle. Sometimes, turning compost more often or using it as soon as it cools rather than warehousing it in the finished state can help reduce the number of them. Covering the pile with a tarp may also help so beetles can't lay their eggs. Most beetles are a gardener's friend, however, and many eat pests such as slugs, so it's well worth welcoming them into your plot!

90. Does adding fresh manure to a compost bin speed up the process of decomposition?

Fresh manure can speed things up but it is not necessary; you can add a shovelful of soil to your compost to help jump-start the decomposition process. Garden soil also contains all kinds of microbes and other good things for composting. A single shovelful of healthy garden soil can contain thousands of different organisms, which can all help to make rich, crumbly compost.

91. I let a pumpkin rot in my compost pile last year and now it's full of seedlings. What should I do?

Pumpkins will grow well on your pile but they are heavy feeders, so you do not want to crowd them. For best results, thin the plants out to be around a metre apart, keeping only the better plants. As they grow, remove most of the pumpkins from each vine so the energy goes to just one or two fruits per plant. Keep an eye on the vines and train them so they don't tangle together. Don't be surprised if the pumpkins you get aren't quite the same as the original parent, but you should get a good crop. If you get time to pot all the seedlings, you could give them to friends, family and local garden societies.

Materials for Your Compost Heap

All sorts of organic matter can be used to make rich compost. As well as vegetable peelings, skins and tops, you can use tea bags and coffee grounds. Young weeds, soft plant trimmings and prunings are also excellent. The compost heap is also the best place for soiled bedding from vegetarian pets, such as hamsters, gerbils, rabbits and chickens. Eggshells and grass clippings can also be added, but bear in mind that the latter contains a lot of moisture, so balance it with shredded paper or crumpled up pieces of cardboard. Avoid meat and fish, bread, wood, glossy paper, diseased plants, invasive or perennial weeds and cat or dog faeces.

Avoid harming the worms in your compost by leaving a layer on top of your beds overnight before you dig it in. This gives them the chance to burrow safely underground.

92. I have a wonderful compost pile with hundreds of worms. How do I avoid killing them when I dig the compost into my beds?

You obviously know the value of these important creatures in the garden! Worms shun sunlight, so to give them a running start – till your garden once, spread the compost over the top and wait overnight before digging again. This will give the worms a chance to head down into the soil, out of harm's way.

Green Manures

Using green manures simply means growing certain plants on vacant ground to improve the soil. This can work in a variety of ways: Some types of plants 'fix' nitrogen from the atmosphere into the soil; others have fast-growing roots that go down deep and bring nutrients up to the surface. You can dig these plants into the topsoil a few weeks before reusing the ground, and the nutrients will be released during decomposition. The good news doesn't stop there — many green manures have dense foliage that covers the surface of the soil, overshadowing it and thus slowing down the growth of weeds. What's more, many have flowers that will attract beneficial insects to pollinate and protect your other plants. There are many plants suitable for this use including mustard and phacelia.

93. Would adding sawdust to my compost pile be beneficial or detrimental?

Sawdust has an extremely high ratio of carbon to nitrogen, which means it takes a long time to break down. It doesn't mean that it won't decompose, but you would need to mix it with a great deal of material high in nitrogen to try to balance it out or use it sparingly as your carbon source. And you would probably have to keep adding more nitrogen to keep the process going. Materials high in nitrogen include grass clippings, manure, fresh green garden trimmings or kitchen scraps. It may be better to use sawdust as a mulch for garden paths, where the fact that it is slow to break down is an advantage; or you could use it as the base for paths and spread something more attractive over it.

94. How long must I wait before adding the compost from my bins to my garden beds? And how do you recommend I add it?

Depending on the technique you use, composting can take from several months to a year or more. Compost is ready when it no longer resembles the original material you put into the pile. If you 'work' your pile, adding both nitrogen-rich and carbon-rich material and turn it often to keep it cooking, the raw material will decompose rather rapidly. If, on the other hand, you just pile up the material and allow it to decompose by itself, it can take many months, even years, to break down. Take a handful of compost and examine it. If it's brown and crumbly in texture, and there are no recognisable plant parts, it's probably ready to use. You can spread a generous layer of compost over the top of the garden bed, leave it overnight for the worms to begin working into the soil, and then dig it in to about a spade's depth. This will help loosen your soil and improve the drainage. Plan to incorporate more organic matter into your garden to further improve the soil every year. It takes a long time to build really good garden soil but it's well worth it!

Compost is ready to spread on your beds when it has broken down into a crumbly texture with no discernible leaves.

95. Is it okay to put our used coffee filters with the coffee in my compost pile?

That's fine. The paper filter (just like plain paper napkins) will compost along with the grounds, kitchen fruit and vegetable waste, and tea bags. However, be sure to avoid meat products and anything fatty, however.

96. Can I use homemade compost to grow plants in containers?

You can use compost in containers but add some vermiculite or sand to lighten the mix a bit and help aerate the compost. It isn't vital, but you'll find adding about one-third in volume is helpful because straight compost can hold too much water.

97. I have just moved into a new house and inherited some old compost bins. The contents are really smelly. What can I do?

When compost develops a bad smell it is usually because there is an imbalance, either because it is too wet or because there is too much nitrogen-rich or green material in the mix. The pile should be slightly damp, like a wrung-out sponge, and there should be a mixture of fresh green material and drier brown material in it. The green would be fresh green grass clippings, for example. To stop the smell you will need to dry the pile out by adding more 'brown' or high-carbon material, such as old fallen leaves, straw, wood shavings or whatever similar material is available. Mix this with the grass clippings and you'll have lovely, crumbly compost in no time!

98. The contents of our vacuum cleaner contains a lot of dog hair. Can we put it into the compost bin?

Dog hair will eventually decompose but it will take a very long time. Instead of composting it, throw it away, or you'll be spreading dog hair all over your garden, where it will remain for a few years.

Don't worry if you've moved to a new house and found a neglected compost heap. With a little tender, loving care it can soon be full of rich and crumbly organic matter.

99. I'm about to start my first compost pile. How do I take care of it?

You are about to embark on an adventure, which will prove rewarding and valuable. You may find this hard to believe, but composting can actually be fun. Here are the basics: Mix together organic matter, such as grass clippings, wood chips, hay, straw, manure, old plant vegetation from the garden and vegetable peelings. Keep it slightly moist by watering it, and keep air in the pile by mixing the materials every so often (called turning the pile), and sooner or later you'll get humus. You'll get it sooner if the materials are about two-thirds 'dry' high-carbon stuff, such as wood shavings, straw and hay, and one-third 'wet' high-nitrogen stuff, such as grass clippings, green vegetation and food scraps (don't include meat or anything fatty because this attracts pests). It will also decompose faster if the pile is fairly large (at least 1.2 x 1.2 m [4 x 4 ft] at the base and 1 m [3 ft] high) so that the interior of the pile is insulated enough to heat up. It also will decompose faster during hot weather, or if it is placed in a sunny position.

In terms of the compost bin or pile, you have many choices, each with its own advantages and disadvantages. You can start out with a simple bin made by rolling wire mesh into a cylinder, wiring the ends together, and setting it upright near your garden. After it's full, you can undo the wires and remove the mesh, then set it up again next to your pile of materials. As you fork the materials back into the cylinder, you'll be turning the pile and mixing in more oxygen for the microbes to use in decomposition. If you do this every couple of weeks, you'll speed up the whole process.

Making Leaf Mould

Many gardens are surrounded by trees and bushes, which will begin to drop thousands of leaves as the summer draws to a close. Rather than adding them directly to the compost heap, consider making your own free leaf mould! Simply collect the fallen leaves and place them in plastic bags, making a few small holes for ventilation. The bags aren't very attractive, so it may be best to keep them out of sight, behind a shed or garage, for example. Alternatively, you can drive four stakes into the ground and surround them with chicken wire to make a bin, and fill this with leaves. After a year, they will have broken down into a rich, crumbly mulching material that can be applied directly to your beds in order to improve the soil structure.

100. How can I quickly encourage worms to flourish in my new compost pile?

Earthworms don't like the heat generated by a working compost pile, so the worms you do see in established piles are a slightly different variety. Composting worms require very good ventilation to survive, and it's also important to avoid adding too much raw onion, garlic or citrus fruit to the bin, because these can harm the worms. There are lots of other beneficial organisms, such as microbes, that do like a warm compost pile and you can introduce them by simply adding a shovelful of garden soil to your compost pile. As they find food to eat they will multiply and help decompose the organic matter you toss into your compost pile.

Irrigation and Water Conservation

Learning how to water plants properly is one of the most valuable lessons for a budding gardener. Get the balance right and your lawns, flowers, shrubs and trees will all grow strongly.

101. Is it best to water houseplants from the roots up or from the soil down?

Either way is acceptable. The main advantage to watering from the bottom is that this method keeps water off the foliage. To some plants, such as African violets, this is important. But watering from the top, if you're careful not to splash water, is just as effective. Houseplants can be watered by immersing the pots in a sinkful of water, just up to the rims. If you set them too deep in the water, the top layer of potting soil will float away. After setting the pots in the water, use a watering can with a spout to direct water over the top of the soil. By immersing the pots, all the potting soil will become saturated. After letting them sit for about ten minutes, allow the excess water to drain, and then set them back on their saucers. Do this once every 10 to 14 days with foliage plants. If you have flowering plants or extra thirsty ones, you may need to water more frequently. A good test is to pick up the pot. If it feels light, it's time to water. If it still feels heavy, the soil is moist enough. Another way to test is to stick your fingertip into the soil. If it is dry 1 cm (½ in) beneath the surface, it's time to water.

Overwatering

People often don't realise that overwatering (drenching your plants every day) can be almost as bad as leaving them to dry out for too long. Overwatering is the number one cause of houseplant death, so never leave plants sitting in water for more than a few minutes or you can literally suffocate the roots. Give plants that are in the ground the opportunity to struggle a little for water, because this will encourage them to put down a healthy root system, which will keep them in good shape if you have to go away for a few days. Allowing them to almost wilt in between drenches can also enhance the flavour of many crops, such as strawberries and tomatoes. However, don't leave them so long that they become stressed; this will make them more vulnerable to pests and diseases.

102. Can we install a drainage system to pull the water away from a damp area?

Controlling drainage and surface runoff and directing water requires professional training and on-site inspection prior to suggesting how to deal with such a problem. For help in designing a system, you might contact a landscape architect or another licensed and certified professional with training in grading and drainage work. Their assistance could prove invaluable.

103. My seedlings start off well but then fall over, even though I mist them regularly. How can I keep them growing and healthy?

Violas can easily be grown from seeds, but be careful that you don't overwater the young seedlings as this can cause a fungal disease called 'damping off', which can kill a whole tray of seedlings overnight.

Based on your description it sounds like your seedlings are damping off due to overwatering, so it's best that you stop misting them. Water only enough to keep the soil slightly moist, like a wrung-out sponge. Also make sure they are in very bright light and have good air circulation. Finally, make sure they are spaced far enough apart from one another to allow light and air to circulate freely between them. Here are some pointers on seedlings you might find useful. As soon as they start to sprout, put them immediately into bright light. Make sure there is also some air circulation where you keep them – stagnant air can encourage fungal growth. Next, make sure the plants are thinned enough to allow for ample light and air to filter through them. Also, do not over-fertilise them. They do not need fertiliser until they have several sets of true leaves. Try watering by dribbling water gently and slowly out of a small can onto the soil rather than spraying them, because wet foliage will also encourage fungal growth. Finally, make sure all of your tools and equipment are clean and that you are using a relatively sterile potting mix. Other causes of damping off can also be too high or low a temperature or too little light. Last of all, you might have luck watering them with chamomile tea when you first see the problem begin to appear.

104. Do well-established shrubs need a lot of water in the summer or can they be left alone?

Shrubs as a rule prefer a soil that is evenly moist, yet well-drained so that it is not soggy or sopping wet. If yours have been in place and growing well for several years, they should not need supplemental watering at this point. However, if you experience several weeks of very dry weather or even worse, drought conditions, it is possible they would benefit from an occasional very deep soaking as opposed to frequent light watering. But in general, if they are planted in a suitable location, they should not need extra water unless they are showing signs of having dried out considerably.

105. My seedlings are very light green and almost yellow in places. Could I be watering too much?

A couple of things come to mind about your seedlings. If they have too much water, the roots won't properly form and the leaves will yellow. Also if they are older seedlings, with at least four true leaves, they may benefit from a weekly application of a dilute fertiliser such as liquid seaweed. Try cutting back on watering and giving them fertiliser and they should soon perk up. Also be sure they are growing in a sunny space with plenty of light.

Once they have developed two pairs of true leaves, seedlings will benefit from an application of diluted liquid fertiliser. Take care not to overwater them.

106. Can a soaker hose be left under the mulch over the winter or does it have to be pulled up?

As long as you drain water from the hose it should be fine during the winter months under a cover of mulch. Frozen water can cause the hose to burst.

107. Should I keep watering perennials and bulbs, such as lilies, once they die back to the ground?

Once the topgrowth of perennial plants is killed back by frost there should be no need to water unless the weather is exceptionally dry. They need a well-drained location (not soggy) with average moisture; in wet soil, they will rot over the winter. A new or established plant would possibly need watering to keep the soil somewhat moist but not sopping wet. In the heat of summer this might be once a week unless it has rained; by autumn, with its cooler temperatures and rainfall, you might not need to water at all. In spring, watering is not usually necessary. Use your finger to check the soil and see if it is damp or not. A layer of several 6–8 cm (2–3 in) of organic mulch, such as shredded bark, can help keep the soil shaded, cool and moist. In the spring, you should see new growth tips emerging and the plants elongating. Again, use your finger to see if the soil is moist or not and let that be your guide for watering.

Once the foliage of perennial plants, such as lilies, dies down for winter, it is not usually necessary to water them. In spring, when the new green growth emerges, keep an eye on the soil and water in dry spells.

Guidelines for Watering Your Plants

Watering plants at key times is vital to their health and development, but there's an art to getting it right. Too much or too little and they can die. Using contaminated water or splashing earth up onto foliage can also cause plants to become sickly or diseased. Fortunately, there are just a few guidelines to bear in mind that can make all the difference. First, try to always water directly to your plants' roots. Secondly, aim to give them a good drench rather than a light sprinkling because this encourages them to put their roots down more deeply where there is more moisture and they are in less danger of getting damaged by the sun. If in doubt, dig carefully under the soil to see how deeply the water is penetrating – you may be surprised to find it has only soaked through the top layer of soil.

Selecting Plants

A key way to avoid the problems caused by overwatering and under-watering is to choose your plants well so they suit the conditions that you have to offer. Some plants can handle drying out and will happily bounce back the minute they get a good drink, while others will quickly wilt and may never recover. If you have a dry, sunny spot, then look for varieties that are known for their tolerance of drought conditions and accept the fact that some plants just will not grow in these spots. You can choose from plenty of other options, such as fragrant and decorative Mediterranean herbs. Similarly, if you have a damp spot, choose plants that grow naturally in these conditions in the wild. There are lots of options that are very eye-catching, such as calla lilies, marsh marigolds, *lysimachia* 'Aurea' and astilbes. All are easy to grow and look great.

108. How do I set up a drip irrigation system?

Drip systems are easy to install. All the components are readily available, and kits will include detailed instructions, such as a grid so you can draw out the area and determine just which kinds of emitters you'll need for your plants. They'll also guide you through the planning and installation process. You may also need a backflow preventer or anti-siphon device, which is required to prevent water from the system reentering your water supply when the system is turned off.

109. Is it true that you should try to water your garden between 11 p.m. and 3 a.m.?

Watering at this time helps to conserve moisture because less will be lost to evaporation. It can also mean that more water is available during peak hours when people are using it for other things. Watering in the early morning hours will accomplish both these goals. There is a concern that some plants may be more susceptible to disease if their leaves get wet and remain wet all night. From a healthy plant standpoint, watering is best done in the very early morning so the leaves have a chance to dry out before nightfall. Watering in the sunlight, however, also gives you a chance to check on their general well-being.

110. I would like to construct a watering system for my plants. Where do I begin?

Start by taking accurate measurements of the beds and sketching them out on graph paper. Then take this with you when you go shopping. There are various kits available and they should detail on the box what area they cover and what you need. If in doubt, speak to a member of staff. Drip systems are easy to install, and can be fitted in an afternoon. Each hour invested in setting up a system could save hundreds of watering hours.

From a healthy plant standpoint, it is best to water in the very early morning so the leaves have a chance to dry out before nightfall.

111. We have a natural spring in our garden that creates a big mud hole. Which plants will thrive in these conditions?

There are a range of options that would appreciate a moist setting. Try perennials such as marsh marigold, Japanese iris, Siberian iris, *Iris pseudacorus*, astilbe, hosta and shrubs, such as small willows and dogwoods. If the spring is an all-seasons water supply, you might be able to open it up slightly and form a small natural pond. This would require consultation with a professional, but might be worth looking into for its decorative value – it could also be a boon for wildlife. You may find that it becomes your favourite part of the whole garden.

112. Is it harmful to spray a vegetable garden with water in direct sunlight?

It's unlikely to harm the leaves, although it is true that the water droplets can intensify the sunlight. If you stop to think about it, most plants survive the sunshine after a rainfall without undue problems. One thing to consider, however, is that overhead spraying is the least efficient method of watering because so much of the moisture is lost to evaporation. It can also contribute to foliar disease problems. So you might want to look into an alternative watering method, such as a drip system, which is far more efficient.

Laying a seeper hose is the most efficient way to water a vegetable garden. The moisture goes straight to the roots where it is most needed, and very little is lost through evaporation.

113. My ficus is dropping leaves at an alarming rate. Does it need more water?

If leaves are suddenly dropping from *Ficus benjamina*, the cause is almost always insufficient water. Try to keep the potting soil evenly moist. Begin by soaking the pot to moisten all of the soil (and remove air pockets) then watering as soon as the top of the soil begins to dry out. Be patient and your formerly healthy plant will regain its health and produce new foliage.

114. What is the best way to lay a soaker hose in a flower bed?

Try burying the hose just 2–5 cm (1–2 in) below the soil surface. Run the hose for an hour to work out how deeply the water penetrates the soil in that time, then carefully dig a hole to check how deep the water has gone. You may need to run the hose for a few hours to get enough saturation – you want the plants' entire root zone to be moist. Run the hose for as long as necessary in the morning. Generally, it's a better idea to water thoroughly less often than to water a little bit frequently. Light waterings won't penetrate the soil, so roots will tend to stay too shallow.

115. Last year my tomatoes got blossom-end rot. Could this be due to lack of calcium or sporadic watering?

Although blossom-end rot can be caused by a lack of calcium, the most common reason for it to actually happen is fluctuations in soil moisture. Using a mulch, amending the soil with ample organic matter, and watering deeply but less often (meaning, water heavily about once every five days in a hot summer rather than a light daily sprinkling) are good steps to take to prevent it.

Sporadic watering can cause a disease known as blossom-end rot, where the bottom of the fruits turn brown. The best way to prevent this is to enrich your soil with plenty of organic matter and apply a good mulch to retain moisture.

116. How do I know if I am watering my vegetable garden too much?

Watering is critical to plants but it is very easy to give them too much. How often you should water depends on how often it rains, how thirsty each type of crop is and how fast water evaporates in your climate. Soil type is another important factor. Clay soils hold water very well – sometimes too well. Sandy soils are like a sieve, letting the water run right through. Both kinds of soil can be improved with the addition of organic matter; it gives clay soils lightness and air while it gives sandy soils something to hold the water.

Generally, however, vegetable plants need about 2.5 cm (1 in) of water a week, preferably in the morning. If you water at night when the day is cooling off, the moisture is likely to stay on the foliage, increasing the danger of disease. When watering your vegetable garden, there is one rule you should follow: Always soak the soil thoroughly. A light sprinkling can often do more harm than no water at all. It stimulates the roots to come close to the surface, where they can be killed by exposure to the sun. One way to determine when to irrigate is to take a soil core sample from near the roots and squeeze it into a ball. If the ball holds together in the palm of your hand, the soil has sufficient water. If it crumbles, apply

When watering your vegetable garden, always soak the soil thoroughly rather than just giving it a light sprinkle. The best time to do this is in the morning.

water. At the crumble stage, the average soil will hold 2–3 cm³ of water per foot. If this water is applied with a sprinkler, determine its delivery by placing three or four cans under the sprinkler pattern to see how long it takes to accumulate an inch of water.

Applying Organic Material to Your Soil

The benefits of adding plenty of organic matter, such as well-rotted manure or compost to your beds can't be overemphasised. Even established beds will benefit from an application of a good layer of organic matter over the surface every year, just before winter. Any time or effort you invest in digging in manure will be returned many times over because you'll need to water and fertilise your plants far less often. By turning your soil into a rich loam, it will hold the optimum level of oxygen and moisture, and it will be easier for your plants' roots to grow deep into the earth. This will help them to cope with weather conditions, such as drought or strong winds.

117. We are experiencing a drought and my fir tree is turning brown. Will a daily application of fertilizer help?

Fertilising will not help a tree in drought stress – it needs water. Unfortunately, a daily light sprinkling encourages surface rooting where the soil dries out the fastest. The best way to water when it is hot is to apply it as a deep, slow soak about once a week or even every five days. Be sure to cover the entire root zone, which may extend past the dripline of the tree. The rule of thumb is 2–5 cm (1–2 in) a week from the hose or the sky. Your goal is to maintain a moist soil without it being sopping wet. You may need to dig down at first to see if the water is actually penetrating any distance at all, especially during very dry spells. Generous watering encourages the roots to grow deep where the soil moisture is more constant. Also maintain 5 cm (2 in) of organic mulch to help conserve moisture and keep the soil cool. This routine is recommended for all newly planted trees for the first year, with added watering in times of dry weather for the next two years.

Water Retention

Savvy gardeners have certain tricks up their sleeves to reduce the amount of time they need to spend watering. One is to use a generous layer of mulch. Covering the soil in your beds and borders with a generous layer of organic matter such as shredded bark, leaves or straw will keep off the sun and can be dug in as a soil improver at the end of the growing season. It has the added bonus of suppressing weed seedlings. These can grow very quickly and will compete with your plants for moisture. Gravel or decorative stone makes a good moisture-retentive mulch for plants in containers, which can dry out very quickly, so consider topping the potting soil in all your pots with a good layer.

118. Do roses need a dry period or can they be watered every day?

Roses, like most shrubs, prefer a good soaking followed by a dry period before another soaking. This allows the water to move down into the soil profile, pulling air with it as it goes. The length of the dry period varies with soil type, soil depth, temperature, the amount of sunlight the site receives and if the shrub is in a container or planted in the soil. In warm weather, watering once or twice a week will probably be sufficient, depending on the temperatures and amount of direct sun. However, in very sandy soil with no organic matter added, you may have to water more often. Container plants may need watering every day. If your plants get a bit too dry for too long, or too wet for too long, the older leaves will turn yellow and drop from the plant.

119. Does it matter that my lawn sprinkler system is in range of my tomato plants?

It is not a good idea to wet tomato foliage unnecessarily, especially in the evenings when it will tend to stay damp longer. This can invite fungal problems. Perhaps your lawn system can be adjusted slightly?

120. I want to conserve water in the summer. Can I reuse my used household water if there is soap in it?

This is very much about balance. 'Grey water' (water from household uses) is fine to use on most plants, but some will be more sensitive than others and the concentration and type of soap

You can use dishwater to water your plants without causing them any harm, especially if you use environmentally friendly dishwashing liquid.

Obviously, do not use any water run through the toilet because of the possibility of contamination. Avoid the use of kitchen waste water that contains grease or harsh cleaners, ammonia, bleach, softeners or non-biodegradable detergents. If using water from the bathtub or washing machine, use only mild, biodegradable soaps.

> If using water from the bathtub or washing machine, use only mild, biodegradable soaps, omit softeners and bleaches and allow the wash and rinse water to mix, if possible.

Omit softeners and bleaches. Allow the wash and rinse water to mix, if possible, to dilute the soap content. Never use a borax-containing product (such as laundry detergent) in water to be

may determine the degree of safety. For years people have used dishwater on plants with few ill effects. If you wish to use grey water on your vegetable garden, a few rules should be observed.

used on a garden because of the danger of applying plant-toxic levels of boron. Always apply grey water to the soil, not to plant leaves, whenever you can.

121. Is there anything we can plant in the dry soil underneath two pine trees?

Any plant with average water needs will always be in competition with the surrounding trees. And the trees will always win! In nature, very little grows under pines. Therefore, you should consider container gardening in this area. You could grow impatiens, begonias or any other shade-loving annuals in large containers under the trees. They wouldn't get competition from the trees' roots, which would reduce the amount of time you need to spend watering.

122. I'm going away for two weeks. What can I do to keep my houseplants healthy?

Simply use plastic bottles filled with water to keep houseplants hydrated. Your success will depend upon how large and thirsty the plants are and how long you'll be gone, so it's worth experimenting to see what works best for you. Start by thoroughly watering each plant. Allow excess water to drain and then insert a bottle of water with the bottom cut off into each container so that the section up to its shoulders is buried beneath the soil (see photo p. 69). When the soil begins to dry out it will wick the water out of the bottle. A large water bottle can keep the soil moist in a medium-sized pot for about two weeks. If you have larger containers or extra-thirsty plants, you may need to use two to three bottles per container. Try it out now so you'll have some idea of how long the water lasts in each one. A layer of mulch around plant can also help.

123. What plants can I use to help stop erosion on dry, sloped ground?

Plants with fibrous roots are best for holding soils in place. Some suggestions include *Clematis paniculata*, shrubby types of dogwood, low-growing types of *Cotoneaster*, juniper and *Euonymus*. Ornamental grasses are also a good choice, as are native grasses. Consider 'artificial' methods too in the short term, such as a layer of mulch.

Although they look very delicate, *Hemerocallis* or day lilies are surprisingly hardy, and there are many varieties that will cope well with drier soils. They also have fibrous roots, making them a good choice to plant on sloping sites.

124. How much should I water newly planted trees in the first three months?

A good rule of thumb is to water deeply once each week. Each tree will need about 2.5 cm (1 in) of water per week (unless it rains – then you may not need to water). Saturated or soggy soils will drive out oxygen and your trees' roots will need air as well as moisture for good growth. The best way to water new trees and shrubs is to make a watering well or water basin beneath each. Scrape out a little soil and mound it up in a circle around the main stem, about 30 cm (12 in) away from the stem or trunk. You'll need a 5- to 8-cm (2- to 3-in) mound of soil to make the basin. When it's finished, fill the basin with water, allow it to drain and then fill it a second time. Once a week is all it takes. This will concentrate the water over the root mass and allow it to trickle down, wetting the entire root system. Over time the mounded soil will erode and the basin will be gone, but by then your tree's roots should be well established.

125. I have many plants in containers. Should I give them all the same amount of water?

There's no set rule for watering plants in pots. Water when they are lightweight or when the top 1.25 cm ($^1/_2$ in) of soil is dry to the touch. As long as your containers have adequate drainage holes the soil will drain well enough to keep the roots healthy. You could upend cut-off water bottles in the containers to help direct water straight to the roots of thirsty plants like tomatoes and squashes.

As long as containers have adequate drainage, plants shouldn't suffer from being overwatered. You can make sure that water is getting to the roots by placing a water bottle with the bottom cut off up to its shoulders in the soil.

126. Is it necessary to water plants in foggy or misty weather?

Shrubs, trees and lawns need about 2.5 cm (1 in) of water per week when they're actively growing, and fog doesn't affect this too much. Most plants slow their rates of growth during the winter months and will require less water than in the summer months. If your plants look healthy, and they were planted more than one year ago, regular watering probably isn't necessary during the winter months. If the leaves begin to wilt, or the plants look stressed, supply water once every week to 10 days at any time of year. Give infrequent drenches rather than daily dribbles.

128. Is it true that watering from the top can wash off pollen?

You can water most plants with overhead sprinklers, and farmers often must. But drip watering is almost always better and more precise. Sprinklers (or rain) may wash away some pollen, but the main concern is disease. Splashing water or wet leaves can cause many plant diseases to spread. Sprinklers also waste some water to wind and evaporation, which is a big concern. Drip watering systems deliver water to the exact place it's needed: the soil at the bottom of the plant. The water is applied slowly and is able to soak in. Water doesn't blow away or run off and leaves stay dry, limiting disease problems. You should consider using a drip watering system.

Using a drip watering system is more efficient than using sprinklers because less moisture is lost to evaporation. It also avoids water and soil splashing onto leaves, which can spread diseases.

127. What type of shrubs can I plant in ground that is waterlogged in spring but dry in the summer?

Although there are some shrubs and trees that will tolerate wet feet in the spring, it's unlikely they would tolerate such flooding and standing water. You might want to consider working with a landscape architect or another professional with specialised training in grading and drainage to see if the flooding can be lessened or the run-off better controlled. Some shrubs and trees that tolerate damp soil include deciduous holly (*Ilex verticillata*), red chokeberry (*Aronia arbutifolia*), 'Henry's garnet' (*Itea virginica*), dogwood (*Cornus racemosa* and *C. sericea*), river birch (*Betula nigra*), red maple (*Acer rubrum*) and willow (*Salix*).

129. Can you recommend some perennials for an area that is hot and dry in the summer, and cold and wet in the winter?

Roses, hollyhocks and mallows are drought tolerant and hardy. Other great choices include lupines, liatris, stonecrop, evening primrose, phlox, achillea, verbascum, shasta daisy, peonies and daylilies. You'll increase the success of all your plants if you improve the soil with organic matter for good moisture retention and adequate drainage. This will also help ensure that the soil is slightly acidic (pH 6.0–6.5), which your flowers and any vegetables will also appreciate. Improving the soil by digging in sand and plenty of well-rotted organic matter is also well worth the time. The beneficial effects are very long-lasting.

130. Our garden is very dry and I've heard that weeds compete for moisture. What's the best way to deal with them?

Many cottage garden flowers such as lupines and phlox are quite drought tolerant. If you water them regularly in their first year, they put down deep roots and thrive in the future.

It's very tempting to buy weed killer when you see it in the shops, but it is rarely worth the expense. Not all herbicides are safe to use on all kinds of grasses or near other plants. The bottom line is that there is no one product that will kill off all weeds and still be safe for your lawn or flower beds. The best approach is to pull or dig the weeds out, starting in just one small area of the garden and working your way all around the plot. After you have removed the weeds you can either lay landscape fabric or several centimetres of mulch over the bare soil to keep new weeds from cropping up. To address problems of dry soil you can enrich it by incorporating lots of organic matter, such as potting soil. The organic matter will hold moisture for longer periods of time, which will help you conserve water. Then you can water deeply once or twice a week and still keep your plants happy.

131. When water from my sprinkler system gets on the leaves of my trees, it causes them to turn brown and die. Is there anything I can do?

It is strongly recommended that you water your trees at the soil level, rather than with a bore-water sprinkler – you are losing lots of precious water through evaporation. You can either set up a drip irrigation system or simply set the hose around the bottom of the trees, and allow water to trickle out until the ground is well saturated. You'll be helping your trees immensely, since more water will reach their roots, where they need it, and not leave deposits on the leaves. In fact, your trees may be turning brown because they aren't getting enough water by the sprinkler method.

Sprinklers are very effective for lawns but are not recommended for newly planted trees. They may not direct enough moisture to the roots where they need it.

Irrigation Systems

Most of us would love to have much more time to spend in our gardens. While going round with a watering can and tending to each plant's needs individually can be very relaxing and enjoyable, it's a luxury that few of us have the hours in the day to enjoy. Fortunately, there are a huge range of automatic irrigation systems available, so there are options for every size of project and every budget. Drip systems and hoses that can be buried just under the surface of the soil are often the most efficient and cost-effective options. What's more, many come with automatic timers so you can set them to come on in the morning. They are also a boon if you are going away, as they can be programmed to work in your absence.

132. My houseplants keep dying. Could I be overwatering them?

Try to keep the soil just moist – never bone dry and not sopping wet. When you water, be sure that the water has actually soaked the soil and not simply run out between the soil and the edge of the pot. Water well, allowing the excess to run off into the saucer but then empty the saucer a few minutes later. Plants use more water when they are actively growing, usually in spring and summer. They also need relatively more water in a brighter or warmer location than somewhere darker or cooler, so get into the habit of feeling the soil to see if you need to water or not. A plant in a large pot will need watering less frequently than one in a pot that is small. A very small pot may need frequent water-ing, because the soil mass naturally dries out quickly. Over-fertilising houseplants can also stress them; make sure you read and follow the label instructions and fertilise less during the winter when the plant naturally grows less.

Many plants are tolerant of under-fertilising, but a plant that is left in the same potting soil and not fertilised for an extended length of time will show signs of being in need of plant food. Also look out for spider mites. These just look like the leaves are drying out, but if you look carefully underneath the leaves you will see very fine webbing there. Wash the plant in tepid water once or twice a week to knock the mites off. Increasing humidity around the plant by setting it on a pebble tray can also help. Fill a tray with pebbles, set the pot on the pebbles and add water to just below the bottom of the pot. The water evaporating from the tray will humidify the immediate area. Another problem houseplants can get is scale. These pests look like flat little brown disks attached to the leaves or stem. During winter they can easily be rubbed off with a fingernail; simply inspect the entire plant carefully under a bright light.

Last but not least, sometimes the plants we purchase have nearly outgrown their pots and they are too crowded. This can make them wilt often and decline in quality. If your plant needs to be re-potted, try to match the same type of potting soil and move it up to a slightly larger pot rather than a much larger pot.

If you have small pots of flowers, you can simply immerse the pot under water to give it a good soak. This ensures that the water doesn't simply run down the sides of the pots where it is wasted.

133. Is it okay to dunk small pots of flowers such as geraniums in a tub of water rather than using a watering can?

You can immerse your plants in a tub to water them as long as you remove them once the soil is saturated and allow the excess water to drain. It can be a quick way to water lots of pots, it uses less water, and it means that the water is evenly distributed with no dry patches inside the pots. In the long term, use larger pots for your flowers, because these retain moisture better.

Plants use more water when they are actively growing, usually spring and summer. They also need relatively more water in a brighter or warmer location than somewhere darker or cooler.

Landscape
Gardening

It's all too easy to assume that the layout of your garden has to remain the way it looks on the day you move in, but there are a multitude of ways you can make your mark on the space – whether you have an afternoon to spare or you want to embark on a much bigger project. In this chapter, you'll discover all the ways you can enhance the setting for your home, and make it into a place where you can relax and enjoy all the other things you want to do.

Planning and Design

If you get the layout of your garden right, it will look attractive all year round, and your main tasks will be as simple as choosing and tending the plants you want to enjoy.

134. What non-invasive plants would thrive in a shady, shallow strip alongside a patio?

The soil's depth and width is just about enough for annuals and perennials but not for shrubs or tropical plants, which tend to have thick roots that could damage your patio. You could plant a mixture of perennials, such as hosta, bergenia and lenten rose, with bright annuals, such as coleus, impatiens, lobelia and pansies.

Aspect and Exposure

Taking note of the features you already have in your garden is an important first step. The area may be full of plants and trees, or it may be a plain, level square of turf. Two key things to consider are aspect and exposure. They will have a strong influence on all your practical decisions, such as what design element goes where, which materials you use, and how high to build your fences. It will also impact on the plants and structures you choose. The aspect of your plot will dictate what times different areas are in the sunshine, and this in turn makes a huge difference to where you site features, such as patios or decking.

135. Is it possible to create a container garden to bring height and colour to the edge of my patio?

If your area is sunny, you might try growing some climbing plants from seed in very large pots or even half barrels. Make sure there are drainage holes in the bottom of the containers and plant the seeds after your last expected frost date. Keep the soil moist but not soggy by watering as needed and provide plants with something to climb up, such as a trellis panel or even some netting stretched between supports. You could try sun-loving plants, such as morning glories and nasturtiums.

136. I'm designing a formal garden and would like *Buxus* for the boundary. Any ideas?

Buxus (also known as boxwood) is a relatively slow-growing shrub and the plants are fairly expensive in larger sizes. Rooted cuttings are cheaper and may be more suitable for a larger project like yours if you're prepared to wait for them to mature. Many garden centres offer them in the spring, but they can also be purchased reasonably by mail from speciality nurseries. Small plants establish quickly and can soon catch up with bigger options.

137. What can I plant in the dry ground between paving stones?

Shallow soil, with the added problem of radiated heat, will create an environment that would be very challenging for most types of plant, especially if the area is in full sun. You will have the best chances of success if you choose some of the smaller-leaved sedums, or woolly thyme, both of which can be extremely attractive and love to ramble between stones. Alternatively, gravel or tumbled slate can look very effective in these spaces and you can choose from a range of colours.

If you are erecting a permanent trellis, you may want to use raised beds and try some intensive planting techniques.

It can be difficult to get plants to grow well between paving stones. Sedums, creeping herbs and saxifrage are all good choices, or you could try using gravel or pebbles to fill the gaps.

138. How should I build permanent supports for climbing beans and squash around my vegetable garden?

There are many trellis designs for trellis using sturdy wooden posts, metal pipes or PVC, along with variations of twine, synthetic netting and wire mesh. They all have different advantages, depending on your budget and visual preference. If you are erecting a permanent trellis, you may want to use raised beds and try some intensive planting techniques to make the most of this very practical construction.

139. My home has a striking, contemporary design, and I'd like the exterior to have a modern look, too. Any ideas?

There are several ways you could go. One might be to use one single sculptural-looking plant and some very large boulders set in a sea of ground cover for a sort of zen effect. Another might be to use lush, bold foliage and vivid blooms for a tropical look. Yet another could be to do a Mondrian-esque design using groups of plants to create a geometric pattern separated by stark, dark-coloured pathways as borders. Since you are trying to do something striking, it is worth giving it detailed thought and careful planning. You will need to take into account the scale of the house and tie it together with the space around it. It may help to consult a professionally trained garden designer who can help you develop something unique and well suited to the architecture, the space and the growing conditions where you are planting. Books and magazines are also a good reference and can be valuable sources of inspiration.

140. Is it possible to buy mature trees to create instant impact?

You can purchase large trees, but their installation usually requires heavy equipment, and this can become expensive as a result. A local garden designer, landscape architect or large garden centre can give you an estimate on an installation. Bear in mind that larger trees can take longer to become established and, in many cases, a smaller tree will catch up to the larger one within just a few years. If you want to create height and visual impact more quickly, a pergola covered with a fast-growing vine would give you more immediate results, with the added bonus of not providing so much root competition for any other flowers and shrubs that you want to plant.

One way of creating a bold, modern look is to choose plants in bright primary colours, such as red, yellow and blue, offset by white paving and geometric shapes.

141. What's the best way to start designing my new garden?

It helps to measure the area carefully first and sketch it out on paper. Then decide where you want trees, shrubs and flowers. Consider where you'll have a seating area and where you'll put paths to connect these features. Do you want a pond, a pergola, a lawn or any other features? Check to see how much sunshine each area receives during the hot summer months, and note on your plan which parts are in sun and shade. Choose plants that you like, based upon their sunshine exposure, and set them in the garden. Most plants have labels detailing their eventual height and spread, so take this into account when you buy them. Then, while they are still in their pots, rearrange them until you're happy with the effect. If you want to enjoy an established look in the minimum of time, it's a good idea to buy three of each annual or perennial flower and plant them in groups rather than just dotting them around randomly. This creates a more natural effect.

When designing a new garden, think about what you want to achieve from the space. If it's a place to relax after work, then seating areas will be a priority, perhaps surrounded by scented plants. If it's a place to play with children, you may prefer a large lawn.

142. Can I use chamomile to grow across a path or will it be patchy?

Chamomile (*Chamaemelum nobile*) forms a soft-textured, spreading mat of bright, light green, finely cut, aromatic leaves. The most commonly grown form has small yellow buttons of summer-blooming flower heads, while others have little daisy-like flower heads. It makes a great ground cover or lawn substitute, especially if mowed or sheared occasionally. Chamomile will continue to spread, so it will fill any gaps you may initially have in the path. If any bare patches do arise, you can reseed each spring, dig and divide the plants, or just be patient and allow the plants to fill in at their own pace. Regular clipping or mowing will keep the plants neat and produce additional lateral growth.

Many gardens are close to nearby properties, but you can still create a private space of your own with the use of clever planting. Using structures, such as a trellis or obelisks, right next to the patio can be more effective than planting tall trees on the boundary.

Ensuring Privacy

For most of us, an element of privacy is very important if you want to be able to enjoy relaxing in the garden. Nobody wants to be seen while they sunbathe, or even get lost in a good book, so it's worthwhile thinking about the positioning of the windows of nearby houses in relation to your plot. Will the person next door be able to watch over your patio while you eat? Or will your neighbours be able to overhear conversations through the fence? You will find it hard to relax in a garden that does not feel private, so it's well worth planning to include hedges, trellis or other measures to help you enjoy a sense of seclusion. Even the soothing addition of a trickling water feature can bring a sense of peace.

143. What decorative plants would offer privacy around a patio?

You might consider some shorter shrubs along with a small flowering tree, such as a cherry or crab apple. This, in turn, could be underplanted with bulbs and ground cover, or perhaps some containers filled with vivid annuals. If you want to create a sense of privacy for the spot, it is often more effective to plant a larger shrub very close to where you are sitting than to plant a hedge or tall tree further out on the boundary of your property. For the same reason, a trellis panel or a large obelisk with a climbing rose can be more effective and makes very efficient use of space.

Your finished design should look like little steps, which also have far more visual impact than a sloping path.

144. Should I use topsoil or sand to build up the level of my garden?

The best option is to use topsoil, and get a three-way mix. This will contain garden soil, organic matter (such as potting soil) and sand. This will be freely draining, but will also have the benefit of being able to retain moisture due to the high percentage of organic material. You will then have the best possible growing medium for any plants that you choose. Time invested now in getting this right could save hours of work in the future.

145. Is it difficult to replace a small lawn with a patio?

The amount of work depends on how formal an effect you want. Ideally, you would remove the sod, create a compacted base layer and then top that with levelled sand, before adding ornamental paving, such as paver bricks, flagstones or other units. This requires a rigid edging system to stay in place. Most supply yards will provide installation instructions for their products. In a less formal setting, you could lay down some weed barrier matting, top that with several centimetres of gravel, and possibly roll it occasionally to keep the surface a bit firmer. The gravel would need to be topped off from time to time because it will settle due to the foot traffic. An edging is also a good idea to keep the gravel from migrating sideways. Either method is usually possible, although time-consuming for the average person who is

Laying paving can be hard work, and unless you're experienced, you may prefer to get professionals to do it for you. However, the results will be longlasting and very low maintenance.

fairly fit. Gravel, sand and pavers are all very heavy. Although hard paving would take longer to lay in the first place, it would require less work in the long run, and will require a lot less upkeep than a lawn, so consider your options carefully.

146. When laying pavers down a slope, should they be kept level?

It's very important to keep the pavers level by building up the soil on the lowest end of each paving slab. Otherwise, you could slip down the slope when the pavers are wet or in frosty weather. Your finished design should look like little steps, which also have far more visual impact than a sloping path.

147. What flowers and shrubs can I plant to attract birds?

There are many ways you could make your garden more attractive to wildlife. The most important things to offer are shelter, food and water. Your ideal planting plan should provide birds with shelter during the winter, a spot to visit for food and water, and possibly a nesting area or materials. Aim to plant a range of deciduous and evergreen plants to allow birds to pick and choose while passing through. In nature, birds seem to prefer the edges of places, such as the line where forest meets field, because it allows a protective cover and an open view, plus the widest variety of plants. You might try to mimic this in your planting by adding some smaller trees, such as serviceberry (*Amelanchier*) and dogwoods, and some berried shrubs. Viburnum berries are very popular, as are fruits, such as raspberries and crab apples.

Sunflowers are very easy to grow, and they attract bees and butterflies while in bloom. Then the seeds are a valuable source of food for wild birds.

Add some flowers that can be left going to seed at the end of summer (purple coneflowers, black-eyed Susans, sunflowers and zinnias are all good choices).

Thorny bushes, such as barberry also provide security from cats. Hang up feeders all year round and bear in mind that clean water is probably the most important attractant you can provide – change it every day in summer and winter for best results. Locate the water source in an area where the birds will feel secure, where they can easily see out around them across low plants or open ground. They also like a perching spot nearby so they can stop and survey the area before approaching the water and relaxing to drink and bathe.

Other important consideration are to reduce the use of artificial chemicals in your garden so that you do not endanger the birds you are trying to attract, and also to allow for some slightly relaxed areas to occur. Nature is never quite so tidy, and the birds use snips of twig and grass and stem to make their nests, and take shelter in brush and twiggy overgrowths. You may need to adapt your trimming schedule to accommodate nesting birds, or accept some insect damage to protect the bird habitat. With luck, you will also find many butterflies frequenting the area as well.

148. Can I use wood ashes to create a woodland path?

As long as you are confident that you won't want to change the placement of your paths at a later date, and that you don't want to plant any acid-loving plants right next to the path, that would be a good way to 'recycle' your wood ashes. However, remember that ashes get messy when wet, so put a thick layer of wood chips over them as this will give an attractive but inexpensive finish.

149. What plants can I use to create a hedge in a shady area with clay soil?

Unfortunately, most shrubs also require a certain amount of sun to do well, and in less than optimum light will grow leggy and thin rather than dense, as is needed for a successful hedge. Since you have a heavy clay soil, you might be better to use a fence and train vines, such as Virginia creeper or clematis up it. Both will tolerate a good bit of shade and could be directed to grow in an attractive shape. Another possibility would be the various evergreen *Euonymus* species. These will grow as shrubs or, when a support is available, will also climb, thus allowing you to keep the planting narrow.

150. Can you offer any tips on planning a raised garden?

Raised beds can be created from brick, stone, or wood or can simply be made by raking garden soil into broad, flat-topped planting beds. Raised beds are common in cooler areas because they help the soil to drain, and also warm up in the spring. They can also help to make the most of a small area by providing height and visual interest.

Any type of plant can be grown in a raised bed. One thing to take into consideration is the size of the plant and the depth of the bed. For example, to grow large shrubs, you'll need a bed with soil deep enough to accommodate those roots but most vegetables will be less fussy than this.

Creating raised beds is a great way to bring interest to a small plot, and you can use trailing plants to soften the edges of the design, creating an established look.

Minimising Exposure to Wind and Cold

Many plots suffer from wind exposure. You can minimise the effect through sensible planting and with garden structures, such as trellis panels. It's worth noting that a permeable obstacle, such as a hedge or an open fence, will do more to improve conditions in windy weather than a solid structure like a wall. This is because the wind is deflected, filtered and slowed down. Forcing it over or around a large object can make it worse by creating a vortex of rapidly moving air, which is uncomfortable for you and your plants. Factoring in exposure to the cold is important when choosing what plants to grow. More tender subjects will prosper in a sheltered position against a warm wall.

the rose as you can without disturbing the roots – 30 cm (12 in) or 50 cm (18 in) away should be okay. The rose can be trained in that direction and tied in as needed until it hooks itself through the trellis.

151. Is it possible to build a trellis behind an established climbing rose?

This depends on where you planted the rose. If it is up against a building, you will need to somehow slide the trellis in behind it. Make sure there is a gap of several centimetres between the trellis and the building to allow for air flow and provide space for the rose canes through it. If it is out in the open, position it so that the wind blows the rose against the trellis framework, or if it is a very windy spot, you might want to set the trellis at a ninety degree angle to the wind so it does not act like a sail. If you want a permanent pillar-type support, simply put it as close to

152. I would like to build a formal garden with beds and brick paths. Any ideas?

Why not make a series of symmetrical square beds in the middle of the plot and place a birdbath or sundial in the very centre as a focal point, with benches at the sides? This classic layout can be used effectively to grow flowers or vegetables and you can then either plant the edges with shrubs or berry bushes. The best way to figure it out is to use graph paper, pencil and a good eraser! If you don't mind spending some money, you can always consult with a local landscaper or garden designer as their years of experience can prove to be invaluable.

Drawing a Garden Plan to Scale

When you're creating a scale plan of your plot, it can be helpful to start with the boundaries and work inward, double-checking each measurement as you go along. Any time you invest at this early stage will be rewarded when you make your decisions, because accurate information will allow you to assess which features you can fit. It will also help you buy the right quantities of any turf, plants and materials. A surveyor's tape measure is the ideal tool for this task. Enlist the help of a friend or relative to hold the tape taught and horizontal (if it flops, the measurements will be inaccurate) and to write down the measurements as you call them out.

153. What's the best way to build wooden windowboxes?

The width of the windows determines the final length of the planter. The depth and height should be large enough to hold enough soil to retain moisture for a few days. To support the weight of the filled box you'll need metal or wooden brackets. Pine is too soft for a project of this nature, so choose sustainably grown cyprus, cedar, teak or mahogany. Cut the pieces to the required lengths and glue them together. Use bar clamps to secure all pieces during drying. Next measure, cut and secure the bottom piece so it has a snug fit. Apply a bead of glue inside the bottom edges of the planter, align the bottom with the bottom edges of front, back and side pieces, then use a mallet to tap them into place. Use screws to secure the bottom piece to the edges of the side, front and back pieces, and for added strength elsewhere. Drill drainage holes in the bottom, spaced about 30 cm (12 in) apart, beginning about 15 cm (6 in) from each end. Once the planter is completed, choose a finish to protect the wood and add colour if desired. Plain wood can turn grey, dry out and rot without protection, so stain or paint is vital to this project's longevity.

154. What cheerful plants do you recommend for beds around a shady patio?

In a mostly shady spot, you could grow a selection of low-maintenance perennials including hosta, heuchera, columbine (*Aquilegia*), bergenia, campanula, lily-of-the-valley, bleeding heart (*Dicentra*), sweet woodruff, gentian, iris, primrose, astilbe and violets. Vivid annuals that are happy in shade include pansies and begonias.

If your patio is often in the shade, you can still grow a selection of attractive plants including hosta, with their large decorative leaves, and cheerful pansies.

When planning a new garden, take into account the practical aspects of the boundaries. In addition to looking decorative, your fence may be necessary for keeping out deer or rabbits.

155. How can I keep deer out of my garden without blocking the view?

Unfortunately, the safest recommendation is a fence because the hungrier deer are the more plants they learn to eat, and a garden is an open invitation. Deer can easily leap over a standard picket fence; it may be safer to make a taller obstacle by using the posts for a decorative fence to support taller extensions, which in turn support wire strands or plastic deer netting up to 2.5–3 m (8–10 ft). This is relatively invisible and usually extremely effective, with the added advantage of not being too expensive.

156. Any tips on planning a garden in the shade that has damp soil?

It is nearly impossible to get grass to grow in the shade, even with careful soil preparation and ongoing care, so it's highly recommended to use ground cover plants instead of turf. You can plant perennials that tolerate soggy soils or, if you know where the water is coming from, you can install a curtain drain to help redirect excess water. Or you could mound up soil in a type of raised island on the wettest areas. Mounding the soil up by 0.5–1 m (2–3 ft) will keep the roots of your plants high and dry and give you more planting options. Some plants that tolerate soggy soils include red maple (*Acer rubrum*), bugleweed (*Ajuga*), serviceberry (*Amelanchier*), astilbe, dogwood (*Cornus*), forsythia, daylilies (*Hemerocallis*), hosta, sweetspire (*Itea*) and maiden grass (*Miscanthus*).

157. Is there a thick-growing hedge we can plant to keep our dog in our garden?

Experience suggests that no hedge will contain a dog who is determined to get out. There is always a gap somewhere! To be on the safe side, it's probably worth it to erect a fence, and then plant shrubs inside or outside the fence to provide a visual screen. You could also grow vines on the fence to soften the appearance.

158. How can I make a path of stepping stones in a muddy area?

Unless a suitable foundation is placed beneath them, any stones you lay will simply sink beneath the mud. You can lay a layer of sand topped with a length of weed barrier cloth down on the soil and place new stones on top. The sand and weed barrier will keep the stones from sinking down into the soil.

159. What fast-growing tree could we plant to offer privacy?

Poplars are always reliably fast-growing and make great privacy screens. They have a colum-nar shape and are deciduous. Evergreen tree options include various types of pine, Chinese holly and Chinese privet. The better you prepare the growing site and care for the trees during their first few years, the faster they should fill the space to provide a screen.

160. What is the best way to lay out a low-maintenance shrub garden?

The standard practice is to put the taller trees and shrubs in the back of the garden, then the lower growing shrubs closer to the front. This way nothing will be blocked from view and everything will be able to perform well. Shrubs, such as weigelas, rhododendrons and azaleas will all grow to be fairly large. Japanese maples are slow growing, and depending upon which cultivars you have will probably remain smaller than the rhododendrons. Choose a range of different shades and shapes of foliage, and take the time to set the plants out so you can decide how they look best before you plant them.

Time Is Precious

Relaxation is the main reason for having a garden for most people. We all relax in different ways, at different times in our lives. Your priorities might be space to play with the kids, somewhere to throw a party for friends and family, or just a space where you can enjoy a comfy lounger chair, a cold drink, and a good book. Unless you're a very enthusiastic gardener, you probably don't want to spend hours working on your plot every week, but most of us really enjoy the time we do spend outdoors. Fortunately, many of the plants and other products available in nurseries have been selected to be suitable for those of us who don't have much time to spare. Landscaping can really help with this; by choosing the right materials, you can save yourself a lot of effort.

161. Which are the most inexpensive options for building paths?

Wood chips are a very economical choice for paths, although they do rot over time. Larger and harder bark chips last longer, but they can be a bit uncomfortable to walk on. Recycling is becoming increasingly popular, and when people redo their landscapes they may offer materials, such as bricks, pavers and pea gravel for free to people who are prepared to collect it. So look on relevant websites and check your local media. Other budget-conscious options for paths include commercial pavers, flagstone, slate and crushed limestone.

Do your research before you invest in new materials for your pathways. It can be possible to pick up pavers very reasonably, if you shop around.

Deciding on Layout

Once your measurements are all sketched out, you can consider how you'll lay out your garden and where you'll put pathways from one area to another. Spend time thinking about how you can create experiences and interest along each stage of the journey. Straight lines and regular spacings of vertical objects will make your garden feel smart and formal, which is ideal if you have a house to match. Alternatively, curves and circles, combined with irregular planting, will give a sense of relaxed, almost accidental informality. You can mix them both in different parts of your layout, but this should be carefully planned at the design stage. Consider creating vistas – perhaps with a seating area or with a birdbath, sundial or statue at the end. Even the smallest plot can be enhanced by a carefully considered focal point.

162. What do you suggest for beginners with absolutely no clue about garden design?

Perhaps the best approach is to do a little reading first so that you have a background on what plants require in terms of growing conditions and soil preparation, and to glean a few ideas about what grows best in your region. Sketch out your ideal garden on paper and visit lots of nurseries and garden centres to take notes on the plants that especially appeal to you so you can include them in your landscape. Start with just one area of the landscape and work your way through the space gradually, sketching your dream garden.

163. How can we discourage squirrels from living on our new deck?

Although they can be fun to watch, squirrels can also be pests. You might try using a commercial squirrel repellent, or a homemade one based on qalia chips available from your nursery. Some people report that a pet dog works as a great deterrent, too. Once you have made your deck less attractive to squirrels, perhaps you can set up another, separate area, possibly even with food for them, that they would prefer to use – sort of a 'bait and switch' operation. Then you can enjoy watching them from a more suitable distance.

164. How can I keep noisy pigeons away from my balcony garden?

One option is 'scare-eye' balloons, which have various markings on the sides intended to frighten the birds. You can also try streamers, which flutter in the wind and scare birds away, or hang unwanted compact discs on wires. Another trick is to use a decoy. These are made to look like the birds' natural predators and could be hung on a wire above your balcony. For best results, move it around from time to time, so the birds don't get too familiar with it! Alternatively, you could have fun making a traditional scarecrow – again, moving it around will help to fool the birds.

165. How do I get rid of a gravelled area so that I can start building a new lawn?

You will need to remove the gravel and then take up the underlying landscape fabric. If this covers a large area, you may need to consider how you'll dispose of all the gravel in advance. It may be possible to advertise it locally and get someone who could use it to take it away for free, or perhaps you could use it elsewhere on your garden. Then loosen the soil down at least 15 cm (6 in) and work in a generous amount of potting soil. Also run some basic soil tests to check the fertility and soil pH. Add fertiliser and amendments as indicated by the soil tests. Then level the area and rake the surface smooth. At this point you will be ready to plant your new lawn or lay turf.

Balcony gardens can be very attractive to birds, because they will feel safe from most of their predators. However, if they become a problem, you can use decoys to repel them.

Trees, Shrubs and Vines

The larger plants in your garden offer height, structure and year-round interest. Once fully developed, they will change the whole feel of the space, so choose them with care.

166. Can you recommend a simple care routine for my topiary shrubs?

Plant shrubs during cool times of the year, and water them regularly, especially in their first year. You will also want to keep your topiary pruned to maintain its shape. Cut away any errant branches and give the entire shrub an overall trim once or twice a year, depending on how fast it grows. If you allow it to lose its original shape it will be difficult to get the look back again, so take your shears to it a little whenever it looks like it is beginning to lose its shape. You'll soon become adept at it!

167. My shrubs need to be cut back dramatically. How should I go about this?

You can certainly renovate overgrown shrubs, but it's a commitment that will take some time. If you remove more than one-third of the live material on a plant, you'll put it under severe stress, making it more vulnerable to pests and diseases. Plan on taking two or three years to prune each shrub into shape, and prune in late spring, after the plants have finished flowering. Just cut back one-third of the oldest branches to a node, where you can expect two stems will grow where you've removed one. This will help them to fill in and look bushy, rather than straggly. If you plan each cut, your shrubs will continue to grow strongly and, at the end of two seasons, they'll be a more manageable size.

Although topiary is a traditional art, it can also look exciting and modern. Shrubs will need to be trimmed at least twice a year to maintain their interesting shapes.

168. When should I prune my clematis plants?

There are different forms of clematis, including deciduous and evergreen types. Some bloom on wood grown the previous year and some on wood grown in the same year. Clematis in the Jackman group of hybrids (such as *C. jackmanii*) bloom on new growth (wood grown in the same year). You'll have to watch where the blossoms occur on your plants to determine if they are on new or old wood. You can prune the Jackman clematis in spring as the buds swell or slightly before. You can prune to within 10–15 cm (4–6 in) of the bottom if you wish. If the clematis flowers on old wood, only prune any dead or broken growth in the spring. Then, after flowering, a portion of old shoots should be cut back severely. Clematis enjoy soil enriched with plenty of organic matter. Give them lots of compost or composted manure. Clematis prefer to have their heads in the sun and their feet in the shade, so mulch is helpful to keep roots cool and to keep competing weeds at bay.

People are often unsure when to prune clematis, but there are two simple rules: If it flowers on new wood, prune it in the spring, and if it flowers on old wood, prune it after flowering.

Clematis enjoy soil enriched with plenty of organic matter. Give them lots of compost or composted manure.

The Benefits of Regular Pruning

Pruning and cutting back trees, shrubs and vines is more than controlling their size, cutting out any parts that are crossing over, or showing signs of damage or disease. Annual pruning also has a more nurturing role; you can use it to keep the plants, such as shrubs and climbers that provide the backbone of your garden in tip-top health. The judicious use of a sharp pair of pruners will help to give them room for strong young stems to grow through. On many shrubs and trees, the flowering and fruiting occurs on this new growth, which is why many (but not all) plants are pruned in spring. For example, hardy fuchsias, hydrangea, mahonia, *Sambucus*, santolina and *Spiraea japonica* all benefit from an early spring trim.

169. Can I grow azaleas in the pots they were supplied in at the nursery?

You should be able to keep your azaleas in the same nursery pots for another year or so but, if you have them sitting on cement in full sunshine, the nursery pot can absorb heat and literally bake the roots. So, you would be better off planting them in a larger container, as the extra layer of potting soil will help to insulate the roots from excessive heat and the plants won't dry out so quickly. For best results, move the plants to an area where they get morning sun and afternoon shade or partial shade. This will help keep the roots from overheating. Water thoroughly when the top 2.5 cm (1 in) of soil is dry to the touch. Sometimes plants in containers develop air pockets around the roots and, even though you think you're watering thoroughly, most of the water will simply pour out of the drainage holes. To make sure there are no air pockets in the soil you can immerse the pot in a larger container of water and let it set for 15 to 20 minutes. When no more air bubbles rise to the surface you can take the pot out of the container and allow it to drain.

170. What fast-growing climber can we plant to hide an unsightly shed?

Vining plants that are suitable for the trellis include Virginia creeper (*Parthenocissus quinque-folia*); Boston ivy (*Parthenocissus tricuspidata*), English ivy (*Hedera helix*) and fiveleaf akebia (*Akebia quinata*). Bear in mind that anything that is fast growing won't just stop when it gets to the size you were hoping for. In future, you will need to prune it to keep it in shape and ensure it doesn't take over the rest of your garden.

Azaleas are a very decorative flowering shrub that can be grown in large containers. For best results, position them in a spot where they only get full sun in the morning.

171. I'm looking for a small, decorative tree. Any ideas?

There are a few ornamental trees you might consider, such as a weeping cherry (*Prunus avium*). This slow-growing dwarf cherry has graceful branches that droop to the ground. Each spring it dons a floral cloak of pure white flowers to rival the elegance of any ornamental. It reaches a height of 30–40 cm (12–15 in), and spreads 15–20 cm (6–8 in). What's more, it's hardy, disease-resistant and tends to be very insect-resistant. Another option is a dwarf flowering almond (*Prunus glandulosa*). This is a spreading, multi-stemmed shrub that grows 1–1.5 m (4–5 ft) tall and 0.9–1.2 m (3–4 ft) wide. Its chief value is in the showy flowers, which are either white or pink, single or double, and appear in mid-spring. You might also consider a dwarf weeping pussy willow. It doesn't flower but gets interesting catkins in late winter or early spring and it isn't too big.

172. How should I start a woodland garden?

Most traditional woodland plants require a soil high in humus, so you will probably need to add copious amounts of organic matter to the soil before planting. You might also want to run some basic soil tests to check the pH, as many of these plants also require an acid soil. There are many options to consider, and you may find that the light varies from place to place and will require some experimentation. Some easier plants to start with might include azaleas, hydrangeas and summer blooming spireas. For bulbs, crocus, many daffodils,

Flowering trees are a boon for wildlife and can help to attract bees to your garden. Ensure you water them well during their first year while the roots are getting established.

grape hyacinths, *Scilla*, *Chionodoxa* and wood hyacinths often naturalise well in woodsy areas. Ground cover plants could include *Dianella* and *Lomandra* but could also feature any other plant that is either a native or prone to naturalising in your area or prone to spread where it is happy. Some to consider might be *Poa*, *Correa*, *Hibbertia* and *Grevillea laurifolia*.

173. How and when should I prune honeysuckle?

Honeysuckle shrubs should be pruned right after they bloom in the spring. The pruning can be as drastic as needed to control size and to shape the plant. Annual pruning should be carried out to thin the plant by cutting a portion of the stems or trunks at the bottom. Shrubs may also be rejuvenated by cutting them to the ground in very early spring; this may be necessary if the shrub has been neglected for a number of years. Honeysuckle vines can be trimmed right after the main spring bloom as needed to control size. For both types, any dead wood can be removed at any time, although the vines tend to leaf out very late in spring so be a little patient before deciding a portion of the vine is dead.

Don't be fooled into trimming back what appears to be dead wood on your honeysuckle after winter. Even perfectly healthy stems may not produce leaves until late spring.

174. Can ivy harm trees by growing up into them?

Ivy can cause all kinds of problems when it is allowed to climb up tree trunks. It can hold too much moisture against the bark, leading to rot. It can cause splitting of the outer bark of the tree due to the sheer force of the growing vines. If it's allowed to climb up very far, it can become heavy enough to cause stress to the tree and it can act as a sail, catching wind and pulling it over. Add this to the potential of strangulation and girdling, and you'll see it would be a wise decision to remove the ivy from the tree. At a minimum, cut enough ivy away to expose the flare of the tree trunk where it meets the ground. It would be even better to remove the ivy within a metre of the trunk. After removing the roots and cutting the vines at ground level, pull what you can from the tree. This might mean that you'll have to cut the intertwining vines and pull them off in pieces, which may take a while depending on the extent of the plant's growth. Any parts of the plant that you can't reach to remove (including the disk-like pads), will eventually weather away. Don't worry too much about removing the pads – they won't produce new plants. And, unless a piece of an ivy vine has got a foothold in a crevice or other moisture-holding spot on the tree, the vine should die off after being cut at ground level.

Although clematis and roses will bloom more prolifically in a sunny spot, they will still do well if they get four to six hours of sunshine a day.

175. What climbers can I plant in a spot with partial shade?

Climbing hydrangea would be perfect for a shady site, and in fact the dainty blooms last longer in the shade than they would in a sunny spot. Trumpet vine (*Campsis radicans*) is another suggestion; it has bright, exotic-looking flowers and is surprisingly hardy. If the spot gets over four hours of sunshine a day, then roses and clematis are also good options. You'll need to provide wooden posts or a trellis for them to climb. Alternatively, you could string some steel wire between sturdy wooden or metal supports and anchor it to the ground so your plants will have some support.

The Value of Shrubs

Although some people may not consider them to be as glamorous as trees and flowers, shrubs are often the most important plants in the garden. They can provide the basic framework that holds the rest of the planting plan together. They are a boon for busy gardeners, as many of them are very low-maintenance. Indeed, if you prepare the soil correctly, by incorporating plenty of organic matter, such as well-rotted manure, before you plant them, many shrubs will need little more care than regular watering — after their first year, most will only need watering during very dry spells. Choose a mixture of flowering shrubs, evergreens and options with red or variegated foliage. This will provide variety and year-round interest, as well as being the perfect backdrop for your flowers.

176. Is there a general rule of thumb for pruning shrubs?

Most deciduous shrubs are pruned according to when they bloom. Early-spring bloomers are pruned immediately after they bloom because they flower on old wood from the year before. Late-season bloomers set flower on the current year's growth and so may be pruned in late winter or early spring before growth begins for the year.

If you have limited space, look out for trees and shrubs that won't exceed a certain height and spread even when they reach maturity.

177. What can I do to help plants grow under my large trees?

Tree roots are naturally attracted to rich, moist soil, so you can't blame them for invading your garden area. You can sink a barrier into the ground on the tree side by digging a narrow trench and laying corrugated panels on their sides. These are typically used as patio or carport coverings and come in 60- to 75-cm (24- to 30-in) widths that are 15–30 cm (6–12 ft) long. They make great barriers for containing bamboo roots and for keeping out tree roots. Alternatively, you could plant in a raised bed rather than at ground level or line the sides and the bottom of your garden with weed barrier or screening material.

178. Can you please tell me how fast 'slow-growing' trees will grow per year, on average?

The ultimate growth rate depends on a number of factors, including climate, soil conditions and general care. However, the nursery industry uses the following guidelines, which may be helpful as a general rule of thumb: on average, trees in the slow-growing category will grow less than 30 cm (12 in) per year. Those in the moderate-growth category will generally grow 30–60 cm (12–24 in) per year. Trees considered to be fast-growing will grow up to 64 cm (25 in) per year. If you are planting trees and shrubs, take their eventual height and spread into account – if the spaces between them look bare, plant annuals as fillers.

179. I would like to plant a fragrant wisteria. What should I choose?

Chinese wisteria is the most commonly grown option. It has extremely decorative long umbels of blooms in lilac, purple or white, but is the least fragrant. If fragrance is what you're looking for, plant Japanese wisteria. Spring is the best time to plant either of these climbers but, if you buy one in autumn, you can also plant it then. Just be sure to keep your wisteria well watered during dry weather for the first year. It may take a while to get established and start flowering, but it will certainly be well worth the wait!

Wisteria is one of the best possible climbing plants you can choose as it is extremely hardy and in good years it will flower in spring and then again towards the end of summer.

180. How should I prune my wisteria to encourage blooming and keep it neat?

Considerable confusion exists about pruning wisteria. The two species most commonly grown are Japanese wisteria (*Wisteria floribunda*) and Chinese wisteria (*Wisteria sinensis*), both of which bloom before or with the unfolding of the leaves. Pruning wisteria extensively during the dormant season may encourage rampant vegetative growth the next spring. Instead, in July, prune out the long, straggly growth except those branches needed for climbing. This is more likely than anything else to induce flowering. Shoots should be cut back one-third to one-half their length. This will induce them to produce the short spurs that will bear next season's flower clusters. Wisterias are normally vines, but pruning can make them take shrubby or weeping forms. Heading back young shoots holds the height at a definite point and after several years, the plant produces a trunk-like stem. Then leaders can be allowed to droop towards the ground. Wisteria will bloom abundantly if planted in good garden loam with full sun, watered well the first growing season and pruned in the summer. Encourage a second flush of blooms in late summer with regular pruning.

> Wisteria will bloom abundantly if planted in good garden loam with full sun, watered well the first growing season and pruned in the summer.

181. Do Japanese maples look attractive all year round?

Also known as *Acers*, Japanese maples are understandably popular. You can choose varieties with foliage in different shades of green or burgundy and it often turns into dazzling shades of gold or scarlet by the end of summer.

Japanese maples (*Acer palmatum*) are very ornamental trees. 'Crimson Queen', for example, has bright red new leaves. The vivid shade persists throughout the summer, changing to scarlet as the weather cools. The tree isn't messy, but does drop leaves just before winter. You can expect a mature height of 3 m (10 ft) and a canopy spread of about 3.65 m (12 ft). Plant in full sunshine, in average garden soil.

It is never a good idea to change the soil grade or build anything over the roots of a tree. The roots can suffocate if you add soil over the top, or the bark can rot.

182. Can I build a raised bed around the trunk of my maple tree?

It is never a good idea to change the soil grade or build anything over the roots of a tree. The roots can actually suffocate if you add soil over the top, or the bark can rot. Instead, why not plant in some containers and group them near the bottom of your tree? You can even add a bench beneath the tree and set a few pots of colourful flowers by it. White foxgloves are ideal.

183. Our variegated weigela now has mostly green leaves. What can we do?

In some case, variegated plants are grafted, meaning the variegated top is literally attached to a robust set of roots. You may find that the roots have overgrown the top grafted section. If this is the case, prune off the green-leafed branches, being careful to get right down to where they emerge from the root itself. Continue to regularly remove any that may appear. In other cases, a variegation may not be totally stable and both variegated and green-leafed shoots will spring off one branch. If this is the case, prune off any green shoots but be careful not to damage the branch itself. Again, check for these and remove them as they appear – they will tend to be more vigorous than the variegated stems.

184. What flowering shrub can I use to brighten up a shady spot?

Variegated pittosporum features beautiful creamy white and green variegated foliage. The flowers go unnoticed against the foliage, but they are pleasantly fragrant, perfuming your garden for weeks with the sweet smell of orange blossoms. It is fast-growing and will need some trimming when young. Best of all, it thrives in sun or shade and is not picky about the soil so long as it is loose and well-drained. This shrub is useful in landscape beds and islands as a background. You can also use it as a natural or formal hedge, and it can be a stand-alone specimen or tree form when pruned properly. It's exceptionally heat- and drought-tolerant.

185. Do bougainvillea plants need to be taken into a greenhouse over winter?

Bougainvilleas will die in very cold weather, so unless you can offer your plant a particularly mild spot that you're confident will never freeze, it would be risky to leave it out. It would be safer to bring it in for the winter, so long as you have a very sunny window for it to enjoy. Leave it in the pot and water sparingly, then take it outside again in spring when all danger of frost is over.

Native to South America, bougainvilleas flower most profusely in very sunny spots. They are very decorative and drought tolerant, but they will not survive a frost.

186. What low-maintenance, tall shrubs or short trees would you suggest for a sunny spot?

For easiest maintenance, the plants need to be well suited to the soil. Heath banksia (*Banksia ericafolia*), *Grevillea* or *Ceonothus* will all thrive in medium soil. All will need some irrigation during the first year, and protection from strong winter winds and sun. Once they are established and growing well, they should be relatively self-sufficient, as long as they are healthy during the growing season. You need to water during dry spells in the second summer. For the first few springs, topdress the soil with 2.5 cm (1 in) of potting soil and cover it with bark mulch. You can continue this practice annually for best results, depending on your energy level!

Researching Trees

A well-chosen tree can enhance a garden, offering privacy, shade and colour. However, it's well worth doing your homework before buying – if they prove to be unsuitable then removing them, or paying for their maintenance every year, can be costly. First consider the planting site carefully – it will need to be away from houses, sheds and greenhouses if possible to avoid potential storm damage. Also bear in mind the eventual height and spread, as fast-growing options could soon block your view, or the roots could damage paths or walls. Finally, think carefully about the ongoing care involved in terms of pruning and dealing with falling leaves and other debris.

187. What is the proper way to trim lilacs?

Lilacs should be pruned in spring right after they bloom. First, remove any dead wood. Next, remove some of the oldest stems by cutting them at the ground, and remove any of the suckers that are thinner than a pencil, also by cutting them off at the ground. If you do this every year, you will always have vigorous new growth and the shrub will stay relatively short. You may also remove the spent flowers, although it is not strictly necessary. An overgrown lilac may be cut to the ground all at once, or it may be renewed over several years by removing a third of the oldest wood in year one, half of the remaining old wood in year two, and the rest of the oldest wood in year three. Always cut it to the ground and, each year, remove the smallest suckers. Then follow an annual pro-gramme as described above.

188. What shrubs can I plant in moist soil under the shade of trees?

There are a number of trees and shrubs with preferences for this type of site. These include *Aronia*, which has nice leaf colour and attractive berries in autumn. Siberian dogwood is another good option and has pretty white-edged leaves and red bark in winter. Witch hazel (*Hamamelis*) has fragrant flowers when little else is blooming. Many hydrangeas will also tolerate quite damp soil. Go to a reputable garden centre in your area and look closely at the labels on the plants that appeal to you. It should be possible to select an assortment that will offer colour and interest throughout the year.

189. Is rosemary an easy herb to grow?

Rosemary is a very decorative shrub that is undemanding and great for wildlife. Depending on the variety you choose, it will grow 0.6–1.8 m (2–6 ft) high at maturity, so it is a good candidate for container growing. Rosemary endures hot sun and poor soil, but requires good drainage. As the plant grows it can be trimmed back by a few centimetres in the spring and again in late summer to help keep it bushy and full of flowers. You may find you are 'pruning' it regularly as you pick the tips of the stems for use in the kitchen.

As rosemary grows it can be trimmed back by a few centimetres in the spring and again in late summer to help keep it bushy and full of flowers.

Rosemary can be grown in containers or in any freely draining soil. The stems are lovely in flower arrangements and the leaves can be added to a number of savoury dishes.

190. When should I start training my new bonsai tree?

Training a bonsai should begin when the plant is very young. It's essentially a regular routine of pinching and pruning the branches to get the shape you want, and keeping the roots in check. You can wait until your plant has at least four sets of true leaves to start training, and you'll need to keep it up for the whole lifetime of the tree. There are many very good books on the subject so you might want to check the shelves of your local library for an overall view of this fascinating hobby.

191. Can you recommend a columnar or pyramidal deciduous tree that won't get too tall?

How about liquid amber (*Liquidambar styraciflua*)? It's narrowly columnar in growth habit with spectacular fall colour. Golden chain (*Laburnum*) is a small tree with a delicate appearance and has yellow flowers in the spring. European white birch (*Betula pendula*), with a strong central leader and weeping branches, is a lovely tree. It likes a sunny, moist site but will adjust to dry soil. Green ash (*Fraxinus*) has a pyramidal habit and is very easy to grow. You could try driving around your area to see what else you like. Usually, gardeners love to share their advice with others and will be happy to give you information about what they're growing.

192. Why have my peonies stopped producing buds?

It is possible that they need to be divided, but more frequent causes for peonies to decline would be lack of sunlight due to the growth of neighbouring trees over the years, and poor fertility due to competing with nearby plants. You might try giving them a topdressing of compost or well-rotted manure and see if that helps things along next year. Another possibility is that repeated overmulching has caused the crowns to become too deeply planted. A layer of 2–5 cm (1–2 in) of mulch is sufficient.

Columnar trees are ideal for small gardens as they bring height and interest while still allowing you lots of space underneath them to plant flowers and shrubs.

193. How can I encourage a climbing rose to flower? It's growing well but not blooming.

Climbing roses bloom on new stems that grow on old wood. Pruning them back in late winter or early spring will encourage new flowering stems. If you didn't prune this past spring, most of the new growth will be at the ends of the main canes instead of all along new lateral stems, which produce the most flowers. Also, to flower freely, roses require full sun. Are your plants receiving at least six to eight hours of sunshine daily? Since the plants seem healthy otherwise, it's possible they might be missing essential nutrients. Nitrogen, phosphorus and potassium are the three major nutrients for all plants. (They correspond to the three numbers on fertiliser packages.) Nitrogen promotes growth of green leaves, and it sounds like your plants are getting plenty of that. Phosphorus is essential for blooms. Roses are heavy feeders during their blooming period. To give them a boost, you may want to apply a fertiliser formulated especially for roses. Just be sure to avoid giving them a high-nitrogen fertiliser, which will encourage foliage growth at the expense of flowers. In general, horizontal canes produce more flowers than vertical canes,

Climbing roses bloom on new stems grown on old wood, so prune them in late winter or early spring to ensure they flower freely.

so you might try encouraging young canes to grow horizontally by gently tying them to the trellis. Also, keep the plants consistently moist and mulch with 5–8 cm (2–3 in) of compost to help maintain soil moisture.

Positioning Your Shrubs

One of the most important rules of growing many flowering shrubs, including roses, is to plant them in an area that receives around four to six hours of sunlight every day, although there are some varieties that fare well in shade, so seek advice from a specialist if your plot is overshadowed. The best soil for planting shrubs is free-draining and loamy in texture — neither sandy nor clayey. If your soil type differs from this, you can improve it by digging in lots of organic material — a few minutes of extra effort at this stage can lead to a healthy plant that gives you years of good service.

194. How do I kill the weeds around my trees without harming the trees?

The safest way to approach any weed problem is to dig them out, roots and all. Any chemical you might use near the trees will certainly translocate through the roots and could damage or kill the tree, so keep weed killers away. When weeding, dig away an area at least 30 cm (12 in) in circumference around the trees. Then, after you have removed all the weeds, place an organic mulch around the trees to suppress future weeds. A 8–10 cm (3- or 4-in) layer of compost or shredded bark will suppress weeds and slow water evaporation. Ensure you don't place it too near the trunk of the tree.

Selecting Climbers

Climbers can make a huge impact so choose them wisely. Avoid invasive species like smile-a-minute vine (*Fallopia baldschuanica*). Fast-growing evergreens like ivies are useful for covering eyesores, but they'll demand regular pruning and their stem roots can damage old walls. Bear in mind that they can also damage trees and other plants if allowed to run riot. If you have a small space, it's better to accentuate features with more easy-going annual climbers and less thuggish varieties, such as large-flowering clematis. Climbing roses are another great choice – many repeat bloom and have the added advantage of colourful hips when they have finished flowering. Honeysuckles are another popular choice and they can smell as lovely as they look, although they'll need regular pruning to keep them in shape.

195. Which easy-grow shrubs would suit a location in partial sun?

Some fairly low-maintenance shrubs that offer a season of interest include peonies, lilacs, hydrangea, roses, *Berberis*, viburnum, *Philadelphus*, mahonia, *Amelanchier*, dogwoods and hebes.

196. Is it possible to dig up maple trees that are 3 m (10 ft) tall and transplant them to another place?

You can transplant maple trees in late winter and early spring. The roots of the tree will extend out beyond the canopy (the tips of the branches), so start digging at that point away from the trunk. Most of the roots will be in the top 30–45 cm (12–18 in) of soil so the hole doesn't have to be deep, but it should start out wide so you can discover the roots without accidentally cutting them off. Carefully dig around as many of the roots as possible and try to leave as much soil as you can around the root mass directly below the trunk of the tree. The less you disturb the roots, the easier the move will be on the tree. When the tree is out, you'll have an idea how large to dig the new hole. After removing the necessary amount of soil, put a small mound of soil in the new hole so you can place the rootmass on top and spread the roots out in the most natural way. Make sure the tree is at the same level that it was growing before, and finish filling the holes around the roots with soil. Give the tree about 2.5 cm (1 in) of water per week during the next spring and summer. It should be established by the next autumn, and rainfall should be all that it will require.

197. I have a beautiful old Virginia creeper growing up my house. Will it will damage the bricks?

Virginia creeper climbs both by means of tendrils with adhesive disks that adhere to brick, stone or tree trunks, and by aerial rootlets that attach only to rough surfaces. It can grow up to 15 m (50 ft) tall and has a loose, open growth pattern. Because it attaches itself by disks and roots, it can cause damage to the bricks on your house, especially if you try to remove it. The disks are nearly impossible to pry off! If there are any cracks in the mortar between the bricks, there's a chance that the roots can grow into them and eventually loosen the bricks. If your Virginia creeper has been in place for some time, it's likely the new growth it develops is attaching itself to the old growth that has already attached itself to the bricks. If so, the damage may be minimal. You won't know unless you attempt to remove it.

Virginia creepers look stunning but they grow very fast and the roots can damage brickwork, so think carefully before planting one.

198. How and when should I prune my overgrown hydrangea shrub?

Generally, you prune hydrangeas after flowering, so exactly when depends on the type of hydrangea you have. *Hydrangea paniculata* flowers in winter and you can prune off flowers any time after winter and save them as dried flowers. You can also prune branches any time after July, but the best time is just before the plant leafs out in spring. If you need to shorten your plant, remove the tallest one or two basal branches every year, which will bring the plant down to size in about three years. Or else cut the trunks back to a side shoot or branch at about 1.2 m (4 ft) above the ground. Both methods will require several seasons to get the plant to its ideal shape. After that, maintenance pruning will be a simple matter.

Lawns and Ground Covers

A sweeping lawn is often the hallmark of a well-tended garden, providing a glorious backdrop to your flowers, shrubs and trees. Ground cover plants can also play a vital role.

199. What should we do about mushrooms on our lawn?

Mushrooms often appear after prolonged rain has caused soggy soils. There will also be something providing a food source for them. Often it's a decaying tree root underground but it might also be due to a heavy layer of thatch at the soil surface. Thatch is basically dead roots and rhizomes and eventually all lawns develop it. If the mushrooms are concentrated in just a small area, use a hand cultivator to de-thatch the area around them and remove them. This consists of getting down on your hands and knees and hand-raking the area around the mushrooms to pull the thatch out of the turf. You'll probably notice smaller mushrooms when you get down closer. To prevent the problem in the future, make sure you de-thatch and aerate your lawn regularly – at least every three to four years. Also, if you use a mulching mower, make sure you mow regularly so that you don't leave clumps of cut grass on top of the lawn after mowing.

Effective Weeding

Once ground cover plants are established, they should grow so vigorously that weeds aren't too much of a problem. However, in the first year or two, hand weeding will be necessary. Take the opportunity to do this in spring, while many garden plants are still dormant. You'll be able to get in and dig any perennial weeds out before they compete with your plants for moisture and light. On patches of bare earth, flushes of weed seedlings can be dealt with very quickly by running over them with a hoe with a sharp blade. Choose a dry windy day and the seedlings will shrivel up. As the season progresses, keep an eye on your ground cover plants and remove any weeds that pop up. If you do this often, you'll soon have them under control.

200. How can I get rid of weeds without damaging my ground cover plants?

It's amazing how annoyingly tenacious weeds can be! If the ones you're dealing with are perennials you'll need to pull them out and mulch heavily under the ground cover with organic matter, such as wood chips. You can repeatedly cut them off to keep them under control, but, unfortunately, you'll need to be very diligent because they usually pop up elsewhere. Herbicides probably won't work in your situation, because the weeds are intermixed with your plants. The herbicide won't distinguish between the plants you want and the plants you don't and will end up killing everything! Once you've factored in the costs and risks, it is usually better to weed by hand.

201. My new lawn is starting to turn yellow although I water it every other day for 15 minutes. Any ideas?

When you water frequently you encourage the roots to remain close to the surface where they are vulnerable. Too much water will encourage fungal diseases and can actually suffocate the roots of your turf, which can turn the blades yellow. So the first suggestion is to begin weaning your turf off such frequent applications of water. Cut back to twice a week and apply water for ten to 15 minutes. Wait 30 minutes and then water again for ten to 15 minutes. This should allow the moisture to percolate down much deeper into the soil and encourage deeper root growth. After adjusting your watering you should see a fast green up of your lawn.

Over watering your grass can suffocate the roots, making it turn yellow and eventually killing it. During really hot weather, it's better to give your lawn a good drench twice a week rather than a daily splash.

202. Is it better to rake up all the leaves off the lawn before mowing it?

Rake them up and then mow the lawn low. While a few leaves on the lawn can be mulched by the mower, a heavy accumulation won't be easy to mow and the mower blades won't be able to cut them into small enough bits to decompose rapidly. Rake and pile the leaves up so they can decompose, or bag them and remove them completely from the landscape before mowing the lawn. Put them in large bags to rot down and use as a mulch on your beds next year.

203. Is Virginia creeper a good ground cover plant?

Parthenocissus quinquefolia is a large, spreading or climbing deciduous vine. It is capable of climbing an oak tree or covering the walls of a building in a solid layer of foliage. If no support is nearby, the vine will spread outwards over the ground as a ground cover. When you plant it, keep in mind that like many vines, this one grows slowly for the first year or two and then grows very rampantly. The leaves turn gorgeous shades of red and orange at the end of summer, so that is another feature to keep in mind when deciding where to plant it.

Ajuga is a surprisingly tough ground cover plant that can help to suppress weeds and grass once it's established.

204 How can I improve a spongy, rutted lawn?

If the lawn is spongy, it may be a result of thatch build up. Check by digging out a sample of lawn. You should expect to see some thatch such as dead stolons and roots but, if the straw-brown thatch build up is in excess of a 1.25 cm (½ in), de-thatching will fix the problem. You can hire power de-thatchers that will rake out the excess thatch along with some of the live grass.

205. How long will ajuga take to spread out over my old lawn?

Also known as bugleweed, ajuga can potentially crowd out grass, but this usually occurs along the edge of a solidly planted bed of ajuga where the plant is extremely vigorous and 'escapes'. Ajuga would usually be planted 30–45 cm (12–18 in) apart for reasonably fast coverage of an area (about two years), and the area would have been first cleared of grass and the soil would have been prepared prior to planting. At this point, you could either lift and replant the ajuga into prepared soil, or you could try the following: mow the grass as short as possible or kill it with a herbicide containing glyphosate according to the label instructions. Cover the area with potting soil, then a thick layer of damp newspapers, then a layer of mulch. This mulch layer should keep the grass from growing back while you wait for the ajuga to grow. It will also rot down and help improve the soil a little bit. Meanwhile, water the ajuga and encourage it to grow out over the mulched area.

206. My creeping phlox looks tired. Should I replant it?

If your plants are quite a few years old, the soil may be depleted after many years of having the same plant taking up the same nutrients. Phlox are heavy feeders in general; the creeping varieties are no exception, though they're often planted in the poor soils preferred by other rock garden plants. Their roots are shallow, so if the top few centimetres of soil isn't rich, they'll start to flag. Enrich the bed with potting soil or aged manure and a slow-release, balanced organic fertiliser, and plant some new phlox. Keep the new planting well watered this season, and next year, after they bloom, trim the plants with garden shears by about a half. This will encourage more root growth and keep the plants neat and healthy. Each season, add more potting soil to the bed and water during dry spells, and the next round should last you a long while.

Creeping phlox is a very attractive and undemanding ground cover plant, but it can benefit from a regular trim.

If your plants are a few years old the soil may be depleted after years of having the same plant taking up the same nutrients.

207. Rather than spending time looking after my lawn, I'd like to plant ground cover. What do you suggest?

Pachysandra and English ivy are two popular options that should fit the bill. You need not remove turf to get them established, but it helps to mow grass very low a few times before planting the ground cover, as this will weaken the grass and reduce its capacity to regrow. You may have friends who'd be willing to give you transplants of either plant, since they're very common.

Lawn Alternatives

Most of us love lawns, and they certainly make an attractive asset, but there's no denying it takes a fair amount of care to keep them in tip-top condition. If you're pushed for time, and there's an area where your grass never seems to grow well, why not look into installing a patio instead? They're perfect for outdoor entertaining, require minimum maintenance, and can be quite affordable if you know where to look. If getting rid of your lawn altogether seems a step too far, creating perennial beds, natural zones or areas of ground cover plants are all easy ways to reduce the time you spend in maintenance. If you're a fan of fragrant Mediterranean-style plants, such as lavender, cistus, thyme and rosemary, why not consider theming your ground cover?

208. I've mistakenly used too much weedkiller and killed my ground cover plants. What can I do?

Pesticides and herbicides can be extremely dangerous and, as you've seen, it is absolutely critical to follow label directions when applying any type of garden chemical. Not only is it a good idea environmentally and health-wise, but it is also the law. Many products should only be used as a last resort as they can do severe damage if not used exactly as stated on the packaging. Contact the makers of the product in question and request assistance from them directly.

Take care when using weedkillers, and always follow the instructions correctly, or else you may end up killing the plants you want to keep.

209. How can I get grass to grow in a shady spot?

It's really difficult to get lawn to grow in the shade so a better option would be growing a ground cover, such as *Vinca* or *Pachysandra*. But, if you have your heart set on growing turf, here are some pointers: since shade is a poor environment for turfgrass, it is essential to develop a good management programme in shady places. First, select shade-tolerant grasses. The fine-leaf fescues are considered the most shade-tolerant of the cool-season grasses. Sow seeds in shaded areas in the autumn. Autumn seedings generally are more successful than spring seedings because they go into the first summer more mature with a better root system and more stored food reserves. In autumn, frequent leaf raking is essential to the establishment of grasses in shaded areas. Leaves left on the lawn shade the young seedlings and slow

Combating Dandelions

Dandelions are one of the most problematic weeds you can find in a lawn. They set seed very easily, and the deep tap roots are difficult to dig up in one piece as they have a tendency to snap off, leaving part in the ground to simply grow back. However, it's worth persevering with these pesky weeds, as if you manage to get rid of them before they have a chance to grow their distinctive 'clocks' you can stop them from spreading. It's also some comfort to know that the young leaves are tasty eaten raw in salads or cooked like spinach, especially if you blanch them first. Never eat leaves from a garden where pesticides or herbicides may have been used. It's also vital to make sure pets don't accidentally consume treated leaves.

their development. Turfgrass growing in shade generally requires less total nitrogen than grass in full sunlight because of the reduced rates of photosynthetic activity. Over-application of nitrogen on shaded grasses reduces stored food reserves and produces thin cell walls, which can cause disease on the turfgrass plants. Late autumn fertilisation of cool-season grasses is extremely beneficial in shaded environments. This is the only time of year when the grass plants under the trees can efficiently utilise the applied nitrogen without competition from the tree for moisture, nutrients and light. Applying nitrogen in late autumn, after leaf drop, is extremely beneficial.

It would also be helpful to raise the mowing height. Increased mowing height induces larger root systems, and healthier plants. Irrigate infrequently, but heavily. An irrigation programme that minimises the amount of time shaded areas are moist is beneficial in reducing disease. Infrequent watering also tends to minimise compaction and reduce shallow surface rooting. Try to reduce use of the area as thin-cell-walled grass plants with little food reserve cannot bear much traffic without sustaining damage. Therefore, any effort to minimise traffic in shaded areas is beneficial. Provide good drainage – poor drainage increases the possibility of disease activity. Finally, remove all leaves and any leftover debris promptly.

210. Is there a ground cover plant that can withstand traffic?

There are few options that will hold up well to traffic, some are woody, such as creeping cotoneaster (*Euonymus fortunei*) and creeping thyme. The herbaceous ones include lily-of-the-valley and creeping potentilla.

211. Can you suggest any low-growing ground cover plants?

Some ground-hugging choices include carpet bugle (*Ajuga*), cinquefoil (*Potentilla*), creeping Jenny (*Lysimachia nummularia*), ornamental strawberry (*Fragaria*), dead nettle (*Lamium*), wild ginger (*Asarum*) and saxifrage. If you have a large area to cover, it may be best to plant them in groups of three or five, or even more, so that you have lots of different interest and you create an established look in the minimum possible time.

The dainty little flowers of saxifrage are held on tiny stems above the foliage, which typically forms moss-like clumps of lime green.

212. Why have my erigeron plants stopped producing flowers this year?

Erigeron, or fleabane as it is commonly known, is a native Mexican plant that thrives in dry conditions and flowers profusely throughout summer and autumn. They do tend to develop into large clumps and, if the plants are overcrowded, they may fail to flower. Since yours is refusing to flower, why not dig them up, divide the clumps into several pieces and replant them? As long as each division has both roots and stems attached they will establish themselves and should flower for you in a matter of months.

The daisy-like flowers of erigeron have a cheerful appeal. They are ideal for growing alongside paths and patios and can even self-seed and grow in the cracks in walls.

213. Can I do anything to stop the roots of my oak tree showing through the grass?

Oak trees are shallow rooted and very sensitive to changes in the soil depth over their roots, so simply adding soil to cover the surface roots could kill the tree. Other shallow-rooted trees, such as maples will simply grow their roots right back up to the surface in a short time, so covering tree roots is not very effective. Grass will not grow in a shady area or in competition with tree roots, so you might consider using a shade tolerant ground cover instead. *Pachysandra* is a good choice. Alternatively, you could mulch the area lightly with an organic mulch all year round, taking care not to pile it around the trunk of the tree.

214. Do wood chips make effective ground cover? Will they control weeds?

This inexpensive material can be a very good form of ground cover. Wood chips will have to be replaced every few years (or simply topped off with another layer), in contrast to materials, such as stones, which are a bit more permanent. There are a number of living ground covers that you can plant after placing the wood chips down, that will grow over the wood chips and eventually hide them. If it's a sunny area, St. John's wort (*Hypericum*), aubrieta or prostrate *Veronica* would do well. If it's shady, try *Vinca minor* or *Saxifraga*.

To block weeds effectively, you can either use black landscape fabric under the chips, covering it with a 5- to 8-cm (2- to 3-in) layer, or use a 15- to 18-cm (6- or 7-in) layer of straight wood chips. Remove any weeds that do appear by hand.

215. When is the best time of year to lay turf? Can I do it in the summer?

Wait until the weather cools after summer, then dig and remove the dead turf you wish to replace. Before re-sodding, work some compost into the ground. It will help hold moisture during dry weather and will get your new sod off to a good start by providing a rich, loose planting area. Try to avoid walking on the new turf where possible for the first few weeks and water well in dry spells and the new grass should romp away.

Compacted soil excludes air (which roots need). You can fix compacted lawns by aerating every two to three years . . .

The cooler weather at the beginning of autumn is the best time to lay new turf, as it will have the longest possible time to put down deep roots before the hot dry weather of the following summer.

216. I think my lawn is compacted. How do I aerate it and why is this useful?

The soil under your lawn can become compacted from foot traffic, and compacted soil excludes air (which roots need). You can fix compacted lawns by aerating every two to three years in either the spring or the autumn. If you rent a power aerator, it will dislodge plugs of soil. Leave the plugs on the lawn (they'll decompose and break down in the rain). After aerating, spread a thin layer of sand or organic mulch over the top of the lawn and then water deeply.

217. My grass got very burned last year. How do I start again?

The keys to starting a new lawn are soil preparation, grass variety and early care. First, the soil; you want to provide a rich, weed-free environment for your new lawn. What you do depends on the size of the area, what you hope to achieve, and how much you want to spend. If the area was a grassy field, you can simply let it grow again, and begin mowing as you would a lawn. By the end of the summer you will have a fairly decent lawn area, depending on the condition of the grass when you started. Regular mowing helps it to grow well. If you are looking for a smooth lawn, you may need to till up the area, grade it, rake it and plant seed. Or you can bring in topsoil, rake it out to a smooth surface and plant. Choose a grass seed appropriate for your use – for your situation a commercial grass mix would probably be best. Your local garden centre should carry a selection. Once you spread the seed, you need to lightly rake it in, or use a lawn roller. This is to ensure that the seed is in close contact with the soil, so it can germinate. You may want to spread some hay lightly over the surface, to minimise erosion and keep the birds from eating all your seed. Finally, keep the new lawn well watered, and try not to walk on it until it is well-established.

If you mistakenly apply too much fertiliser to your lawn, it can result in patchy streaks, so take your time over this job and always follow the instructions carefully.

218. We recently fed our lawn and now it looks worse. Any ideas?

When streaks develop after fertiliser application, it usually indicates,the fertiliser was applied in overlapping passes with the spreader. To avoid this in the future, divide the amount of fertiliser you want to apply in half. Fill the spreader with half the fertiliser and apply in a north–south direction. Then fill the spreader with the second half of the fertiliser and apply in an east–west direction. This will ensure a consistent amount of fertiliser will be applied to all parts of the lawn. If you apply in only one direction there is a chance of overlapping and ending up with green and yellow streaks in the lawn. With regular watering and mowing, the streaks will eventually disappear.

219. Can I remove clover that's mixed in with my wild flowers?

There's really nothing you can apply to a wild-flower bed that will target the clover without harming all the other flowers. Digging the plants out is probably the best approach. However, clover attracts lots of bees and other valuable wildlife so it may be better to learn to like it!

220. How do I plant a wildflower meadow?

Starting a wildflower meadow takes some effort, but the results can be spectacular. In general, first you need to control the existing vegetation. Then the soil needs to be worked to loosen it and make a seedbed. Next, any weeds that germinate in the seedbed need to be controlled and the soil worked lightly again. This may have to be done several times to eliminate the majority of weed seeds within sprouting distance near the surface. Finally, the wildflower seeds can be planted, or you can plant small seedlings or even larger-sized starter plants. The planting will need to be watered (and weeded) until it becomes established. You may want to consult with a local native plant specialist as to the types of wild flowers that would be most likely to grow naturally in your area, or which ones could be planted there and become self-sustaining successfully. Alternatively, plant a mix suitable for the location; over time, the plants will 'self-select', leaving only those that are well adapted to your particular site.

You can buy various seed mixes for different types of wildflower meadows. Some are suited to different soil types, others may be more attractive to birds or butterflies, so do your research before buying and select the right one for your needs.

Mowing the Lawn

If you mow your lawn regularly in spring, summer and autumn, it will grow far more strongly. Always adjust the cutting height to the growing conditions, so that you can take more off when the grass is growing fast and less off if growth slows (such as during dry spells). If your lawn is large enough, you might prefer to leave an edge or bank to grow a bit longer. This will provide shelter and wild flowers for insects and birds. If you have the space, you might even choose to plant a wildflower meadow. This can look very striking next to an area that is neatly mowed and, once established, it can often be quite a low-maintenance option. Wildflower meadows will attract a range of wildlife.

221. Is clover good for the lawn? I heard it's a nitrogen source.

Clover is a legume, and all plants in this family have nitrogen-fixing nodules on their roots. The plants take nitrogen from the atmosphere and store it up. Clover that is used for cover crops (usually crimson clover, *Trifolium fragiferum*) should be turned into the soil before it flowers and sets seed. When the plants are turned under and begin to decompose, the root nodules release the nitrogen, which enriches the soil. The clover that appears in lawns is usually *Trifolium repens*, or white clover. It also fixes nitrogen in the soil. Clover in the lawn is rarely mowed down often enough to keep the flowers from producing seeds and that's why it becomes such a pest. Both kinds of clovers also spread through spreading stems that root easily – a good thing for a cover crop, but not so good in the lawn.

222. What advice would you give a complete beginner on lawn care?

Good lawn care includes regular fertilising, watering and mowing. A thick, healthy lawn will crowd out most weeds so here's how to get the upper hand. Grass needs to be watered once or twice a week, depending upon weather. Deep soakings are preferable to daily sprinklings. Plan on applying 2.5 cm (1 in) of water per week to your lawn. You can use a 'weed and feed' product if you have weeds in your lawn now, or you can simply dig the weeds up and re-seed any bare areas. Mow as often as necessary to keep your lawn at around 5 cm (2 in) in height. The general rule of thumb is to remove no more than one-third of the grass blade when you mow. So, mow when it is 8 cm (3 in) high and take off no more than 2 cm of grass. This may involve mowing more than once a week during spring when it is growing very quickly.

223. How can I repair a bald spot in my lawn?

Start by raking out the bald patch and digging in a little compost. Then spread grass seed over the spot and keep it moist until the seeds germinate (usually seven to ten days). After the new grass is up and you have mowed the lawn two to three times, the roots will be established enough that you can carefully remove any weeds that have popped up. Keep your lawn watered and mowed regularly and it should grow lush and thick. Keep a hand trowel handy so you can dig up any weeds as soon as possible.

Although clover and daisies look quite pretty in the lawn, they can become invasive, so try to mow regularly to help prevent plants from setting seed.

224. How can I improve the scruffy edges on the side of my lawn?

Your lawn should be mowed frequently enough so that no more than one-third of the leaf blade length is removed during any one mowing. During periods of active growth, many lawns will require mowing at least once a week. The direction of mowing should be altered every one to two mowings. Mowing at right angles to the previous direction will help prevent the grass from repeatedly being pushed in one direction and laying over, an important consideration at high mowing heights. Also, if scalping areas of the lawn is a problem, the different mowing directions will help minimise continual scalping in any one area. Edging and trimming are the finishing touches of mowing, kind of like getting a shave after you've had a haircut. Edging and trimming are pretty close to being the same thing. Some tools are called edgers because they're designed to trim the lawn along a hard surface, such as a driveway. Edgers cut a nice clean edge, but leave some dirt and grass debris that you need to clean up. On the other hand, you can use trimmers anywhere – along a hard surface, in tight spaces, next to planting beds and so on. Trimmers also leave some clippings that you will need to sweep up.

The edges of your lawn need particular care as they can suffer from always being mowed in the same direction, which can cause the grass to lay over.

225. How do I decide between a push-mower and a self-propelled mower?

Either type will be efficient on an average-sized lawn. Self-propelled mowers take less effort to use. The wheels are power-driven, so the engine does the work and you just walk behind and guide the mower. Push mowers require a little more physical effort. So, if your lawn is large, you may want to invest in a self-propelled mower. It's a personal preference, so choose the one you are most comfortable with.

Maintaining a Healthy Lawn

If you take an hour or two to give your lawn a helping hand in spring, it could save you much more time later in the year. After cold, wet winters, grass roots are likely to be struggling to recover. You can make a big difference by spiking the lawn to open up its texture. Depending on the size of the space, you can use a garden fork or get a tool designed specially for the purpose, which takes out cores of earth. Push the fork in as far as it will go and wiggle it gently back and forth. Next scatter sharp sand over the area, and brush into the holes. This will help to improve drainage and aerate the roots. Don't worry if this looks a little untidy at first, it will soon be an expanse of fresh, green grass.

226. How can I propagate my ground cover plants?

You should be able to dig and divide each plant quite easily so that you can grow lots more. Just cut into one with a shovel, taking a large piece of the plant, with roots attached. Examine the root system so you can see how it grows. Then divide the shovelful so that each division has both roots and foliage. Replant in a similar spot in your garden, or pot up each division in a separate container and keep the divisions well watered. They should re-establish their roots in a few short weeks. You'll know they have rooted successfully when you spot new growth.

Perennial ground cover plants, such as hardy geraniums can easily be propagated by digging up a part of the plant with its roots intact and carefully teasing it out into a few new, smaller plants.

227. How hardy are heucheras?

These perennial plants are surprisingly hardy and extremely versatile. There are lots of new varieties, which can have interesting blends of colours, such as red, maroon and lime foliage throughout the growing season. The mounded, attractive clumps remain compact, measuring a tidy 20–30 cm (8–12 in) across and 45 cm (18 in) tall when in bloom. Wiry flower stems bearing numerous small, bell-shaped flowers appear in the late spring and continue throughout the early summer months. Most heuchera cultivars perform best when grown in partial shade. Heucheras are commonly used as accent plants, border plants or components in mixed containers. The blooms attract both butterflies and bees to the garden, and they can also be used as cut flowers. An added bonus is that these plants are also resistant to deer.

228. How can I improve a patchy lawn?

It's possible the lawn has been neglected for some time and all you need to do is put it on a regular fertilising, watering and mowing schedule to get it to green up. To have the healthiest, greenest lawn possible, water deeply once a week (twice if the weather is really hot) to force the roots to penetrate deeply. Deep-rooted grasses don't need as much water as those that are shallow rooted, and won't turn brown as easily. (Frequent, light watering will keep the roots close to the surface, making them dry out faster in warm weather and require even more frequent watering.) Put your lawn on a regular fertilising and mowing schedule, too. Fertilise four times a year with a balanced product. Mow when blades are around 5 cm (2 in) high – if you let the grass grow really tall and then mow, you'll take off too much of the living tissue and scalp the lawn. Finally, rake out the dead grass and debris, then reseed those areas.

229. I'd like to plant creeping thyme as a ground cover. Any tips?

Thyme seems to thrive on abuse, but don't let that stop you from providing reasonably good conditions in your garden. All plants appreciate loose, well-draining soil, so amending it with organic matter before planting is a good idea. Rosemary is another rugged plant that will grow in poor soil, but good drainage is a must. Both rosemary and thyme will look best if given water on a regular basis. The prostrate dwarf rosemary grows to 0.6 m (2 ft) tall with a 1- to 2.5-m (4- to 8-ft) spread so it is another option for ground cover.

If your lawn is looking a little tatty, get into a regular routine of fertilising, watering and mowing and it should soon look fresh and green again.

230. How long should a petrol power mower last?

Seven to ten years is about all you can expect from a power mower. You can run it longer but eventually the repair bills will cost more than the mower is worth. Even with excellent care they do wear out. Unless you invested a fortune in it when you first purchased your mower, you may simply want to replace it. If you did invest a lot at purchase, it may justify having it repaired for another few years.

231. Could we use red clover as ground cover?

Although not widely used, red clover is a short-lived plant that is a useful ground cover. It thrives in fertile, near-neutral pH soil, and does require regular irrigation until established. To give your clover the best chance possible to compete with weeds, till a couple of times prior to sowing seeds. This encourages weed seeds to sprout, and the next pass of tilling a few days later kills them.

Garden Features

Even the smallest garden can be enhanced by a feature or two, while larger plots give you scope to substantially increase your enjoyment of your outdoor space. From a simple hanging basket to a flowing stream, you can create your own lush oasis.

232. Why haven't my water lily leaves grown up to the top of the water?

If you set them too deeply in the water, they may not have the strength to grow to the top. Generally, the stems grow just long enough for the leaves to rest on the top of the water, so don't worry about the leaves growing up and out of the water. You'll need to place your lilies in a shallower part of the pond, or buy a platform to place the pot of lilies on. Take care that this is not made of a material that can damage your pond liner. Don't worry if you see fish appearing to nibble at the edges of the lily leaves – they generally like to feed on the algae that forms on the leaves, but this won't hurt your plants and in fact can aid photosynthesis and get them more energy.

The Garden Pond

Using either a rigid or flexible liner are the two main options for garden ponds. Rigid liners have a preformed shape. This is often irregular but can sometimes be geometrical, such as a circle or square. If used in the ground, this design requires an excavation exactly the same shape as the liner, which is then dropped neatly into place. Flexible liners give you the option of making a pond of any shape and size, allowing you to create a much more natural effect. The sheets are made of waterproof material, such as PVC or butyl rubber. To avoid damaging it, remove all stones and sharp objects from the excavation and consider installing a protective layer of sand or landscaping fabric between liner and soil.

233. How many plants should I put in a hanging basket?

The answer depends on what kind of plant it is and how impatient you are for that 'full' look. It also depends on what size of basket you are using and how advanced the plants are. Three mature pansies could fill a regular-sized basket, but five young plants would probably be needed to make it look nice early in the season. Plants are placed quite close together in hanging baskets, much closer than they would be in the garden. You could try taking the basket with you when you purchase plants so you can plan the perfect mix and composition. Although options containing just one type of bloom can be very effective, you may also want to consider using a mixture of large-flowered and more dainty varieties, as well as plants with trailing foliage, as this can create a longer season of interest.

234. Can you give us any ideas on making a gazebo?

These structures need to be sturdy enough to withstand wind and support any plants you intend to grow on them. They should be made of a weather resistant material or routinely stained or painted to protect them from the elements. The design should complement and tie in with your house style and any fencing or other similar features in your garden. There are many differ-ent techniques from simple to elaborate and you could start from scratch, use a kit or get someone in to build and install it for you. You should try looking at a book or two and find a style you like and work from there. Local companies may be able to show you photos of finished designs.

Add height and interest to a seating area by building a simple gazebo. In summer you can hang baskets of flowers, such as scented petunias from the beams to enhance the effect.

235. How can we shade our deck?

Along with trees, you might want to consider a trellis with deciduous climbing vines to help shade your deck. Some of the most well-behaved 'patio

> Gazebos should be made of a weather resistant material or stained or painted to protect them from the elements.

trees' (so named because they don't have many bad habits) include paperbark maple, trident maple, dogwood, *Stewartia* and crape myrtle. *Acacia* and *Laburnum* might be nice, too.

236. How can I create an oriental garden? What plants should I choose?

Garden design is always easier when you have a theme! In oriental gardening, the key is to remember that 'less is more' and to be very selective in the special features you decide to use. Evergreens are usually important, as are spring-flowering trees. Ferns, hosta and other fairly subtle foliage plants are the accents. Moss is very commonly found, as is bamboo. Chrysanthemums and peonies are traditional, and happily you can include almost any flower you prefer as long as it is used with some restraint. Mysterious pathways, stepping stones, stone lanterns, simple benches and water features, such as ponds and quiet fountains are often chosen. Another feature with great importance is stone: the larger the piece the better, or at the opposite extreme, the illusion of water can be created by small rounded stones placed to mimic the channel of a stream.

237. Can you please recommend some plants for my first pond?

To keep a healthy balance in your pond you will need a good number of oxygenators, as well as plants to shade about two-thirds of the surface. Hardy water lilies will do this nicely. You may also choose to add large architectural plants, and some floating plants, such as water hyacinths, which are lovely although they are not hardy. You will also have to decide if you want your pond to be more of a pool of water or more of a large container for water plants – it's easy to add too many! Plants will also help keep your pond algae free and the water clear. Remember though that water lilies prefer still water so need to be placed away from any fountain you may have. Around the pond, some gardeners find that a combination of rocks, dwarf conifers and creeping plants, such as thyme suit their garden; others prefer a more floral effect and use all sorts of sun-loving perennials, such as daylilies, sedum, purple coneflower, small grasses and achillea. It's really up to you because your pond can be surrounded to integrate with the rest of your landscape in almost any style.

Water lilies are easy to grow and generally undemanding, but they have a definite preference for still water, so try to site them away from a fountain or waterfall if you want them to bloom.

238. What's the best way to plant in pots and what's best for drainage?

As long as your pot has drainage holes (which are vital), in most instances it is not necessary to add pebbles to the bottom of the pot. One of the reasons for this is that the plants usually need every inch of space for soil! Do keep in mind while planning your container garden that the larger the pot the greater the root area and moisture-holding capacity will be. Also check each plant's soil preferences, since some (especially among the trees and shrubs) are particularly sensitive to either moisture levels or pH. Finally, if you plan to keep them after next summer, think about how you will be protecting the plants during the winter.

239. How do I plant a cutting garden?

A cutting garden is a fantastic idea and allows you to create beautiful vases of flowers for your home very reasonably. It's a good idea to include a mixture of both annuals and perennials. You can plant several shades of one colour, or plants with several different flower colours and shapes to add variety to your flower arrangements. As with any garden bed, dig the soil to remove weeds, then amend with aged-compost mix, peat, aged manure or leaf mould to help loosen the soil and enrich it. It's best to find the sunniest site possible because most flowering plants require six to eight hours of direct sunshine each day. Plants that provide the best flowers for cutting include snapdragon (*Antirrhi-*

The larger the pots you use, the better their ability to hold moisture in the soil – something that is important for fast-growing flowers, such as *Thunbergia*.

num), calendula, China aster (*Callistephus chinensis*), cornflower (*Centaurea cyanus*), spider flower (*Cleome hassleriana*), larkspur (*Delphinium*), cosmos, dianthus, lisianthus

> As long as your pot has drainage holes, in most instances it is not necessary to add pebbles to the bottom.

(*Eustoma russellianum*), strawflower (*Helichrysum bracteatum*), phlox, scabious (*Scabiosa*), *Alstroemeria*, aster, chrysanthemum, coreopsis and dahlia.

240. When should I plant seeds in my greenhouse? Is there a general rule?

Seeds are usually started in a greenhouse about six weeks before you plan to set them out in the garden. Greenhouses are typically used from autumn through spring for protecting tender plants and seed starting. The summer months can often be too hot to keep plants in a greenhouse, unless you have very good ventilation! If you know when the last frost is predicted in your area, you can work back from then for many types of flowers and vegetables. More hardy varieties can be planted in autumn and overwintered in the greenhouse to give you a head start the following spring. Make a list of all the things you'd like to grow and take note of all the sowing times. This will help you to keep your greenhouse productive for as much of the year as possible.

The Greenhouse

If you want to grow vegetables or flowers from seed, a greenhouse is vital. Not only does it give you a few precious weeks at the beginning and end of the growing season, it can offer a sheltered place for you to enjoy your hobby even if the weather's bad. If you can, it's wise to site your greenhouse in the sunniest spot you have available as sunshine is essential, and you can always fit blinds to add more shade during the summer. Avoid anywhere too shady, cold or damp, and consider shade cast by overhanging trees, fences and walls. Also avoid any lower parts of your plot or the base of slopes, as these can be frost pockets in winter.

241. What beds would you suggest for a gardener who has back trouble?

Raised beds are ideal for gardeners with back trouble. They're typically built to dimensions of stock wood sizes, such as 4x8, for economy's sake. The overall dimensions and the height are determined by personal preference; however, there are some factors to take into account. A common height is only about 20–30 cm (8–12 in) due to the construction difficulties of going higher. The cubic space within the box must be filled with soil mix, which can be a considerable expense if you are purchasing the fill. The higher the bed, the faster it will drain and dry out, so you will need more frequent watering. The narrower the bed, also the more frequent the watering as there is more soil closer to the edges where it dries out faster. Next, the taller the bed the stronger the sides need to be due to the weight and pressure, and the stronger, deeper set, and closer together your support posts will need to be. Local building code specifications for retaining walls would be a good start in terms of determining what is required for construction design; you might also want to consult with a contractor. In terms of wood, treated wood is no longer routinely recommended for vegetable garden sides. Redwood, cypress or cedar are naturally longlasting, there are also some recycled plastic products that are worth considering. You could also use regular pine boards will last a number of years. Bending is a concern for you, but given the above considerations you may find that it is preferable to use a kneeling bench or other means of sitting closer to the ground so that the bed does not need to be quite so high. You could also make a wider edge or bench seat on the sides of the bed so that you can sit on it while you work.

One advantage of growing climbers, such as clematis, on a trellis is that even if they are pruned back extensively they will usually recover.

242. What can I grow over a metal fence?

You can easily grow tall and productive raspberries and blackberries on a chain-link fence, provided the area gets full sun or partial shade, at most. The brambles will grow best if the soil is rich and well-drained and protected from dog activity. You can grow grapevines or Virginia creeper on the fence, too, but grapes won't be very productive unless trained properly, and a chainlink fence won't provide the kind of support they need long-term – and as vines grow into large trunks, they can contort and damage the fence! If you're interested in managing the berries for vigorous growth and fruit production, you'll need to prune out the canes that fruit in a given summer that same autumn, leaving the newly grown canes to fruit the following summer. Being deciduous, brambles won't provide much of a screen in winter.

243. Can I prune a clematis back to the ground in order to paint my trellis?

Without knowing what type of clematis it is, it is difficult to give a pruning recommendation. As a general rule, clematis are said to sleep the first year, creep the second and leap the third. If you feel it is getting out of bounds, trimming it back lightly is unlikely to do it too much harm, especially if you fertilise and water the new growth and protect it from slugs and snails.

244. How should a sundial be placed?

That's a good question. People often assume that the arrow should be pointed in a certain direction, such as North, but the easiest way to work it out is to place the sundial so the time showing (where the shadow lands) matches the time of day (according to a watch or clock). Then you can go out and check it at different times of the day, to see if it is indicating the proper time. This is the most accurate way of being sure it is placed correctly!

Although sundials can be quite accurate (on sunny days) their main appeal is their ornamental value. They are ideal for formal gardens.

245. What can I plant in a windowbox?

There are lots of decorative flowers you can choose for your windowboxes. One idea that might appeal is to choose scented plants that will fill your rooms with a fresh fragrance. You might try one of the smaller forms of scented stock, or possibly a fragrant form of nicotiana (although avoid the taller-growing varieties). Another good flower to try would be one of the fragrant petunias – many of these are particularly appealing at night, so it's worth having your windows open in the evenings to enjoy the lovely scent.

246. Any tips on building raised beds?

Most flowers and vegetables will grow as well, if not better, in a raised bed as in a conventional garden plot. You can simply mound up the soil into long, flat-topped hills to create your raised beds. Choosing a building material can be tricky. Many people prefer not to use treated pine for growing vegetable crops, fearing the chemicals used to treat the wood will leach out. But there's no such concerns for flower beds. Raised beds made from untreated pine will last a few years but will rot and need to be replaced. Options made from recycled plastic may not be quite as attractive but they're certainly long-lasting. Or, you can use bricks or concrete blocks to make a more permanent raised bed. Once you decide on the building materials, choose the sunniest site available and, if there is existing vegetation, dig the area to roughen it up. It isn't necessary to remove the debris because you will be putting new soil over the top. Then simply lay your lumber or concrete blocks out in a square or rectangular pattern and build up each level, securing the wood together with screws or the concrete with metal posts driven through the top holes. Fill with a mixture consisting of about three-quarters good topsoil and one-quarter made up of aged compost, well-rotted manure or shredded leaves or grass clippings. Depending on the soil type, you may want to add some lime to raise the pH or some bonemeal for phosphorus. Some root vegetables, such as carrots, require deep soil, so either make the beds quite deep (60 cm [24 in] is the minimum) or build them up over existing garden soil. You can purchase garden material in bulk and have it delivered. The more you purchase, the cheaper each unit will be.

247. How can I grow ferns? Are they hard to keep alive?

There are exceptions, but most ferns are usually happiest in shady areas in cool, moist soils. They don't like being left to dry out, so ensure that you keep them well watered and protected from hot sunshine. The new fronds develop in the centre of the plant and the older, outer fronds will eventually die down and can be pruned off the plant. If you plant newly bought ferns, some new growth should be visible within two to three weeks. They will relish the moist atmosphere at the side of a stream, pond or waterfall and may even self-seed over time.

Ferns have a reputation for being difficult to grow, but as long as you can offer them a shady spot with moist soil, they will romp away.

Adding a Water Feature

Most of us want to include some sort of water feature in our gardens, with good reason. Water can add a sense of movement and magic, and is often the ideal accompaniment to an area of deck or paving. A pond or fountain makes a great focal point and they are also a real draw for wildlife. Ponds and waterfalls work well next to seating areas because they are a great spot for relaxation. The constant gentle gurgle of a fountain is a great way of masking unpleasant noise, such as traffic on a nearby road. A raised pond is also a clever way of adding vertical interest to your plot, and can even be used to provide a seating area if the walls are wide enough.

248. Should I cut water irises back in winter?

The foliage of some pond plants, such as irises can start to look a little tatty by the end of winter. If so, trim it back carefully with sharp pruners.

By the end of winter the foliage of irises may be a bit ragged and in need of cutting back, but that will depend on the specific type of iris you are growing and how cold and windy the weather is likely to be. In warmer climes, irises can be trimmed at the end of winter when their appearance can be better assessed. Avoid cutting the foliage in spring as it is needed to provide nourishment to support the growing flowers. If you absolutely have to trim it, be prepared for no blooms.

If your spot is sunny you might grow junipers, creeping phlox and sun-loving herbs, such as the various creeping thymes.

249. Is a coldframe suitable for growing flowers from seed?

These structures are ideal as you can cultivate hundreds of plants in a very small space. However, if you have room, it's worth building the frame larger that you think you'll need to as it's very easy to fill it up! Design it to allow a hinged or removable top, as warm sunny days will cook your plants, even in early spring. Building a high-quality, 'permanent' cold frame can cost quite a bit, depending on the size and choice of materials – an alternative is to make one from a kit. On particularly cold nights, you may need to add a cover (like a blanket) to hold heat.

250. What can I grow in a rock garden?

'Rock garden' means different things to different people. To some gardeners it is a label for a special planting of alpine plants or dwarf conifers, for others it is a catchall for plants which like good drainage. If your spot is sunny you might grow junipers, creeping phlox and sun-loving herbs, such as the various creeping thymes. If it is shady, you might consider a ground cover, such as creeping myrtle or ajuga. As you gain confidence and experience as a gardener you will find there are many plants for a slope and rocky ground.

251. What is the Three Sisters design?

Beans, corn and squash are the traditional crops in a Native American Three Sisters garden. One planting method is to form mounds of soil about 0.3 m (1 ft) high and 1 m (3 ft) in diameter, spaced about 1 m apart from each other. Once the soil has warmed, plant the corn first. Wait two to three weeks before planting the beans and squash, to give the corn a head start. The corn should be at least 7–10 cm (3–4 in) tall when you plant the others. Traditionally, climbing pole beans were planted that used the corn stalks for support. In turn, the beans fix nitrogen from the air and provide it to the corn. The large leaves of the squashes shade the ground to retain moisture and help keep the weeds down. Planting these three crops together can certainly save garden space, and as long as you provide full sunshine and adequate water, your Three Sisters garden should thrive, even in a small space.

252. What's the best way to build a coldframe?

Basically, a coldframe is a rectangular box with the back higher than the front, that is covered with a transparent roof. You can make one using scrap lumber and old windows to reduce your costs. The windows available will determine the dimensions for the bed. A glass sash is the easiest to use because it has a conventional frame covering. You'll be building a box with the wood and securing the glass windows on the top of the box. The back wall (generally the north wall) should be at least 50 cm (18 in) tall, measuring from the top to the bottom. The front wall (generally the south wall) should be about 30 cm (12 in) tall. A 1.8-m (6-ft) frame is a workable size but you can adjust the size of the frame according to the amount of wood you have. You can add weather stripping at the joints to help retain heat and make the frame even more efficient.

Cold frames provide an excellent growing environment for young plants, and they can be built quite simply or bought in kit form.

253. Do you have any suggestions for building a small outdoor fountain?

Building your own is fun and not too difficult. You will need a pump, plastic tubing to fit the outlet on the pump, a basin to hold water deep enough to cover the pump (this container can be anything from a decorative bowl to a plain old bucket, depending on your taste), and an electrical outlet with a ground fault interrupter (GFI) for safety. Basically, the pump re-circulates the water from the basin and spits it out the end of the tube. The water then trickles back into the basin and the cycle starts again. You can arrange the tube over or through any type of decorative set-up you like (for example, you could hide the tubing in a little pile of rocks so the water spills over the top of the rocks and looks nice), but make sure the water coming out of the tube returns to the basin. Play with the height and width of the 'fall', and the arrangement of items for the water to run over or hit, until you like the look and the sound of your fountain. Replenish the water (some is lost to evaporation) as needed so the pump is always submerged.

254. Where should a birdbath be placed?

That is a very good question and depends to some extent on which birds you wish to attract and which birds are in your local area. For the most part, however, birds like to be able to perch safely near the birdbath (as in shrubbery or small trees) with a good view of the area to check for possible dangers and predators, then bathe with a natural protective open space (as in open lawn) between them and any possible hiding places or attack routes for their predators. Different birds have different comfort zones and preferences, which makes stating a hard and fast rule somewhat challenging. If you have sufficient space and resources, it is best to provide several birdbaths in different locations and then see which ones the birds like best. Then you can sit back and watch their hilarious antics!

Birds need fresh water both for drinking and washing every day, and so by providing birdbaths you can make a real difference.

255. How should I lay down plastic in order to prevent weeds?

If you're concerned about weeds growing up through the soil in your raised beds, try laying down woven weed barrier cloth rather than plastic. The cloth will allow soil to drain, whereas plastic will turn the planter into a tub – most plants do not like constantly wet feet. If you're planting flowering annuals and perennials, the soil needs to be only about 30 cm (12 in) deep. If you're planting woody ornamentals, you may need up to 90 cm (36 in) of depth. Bulbs will be happy with 20–25 cm (8–10 in) of soil.

256. How can I create an attractive sitting area?

First, you need to figure out how much sunshine and shade the area you have in mind gets so you can choose appropriate plants. Then you'll want to sketch your ideal sitting area out on paper. Decide where you'd like to place a bench or some chairs and what you'd like to see when you look out onto your new garden. The next project is choosing plants that appeal to you and will grow well in the sun or shade exposure (lots of home-work here!). Then, once everything is down on paper, you'll want to prepare the planting beds. Start spreading 10–12 cm (4–5 in) of organic matter over the beds. You can use compost, aged manure, shredded leaves or whatever organic matter is readily available in your local area. Dig this organic matter into the soil 20–25 cm (8–10 in) deep. Plant your perennials and shrubs and mulch over the bare soil between the plants with additional organic matter. A 5–8 cm (2–3 in) layer will help slow water evaporation.

When planning where to site a garden bench, think about how much sun the particular spot gets and choose plants accordingly.

Decorative Plants

A garden seating area is not complete until you've added plants. These can be grown in pots or kept in beds and borders to edge and define the space as an area for relaxation. The advantage of container growing is that you are able to move the plants around as the occasion dictates, letting them take centre stage when they are at their best perhaps, or bringing tender varieties inside for the winter. Containers need regular maintenance in terms of watering. Even in large pots, few plants will survive purely on the water that falls as rain. When choosing plants, you should first and foremost consider the conditions you are offering. The amount of sunshine the planting area receives through the day, whether it is exposed to strong winds, and how cold it gets in winter are all key factors.

257. What's the best way to install a pondless waterfall?

It's easier than it looks to create a stunning feature, such as a waterfall, and building one is a fantastic way to attract wildlife to your garden.

Once you have all the supplies you need from a good garden centre, the next step is to actually install the parts. Dig a hole, put the tub in the hole and backfill with the soil you dug out. Get the tub as level as you can, but leave it elevated about 10 cm (4 in) above ground level. Fill it with water to help it settle. At this stage the water will be very muddy, but don't worry, you will be able to pump it out later and replace it with fresh, clean water. Then use the hose to wet the soil you used to backfill. That makes it settle into all the air pockets and makes your tub stable. If you don't have it filled with water, the tub will float up while you are hosing the soil into place and you will have to start digging all over again. Now that you have the tub in place, it's time to put your pump in. Ideally, put the pump somewhere accessible so you can get to it later, because it will need cleaning periodically. Connect a long piece of flexible tubing to the

Combining Features in a Garden

Creating the garden of your dreams is about much more than simply selecting all your favourite plants. It's also important to think about all the features you want to include and look at ways you can incorporate them into the space. As well as practical items, such as greenhouses, coldframes, trellis and decking, consider the more decorative features, such as summerhouses, arches, ponds and pergolas. These can all enhance your enjoyment of the garden and encourage you to spend more time outside relaxing. After all, if you've just invested a few hours tending your lawn and planting flowers and vegetables, it's only fair that you have a comfortable area to admire the fruits of your labours!

pump and lay it outside the tub. This tube is what the water will go through to get up and over the waterfall or through the rocks, so be sure the tubing is long enough. Next, place big rocks, any kind you like, in the tub. Put big ones on the bottom, smaller on top. Remember, you will have to get to the pump to clean it at least twice a year, so cover the pump in a way that means you can remove it easily. Put topsoil around the 10 cm (4 in) of tub that you left sticking up. You will plant in that later. On the top of the topsoil, cantilever flat rocks over the top of the tub so none of the tub is showing. Now you are ready to either build a waterfall using flat rocks or use a rock with a hole drilled through it. Push the tubing through the hole and let the water bubble up and back down into the tub. Or, build a stack of rocks with the tubing running up through the centre so the water bubbles up through the top of the rocks and down into the tub. Plug in the pump. All that's left is to choose some pretty plants, such as hosta, for the edges.

258. What can I plant around a gazebo?

As long as each area gets at least four hours of sunshine a day you can plant the same sun-loving perennials all around the gazebo. If one side gets more shade than sun, you'll need to choose shade-lovers for that part of the border. You can plant gazania, dianthus, garden phlox, astilbe or bleeding hearts in the border.

When choosing plants to brighten up a gazebo, bear in mind that one side is likely to be much shadier than the other, and select flowers accordingly.

259. Any tips on planning a kitchen garden?

If you have plenty of room, a greenhouse is a good option as you can use it to raise lots of plants from seed, and it will provide the ideal conditions for growing sun-loving options like tomatoes and chillis. It's also a good idea to plant fruit trees, which should be 3 m (10 ft) apart if they're semi-dwarf (mature height and width 2.5–3 m [8–10 ft]). Most edible plants need full sun to produce well, so choose a spot for them well out of any shade the southern border trees might cast. The exceptions are some veggies, such as lettuce, spinach and some herbs, which tolerate (and even enjoy) shade from hot summer sun. Plant the taller trees at the northern side of the garden so they don't shade others. Then put taller fruits, such as raspberries north of tall veggies like asparagus, and then place other vegetables on the southernmost edge out of the shade.

260. How can we make our new stone wall look established?

Lichens and moss do look nice on a stone wall, but in the sunshine you may not be successful in getting them to grow. If there's moss or lichen nearby, you may be able to transplant some pieces to your stone wall. Try mixing regular baking yeast in water to make a runny paste, brush it into the crevices of the rocks, and then plant the moss

> Mix moss with either buttermilk or yoghurt (the kind made with live cultures in it) in a blender, then paint that onto the surface.

or lichen pieces in the yeast. Start in the shadiest areas you can find, and maybe the moss will take hold. You might want to consider other plants, such as a small-leafed ivy, that will cling to a stone wall and soften its edges.

261. How can I encourage moss to grow on my new fence?

In many cases, moss will appear on its own if the conditions are right for it to grow. To introduce moss, the old rule of thumb is to find some moss growing in a similar situation (on a similar type of surface in similar lighting), mix it with either buttermilk or yoghurt (the kind made with live cultures in it) in a blender, then paint that onto the surface. The area should be damp and humid for best results. Most mosses grow well in the cooler, moister months and, by taking it from a nearby source, you will know it is suitable to your area. Since your fence is wooden you might not want to keep it wet as this may cause it to rot and deteriorate. It may also be difficult to get moss to grow on it if it is made of treated wood. Instead, you might consider using a soft sage-coloured or mossy-green-coloured stain, or applying several colours in a mottled effect. This, combined with a climbing plant or two, should give a similar visual 'feel' and be safer for the fence. It is also faster and more predictable.

Stone walls can provide a great opportunity to grow tiny, drought-tolerant plants, such as saxifrages, thymes and sempervivums.

262. What can I plant to cheer up some steps in full sun?

The conditions you describe are probably very hot, dry and bright in warm weather, so you'd get the best from flowers that enjoy these conditions, such as *Portulaca*. Some species of sedum and ice plant are succulents that would also do very well. Other colourful annuals include marigolds, nasturtiums, California poppy (*Eschscholzia*), verbena and everlasting flower (*Helipterum*). To help the soil maintain some moisture in these conditions, mulch the surface of your pots.

263. Are wood chips or sand better for a play area?

Try wood chips. They're spongy and soft, and although some of the smaller particles may cling to your children's clothing, at least they won't have to share their play area with anything the neighbourhood cats might leave behind. (Cats love to dig in sand but they generally stay away from wood chips.) The wood chips will need to be topped up every year or two.

Make the most of a sunny spot by adding lots of containers of sun-loving plants, such as verbena.

Selecting Plants for Your Containers

Whether you're filling planters, pots or hanging baskets, it's useful to consider what containers you are putting where. Making a few notes before you go shopping will help you to decide on the types of plant you need and how many of each to choose. Look out for drought-tolerant options, such as geraniums and verbena if you have a sunny spot. For containers in shade, consider begonias, fuchsias and impatiens. Select your container and decide what plants will suit it, placing the potted plants in position to finalise the design. Fill containers with potting medium, then carefully tip the plants out of their pots and plant. Firm in well and water, ideally by immersing it in a larger container of water for a couple of minutes.

Flower
Gardening

When it comes to choosing plants, it's all too easy to just snap up a random assortment of the ones that happen to catch your eye while you're shopping. Then you get them home and have to try to shoehorn them into the spaces you have available. But with a little planning and forethought, you can avoid costly errors and create a garden that is balanced and structured, both in terms of the height and shape of your plants, and their colour and interest. You can create a constantly unfolding landscape that always has something new to offer.

Perennials

Perennial plants represent a very wise investment of time and money. Choose the right spot for them and once established they'll come back bigger and better each year.

264. What is a perennial? How long will it live?

This term refers to any plant that lives for three or more years. There are woody perennials and herbaceous perennials. Woody perennials can be evergreen or deciduous. Evergreen perennials retain their leaves all winter long; deciduous perennials lose their leaves in the autumn and grow new leaves in the spring. Herbaceous perennials die down in the cold weather and sprout new stems and leaves in the spring time.

265. What do I need to consider when choosing perennials?

The old adage of 'right plant, right place' is a good guide. First, determine the amount of light the location receives, as well as the soil type in regard to how much sand, silt, clay and organic matter it contains. This will affect its degree of soil-moisture retention. The characteristics of the site will help you narrow plant choices to those that will thrive there. Design considerations such as height, width, colour and when it blooms usually come last on the list, because if the plant won't thrive on a particular site, there isn't much point in planting it! In practical terms, once you are familiar with plants that do well in your area, choose the ones you like and experiment a little to get the mix that works for you. Keep in mind, too, that if your heart is set on growing a plant that isn't suited to the soil you can modify the site to accommodate the plant to some extent. But it's a lot more work than just choosing something that will thrive there in the first place.

Planning for Perennials

Take your time to make the conditions just right. Your perennial border is a feature that could look great for decades to come, so why not get a load of mature organic matter delivered and dig this into the beds. If your soil is heavy, it's also worth digging in sand to improve drainage. You'll also need to consider how much sun or shade the space gets and bear in mind that this can be affected by any shrubs or trees you have. You'll need to choose different heights of plants for the front, middle and back of the border. Don't be fooled by the heights plants are at the garden centre, as this can change very quickly. Always look at the label for the eventual height and spread. Don't be afraid to move plants if need be.

266. Any tips on planting aquilegia?

Colombines are a classic cottage garden flower, and their historic popularity is reflected in the large number of common names for them, which include 'doves at the fountain'.

Aquilegia, or columbines, are perennial plants that like full sunshine or filtered shade. They have lacy foliage and beautiful, often pastel-coloured flowers that can reach up to 8 cm (3 in) across. They need well-prepared soil,

Organic matter, such as compost, leaf mould, or peat moss will help retain moisture and supply nutrients to the plant roots.

so add some organic matter and dig it into your garden bed before planting. Organic matter, such as compost, leaf mould or peat moss will help retain moisture and supply nutrients to the

plant roots. Sprinkle seed, or put young plants in the soil in the early spring for summer bloom. Be sure to keep the area well watered until the plants are established, then supply water once or twice during the week. Cut the flowering stems down when the flowers fade, and the plant will bloom again. You can save seeds to sow, or let the seeds mature on the second flush of bloom and the seeds will scatter themselves in the garden. Move any seedlings that pop up in the wrong spots.

267. What type of mulch is best for my perennial garden?

Nearly any type of organic mulch can be used in a perennial garden and will help keep down weeds, moderate soil temperature and retain moisture. It will also assist in fertilising the soil as it breaks down and will help to improve its structure. Many people prefer to use double-shredded hardwood bark or partially finished compost or leaf mould, as this looks attractive. Grass clippings can be used in a thin layer but may mat and repel moisture if used thickly. Very fine mulches may also blow away. Most people just use what is locally available and at an acceptable price. Woodier mulches, such as shavings, as opposed to bark, will tend to tie up nitrogen in the soil temporarily, so if you use one of those you may need to supplement the nitrogen somewhat at first, or else allow the wood mulch to age for at least a year before you use it. With a little trial and error you will find what works best for you.

268. What is the difference between a daylily and a true lily?

Daylilies are members of the genus *Hemerocallis*. They grow from crowns (not bulbs) and have many long, narrow leaves that originate from the crown. The flowers grow on long stems that also grow from the crown. On the other hand, members of the genus *Lilium* grow from bulbs. The leaves are short and narrow and grow along a stem on top of which sits the flowers. Both are related in that their flower parts come in sets of three or six and their leaves are strap-like. They are members of the family Liliaceae.

269. How do I care for a cranesbill?

The perennial geranium, or cranesbill, blooms profusely over a long summer season, providing that its basic cultural requirements are met. It grows in full sun or partial afternoon shade and needs constant moisture. Water before the soil begins to dry out and mulch over the soil with organic matter, which will release nutrients as it decomposes, and you'll be rewarded with a vivid show of flowers. Snip off any dead blooms as they appear, as this will encourage plants to flower stronger and for longer.

Perennial geraniums are a boon for any mixed border. As long as you provide plenty of moisture, they can bloom for months on end.

270. Are there any perennials that rabbits won't eat?

Unfortunately, rabbits seem to eat just about whatever is available. A fence is usually the most reliable form of protection – you can use chicken wire, 0.6 m (2 ft) high and buried about 15 cm (6 in) deep. A pet dog or cat can be a good deterrent, too. Some gardeners report success using some of the commercially available repellent sprays, applied and reapplied according to the label directions. You can also try some of the home remedies such as cayenne pepper mixed with garlic and sprayed around the lawn, or dog or cat hair sprinkled on and between the plants. You can even try to scare them by burying empty drink bottles with the tops poking up a few centimetres above the ground (they whistle in the wind). Using a combination of things and changing them often may work, but the only real guarantee is a fence.

Herbaceous perennials, such as aquilegia, have foliage that dies down over winter. New growth pops up in spring, followed by the flowers.

Unfortunately, rabbits seem to eat just about whatever is available. A fence is usually the most reliable form of protection . . .

271. What is a good evergreen plant for a hedge behind a perennial bed?

Traditional hedging in such a location would include boxwood, for a low clipped hedge, or yew, for a more massive background. You could also use germander (*Teucrium*) or Japanese holly.

272. How should I protect my aquilegia in winter?

Also known as columbine, the foliage and stems of these perennial plants will die down to ground level with the first frost. At that time you can prune away the dead plant parts and mulch over the top of the soil with a few centimetres of compost or other organic matter to help suppress weeds. By the springtime, you'll see that new stems and foliage have emerged and your plants will flower later in the season.

Also known as rock rose, cistus is a low-growing shrub that is very useful for the front of a sunny border.

Planting Perennials

It's well worth taking a little extra care when planting perennials. Remove each plant from its pot and soak in water for around ten minutes before you plant it. Then gently tease the roots out so they point downwards. This helps to get plants off to a flying start and prevents the roots simply growing round in a circle. It's easy to get carried away with wanting to grow a huge selection of plants, but if they're dotted around randomly, they won't make much impact. Always plant perennials in drifts of three, five or seven plants, if you have room. This way you'll get an established look very quickly, with a pleasing and natural effect. This also makes them easier to tend as well as providing supports for taller plants.

273. Can I grow cistus in a spot that only gets sun for a few hours a day?

Although cistus prefers growing in all-day sunshine, growing it in full-afternoon sunshine should be just fine. Try to keep this plant on the dry side to help it bloom more readily. Providing reflected heat (such as from a building, wall or fence) will enhance its performance.

274. Is it wise to put weed matting around my perennial plants?

Landscape fabric will help to keep weed seeds from germinating, so if you are very busy or you have a problem with weeds, it can be a good idea. Putting a decorative mulch, such as chipped bark, on top will help to conceal it.

275. How should I care for perennial poppies?

For best results, plant them in full sunshine in average-to-poor, well-draining soil. Poppies require excellent drainage. You can achieve this by digging an 45-cm-deep (18 in) planting hole, adding a layer of gravel, then mixing some compost in with native soil to fill the planting hole about half way. Then put more soil in and plant the poppy, gently tamping the soil around the roots. Water well after planting, then water only during the hottest summer months. Disbud after blooming, and stake the plant if it's in a windy area. When frost kills back the foliage, cut it from the plant then mulch well to help protect the roots during winter. Remove the mulch in the spring as the soil warms and sprouts begin to grow. Poppies do not need to be fertilised, and do not like to be moved once they've become established.

276. How do I grow delphinium from seed?

Delphinium seeds can take 15 days or more to sprout and they need darkness to germinate, so cover the seed flat with a layer of moist newspaper. Check daily, and place on a sunny windowsill or under lights as soon as you see the shoots. It can be helpful to start your delphinium seeds (or buy your plants) in late summer, plant them into the garden in early autumn, mulch them for the winter (if your ground freezes considerably), and expect a knockout show early next summer. Hopefully, your plants will get bigger and stronger each year. A summer mulch will help keep the soil moist and cool.

277. Any tips on caring for lupines?

Lupines are very beautiful, but sadly short-lived, perennials. You can prolong their lives by cutting off the spent flower stalks, but their flowering often declines after a few years. They will not form massive clumps like perennials such as phlox do, but they may self-seed if you leave a few seed heads on at the end of summer.

The stately spires of delphiniums are perfect for bringing height to the back of the border. Varieties are available in intense shades of blue and turquoise, and there are also white, pink and purple options.

278. What perennial flowers are deer proof?

Sadly, no flowers are completely deer proof but there are some that only seem to be eaten as a last resort! These include red valerian, wall flowers, achillea, nepeta, ajuga, coneflower, campanula and astilbe. Putting up tall fencing is the only absolute way of keeping deer from browsing in your garden, but you might try a deterrent. You can buy nasty-tasting mixtures that will usually keep deer from taking more than a bite or two.

279. Which perennials bloom in the first season from seed?

If you start the seed indoors around eight weeks before planting them out, the following plants should all flower in their first year, and then continue to improve with age: yarrow (*Achillea* 'Summer Pastels'), aster, blue Cupid's dart (*Catanache caerulea*), tickseed (*Coreopsis grandiflora*), perennial larkspur (*Delphinium belladonna*), purple coneflower (*Echinacea purpurea*), blue flax (*Linum perenne*), lupine hybrids (*Lupinus*), rose campion (*Lychnis coronaira*) and 'fastigiata' hollyhock mallow (*Malva alcea*).

280. Are there any perennials that thrive around Black walnut trees?

Black walnut (*Juglans nigra*) has a reputation for being allelopathic. This means that it inhibits the growth of other plants. Small amounts of juglone are released by the tree roots, but a far greater amount of this growth-inhibiting chemical is found under the canopy of the tree. Some plants that are tolerant of juglone include daphne, astilbe, bellflower, hosta, phlox, primrose, snowdrop, sweet woodruff and *Trillium*. Since your walnut tree is there to stay, try to plant one of the less-susceptible plants in the vicinity of the trees roots or canopy. You could create a pretty cottage-garden effect with a mixture of plants.

Although deer will eat most flowers if they're hungry, they tend to avoid red valerian. However, the safest way to protect your plants is to put up a fence.

281. Any tips on growing phlox?

There are several types of tall phlox and they are all lovely summer blooming garden plants and are all treated more or less the same way. They prefer full sun, good air circulation and an evenly moist yet well-drained and rich soil. You may find it beneficial to thin the emerging bloom stems in spring so as to allow space for good air circulation during the summer. The plants do best on a deeply prepared soil and will appreciate some balanced fertiliser or compost in early spring. It's a good idea to keep an eye on the watering and mulch them with several centimetres of organic mulch to help maintain soil moisture since they will bloom best with adequate water. Finally, remove spent flowers and at the end of summer do a careful cleanup of old stems and foliage, especially if there was any problem with mildew during the growing season.

282. What is the difference between a perennial and an annual?

An annual plant is one that grows, flowers, and sets seeds all in one season before dying. A perennial is a plant that lives for two or more years, growing, flowering and setting seeds. Some perennials are woody, meaning their tops remain above ground even during the winter months. Other perennials are herbaceous, and their tops die down in the winter but new stems and foliage appear the following spring. Many annuals self-seed and you may have new plants coming up the following spring in a bed that was growing annuals the previous year.

Perennial geraniums live for many years and survive in cold winters by storing all their energy in their roots. Annual geraniums are unable to survive cold weather and will usually be killed by the first frost.

Cutting Perennials Back

Perennials can be cut back at different times. Some should be trimmed just after they flower, to encourage them to produce more blooms later in the season – hardy geraniums will benefit from this approach. Some others such as phlox can be cut back to stop mildew (which can be bad if you have a warm, wet summer). At the end of summer take a while to look at your plants and trim back any parts that look too scruffy, but don't be too eager to cut your perennial plants back in autumn. Even after they've finished flowering many perennials can provide beautiful structure to the garden, and they can look fantastic when covered in frost or snow. Also bear in mind that their seed heads can be a great source of food for wild birds. What's more they can offer shelter to beneficial insects such as ladybugs.

283. How often do perennials need to be pruned and divided?

The answer depends to some extent on what the plant is, but in most cases pruning it back too often will eliminate the blooms and may weaken and possibly kill the plant by limiting its foliage and thus its energy. Division is one way to control size, and is necessary with certain perennials. Others will reach their mature size and stop expanding, so with these ones a better approach might be to plant them at a more appropriate spacing to begin with, perhaps temporarily filling the spaces in between with annuals.

284. Are there any perennial varieties of sweet peas?

Lathyrus latifolius is a perennial sweet pea. It usually has pink or white blooms and is a good cut flower. *Lathyrus odoratus*, which is the more commonly known sweet pea, is an annual. It tends to have larger, more decorative blooms and is usually scented. However, you will have to plant new seeds every year. If you're a fan of the flowers, why not grow both?

285. Does geum repeat bloom?

This perennial should produce lots of new flowers over a long season (often from May to September) if dead blooms are removed regularly. The plants grow best in full sun to part shade in ordinary garden soil that has good drainage. Cut back the spent flowers and their stems and new flowers will follow in a few short weeks.

Once your geum flowers have died, cut the stems off and more blooms should appear a few weeks later.

286. Is it possible to split peonies?

If your peonies are getting too big, or you want more plants, you can carefully divide them. However, they may take a year or two to flower after this as they resent being disturbed.

These plants can be divided to start new beds in late summer. However, you'll want to be as gentle as possible with peonies as they are

> Be as gentle as possible with peonies as they are sensitive and may take a couple of years to bloom after dividing.

sensitive and may take a couple of years to bloom after dividing. Unlike many perennials, peonies can go for many years without needing to be divided. To divide them, separate a portion of the clump by inserting a spade and making a vertical cut into the root ball. Dig up this portion, and replant in a carefully prepared bed. (Fill in the hole left next to the parent plant with rich soil.) Or you can dig up the entire peony plant and prune off a section of the root ball. Then replant both sections in prepared beds, taking care to plant the crowns no deeper than 4–5 cm (1½–2 in) below the soil surface. If they are too deep they are unlikely to bloom.

Many perennials can be bought very reasonably in spring as bare-root plants. Dicentra, or bleeding heart, can be found in pink or white and is far tougher than it looks.

287. How should I begin a perennial garden?

Your first step should probably be to obtain an accurate soil test to see what you have to work with. Most new planting areas appreciate a hefty addition of organic material such as mushroom soil mix, leaf mould, material from your own heap, or composted cow or horse manure. Also, it's very important to make sure your soil is loose, not compacted. You want good drainage as well. This can be achieved by adding sharp sand to the bed. Take a look at gardening books and magazines to see what plants strike your fancy.

light application of an organic liquid fertilisers, in accordance with the label instructions, to help them along. If possible, plant out new perennials on a cloudy day or in the rain to minimise stress. Should extreme cold threaten at night, cover them with a mulch such as straw or old leaves, or even an upturned cardboard box, to protect them. In the day, remove the box to avoid overheating. It can also be helpful to shade them slightly (leaves or straw work fine) and protect them from drying winds for the first few days to allow the foliage a chance to green up gradually. Once they are in the ground, keep the soil evenly moist but not soggy until they become well established. Using several centimetres of organic mulch around the plants, without touching the stems, can also help conserve moisture and keep down annual weeds.

288. How should I plant bare-root perennials such as *Dicentra*?

These are usually available in spring when the weather can be very variable! Fortunately, most of them are very tough and resilient plants and are likely to have sufficient root reserves to overcome any initial difficulties. Plant them as soon as you can and keep them well watered and mulched, and provide a bit of extra potting soil or possibly a

289. Can I use a lawn mower to trim my perennials at the end of summer?

Wait until after frost kills the tops of the perennials. When they experience a frost, the plants go into dormancy in a natural way. If you cut or mow down the foliage while it is still green, the plants will use up energy trying to regrow. Once the plants are dormant, it's simple to cut the dead foliage off with secateurs.

290. If you plant a perennial in a pot, will it come up yearly?

The problem with planting in containers is that the roots of your perennials can freeze solid during the winter months. You can protect them by burying the pot in the ground or wrapping bubble wrap or a garden insulation blanket around the outside of the pot to keep the roots from freezing. If you can't do this, you might prefer to just plant annuals with the expectation that you'll have to replant every spring.

291. How can I grow some scarlet-plumes from seed?

There are many different types of scarlet-plume. *Euphorbia lathyrus* is an annual and is planted in early spring as with any other typical annual. Most of the named scarlet-plumes, however, are propagated from cuttings or divisions. To start the perennial types from seed, chill the seeds for a week (place in a plastic bag or closed container with some slightly moistened peat moss and place in the refrigerator), then soak in water for several hours and plant in a warm, well-drained soil mix (temperature of 24–27°C, or 75–80°F). The seeds should germinate in two to three weeks.

There are many perennial euphorbias, from low-growing varieties to impressive, shrub-like giants. Wear gloves when pruning them as their sap can be irritating to the skin.

292. Do I have to stake tall plants or will pinching them back help?

Pinching back will probably stop plants from flowering altogether so it isn't recommended. The stems on some perennials are naturally tall and pinching them back will only result in short, bare stems. There are some nearly invisible stakes available. They are green and most will be hidden by the foliage as the plants grow. Look out for designs that consist of two green stakes with a circle on top for the flower stems to grow up through. The plants remain upright and the leaves disguise the entire thing.

293. How do I grow the perennial wallflower?

Erysimum, commonly called wallflower, is a colourful perennial but is often grown as an annual. As longs as winters aren't exceptionally cold it will perform reliably as a perennial. Provide full sunshine and regular water during the growing season. If it starts to look scruffy after a few years, it's best to dig it out and put in new plants.

Perennial wallflowers are very easy to grow and provide welcome colour in spring. However, they have a tendency to get untidy over the years and so you may choose to replace them from time to time.

294. How do I grow violets from seed?

The seeds for violets need to be pre-chilled for two weeks prior to sowing. Since the seeds are small, you can place them between the folds of a barely damp paper towel and seal them in a plastic bag before placing in the refrigerator. (For larger seeds that need pre-chilling, simply mix them with some moistened potting soil, seal in a plastic bag and place in the refrigerator for the prescribed length of time.) After the chill period, sow the seeds 0.2 cm (¹⁄₁₆-in) deep in moistened seed-starting mix and cover the trays or pots with plastic wrap to help hold in the moisture. Place the trays or pots in a warm area, such as on top of the refrigerator. The seeds should germinate in 14 to 21 days when kept at 18–24°C (65–75°F).

Some perennials, such as violets, need to have their natural growing conditions imitated before they will germinate. Therefore, you'll need to cool the seeds and then place them in a warmer environment so they react as if winter is over and spring has come.

295. Which perennials bloom in late summer in shade?

You might try some of the bolder foliaged hostas that bloom later in the season, along with some of the lesser-known upright shade-lovers, such as Solomon's seal (*Tricyrtis*) and *Cimicifuga*. You might try training a climbing hydrangea up behind them. Another way of adding height and interest would be a pedestal with an ornament or container on it, or perhaps a series of containers on your back fence. For the containers, impatiens and small or variegated forms of English ivy are classic accompaniments to shady perennial beds.

296. Are foxgloves perennial? Will they return next year?

Foxgloves are usually considered a biennial. In the first year, the plants grow only a rosette of foliage on the ground. In the second year, they bloom and set seed and then usually die. If you allow the seeds to ripen on the plant, they will self-seed and new seedlings will emerge the following spring, creating a seemingly perennial patch. These plants do best in a rich soil that is evenly moist (but not soggy) and in morning sun, filtered sun or full sun (but only if the soil is moist enough).

297. What's the best time to plant a perennial garden?

You can plant perennials at any time when the ground isn't frozen, but early spring and autumn offer the best chances of success because the ground is more moist.

Bare-root perennials are usually planted in very early spring when they become available, but container-grown perennials can be planted from spring through to just before the first frost. Early spring and very early autumn are typically the preferred times for planting. Planting too late in the autumn does not allow enough time for the plants to become securely rooted before the freeze and thaw cycles begin. The resulting heaving ground can dislodge the plants. Planting in midsummer causes undue heat stress but can be accomplished successfully if you are very careful about watering.

Researching the Right Perennials

Perennial plants are among the loveliest flowers you can grow. Although they need a certain amount of staking, weeding and deadheading, they are relatively low-maintenance compared to an area filled with bedding plants. What's more, the plants will get bigger and better every year, if tended well. In fact you may need to divide clumps every five years or so, but this task means that you get more of your favourite plants for free. Given that they are a long-term investment, it's well worth doing a bit of research before you start planting. Consider what sort of soil you have. If possible, dig over the whole area (a little at a time is often the best approach). Remove any large stones and weeds.

Annuals and Biennials

Some gardeners are nervous about growing flowers from seed, but once you try it, and see how easy it is, you'll never look back. It's a very rewarding way to fill beds and borders with bold colour.

298. What marigolds should I plant with tomatoes?

French marigolds can help repel nematodes, so if your tomato plants are historically attacked by soil nematodes, planting marigolds next to them can be beneficial. *Calendula*, or English marigold, has similar repellent properties but is commonly used to repel tomato worms. Not only is companion planting a lovely way to bring bursts of colour to a vegetable garden, it can attract a host of beneficial insects in addition to repelling destructive insects.

Both English and French marigolds can be very helpful if planted next to your tomato crops as their bold colours attract useful insects.

299. Can I plant annuals in situ?

If you prepare the growing site first, you can plant annual seeds directly in the ground. For real success, take your time when you prepare the planting bed – you'll be greatly rewarded for any extra effort you put in. Start by removing any weeds in the area and digging down into the soil with a shovel to loosen it up. Then spread 8–10 cm (3–4 in) of organic matter (such as compost or aged manure) over the top of the bed and then dig it in to a depth of about 20 cm (8 in). Rake the soil smooth and then plant. The organic matter will help loosen the soil, help it hold moisture, and release nutrients to the roots of your plants. Sow your seeds as directed on the packages and then carefully sprinkle the bed to help settle the seeds. Once your plants are up and growing you can place another 5–8 cm (2–3 in) of organic matter over the top of the bed to help suppress weeds, moderate soil temperatures and slow water evaporation. Keep your new plants watered well and they should bloom their little heads off!

300. Do zinnias self-seed? I'd like to grow them next year.

Zinnias are considered annuals and as such need to be started each year. The seeds form inside the flower head once the petals fade and the ripening process is completed. Usually the seeds are mature when the spent flower is completely dried up. The seeds tend to stay stuck in the flower form so, if you want to save your own seed and plant them next year, you may need to pull the heads apart gently to separate them. Although they do self-seed occasionally, they are not reliable, and over time the more unusual colours seem to disappear, so you may prefer to simply buy a new packet each spring. This will also give you the chance to try out different varieties.

301. What long-stemmed flowers are suitable for cutting?

Sunflowers are great cut flowers and come in a variety of 'happy' faces that seem to draw people to them. You may prefer to choose those that are pollenless, so they don't drip pollen on surfaces. Although seldom long-stemmed (unless you train them carefully), most people love the scent of sweet peas, which make lovely little 'nosegays'. Stock is another that has a spicy scent and so makes a good cut flower. Salvia and larkspur are two more fantastic plants to consider, and larkspur is an easy and colourful annual to grow from seed.

Some annuals such as zinnias can have disappointing results if you try to grow them from saved seed, so you may prefer to buy new seeds every year.

If you prepare the growing site first, you can plant annual seeds directly in the ground. For real success, take your time when you prepare the planting bed — you'll be greatly rewarded for any extra effort you put in.

302. Is it possible to grow French marigolds from seed?

The botanical name for French marigold is *Tagetes patula*, and you sometimes see a type of marigold for sale labelled simply 'tagetes', which refers to the tall version of these plants that have small orange or yellow flowers and a sharp, almost citrus fragrance. Marigolds are a relatively easy crop to grow from seed and have no unusual requirements. In fact you may notice seedlings popping up in late summer where the earliest blooms of this year's plants set seed. For best results, start seeds indoors in early spring. Sow them in a sterile seed-starting mix and keep the soil evenly moist, but not too wet. When seedlings emerge, place on a sunny windowsill or under fluorescent lights, keeping the lights just an 2–5 cm (1–2 in) above the tips of the plants. Continue to keep the soil moist, and thin seedlings to one plant per pot (if you've used small containers or 'six-pack' trays). Repot them to larger containers if the roots become crowded. Transplant to the garden when all danger of frost is past.

French marigolds are very easy to grow and will bloom for months on end if you water the plants in dry spells and remove the dead flowers.

Nurturing Seedlings

The most important thing to remember when growing annuals from seed is to make sure that your hands and the containers are meticulously clean before sowing; this will lessen the danger of plant diseases spreading to your seedlings. Remember to label everything; one seedling can look much like another, and although you may be convinced you'll remember which is which, it's all too easy to mix them up at some point. Choose compost that is free-draining and suitable for seedlings. Although all seeds need moisture to germinate, too much can be fatal; the best way to water seeds in pots is to do so by allowing the water to seep upwards via capillary action. To do this, place the containers in a large tray filled with 2.5 cm (1 in) of water, and remove once moisture has risen to the soil's surface. Don't let them sit in water for more than a few minutes or the roots could start to suffer.

303. Is *Rudbeckia* an annual or not? I've heard differing opinions.

Some forms of this plant, such as Indian summer rudbeckia (*Rudbeckia hirta*), are annuals in cooler climates. So although this variety will bloom all summer if you keep the spent blooms removed, it won't survive cold winters, although most other species of *Rudbeckia* do. You can expect that it won't come back the following spring, although if you have an especially mild winter, you might be pleasantly surprised.

Most *Rudbeckias* are perennial and will come back every year, but there are also some annual forms that will be killed off by a cold winter.

304. What late summer flowers can I grow for a wedding?

You could try gerbera daisies, which are most reliably grown from purchased plants set into the garden in full sun with a rich soil and regular watering. They really like long days and hot weather and may slow down by the end of summer. A safer bet would be dahlias which are very fine for cutting and come in all sorts of colours, shapes and sizes. Some of the more reliable later annuals include cosmos (available in pinks, yellows and white), tithonia (which has orange flowers), salvia (available in red and blue), zinnia (all shapes, colours and sizes), and gloriosa daisies (gold and autumnal tones). It's also worth considering some plants to grow for foliage.

305. What fast-growing annuals can I plant in patio pots?

Most common annuals take ten to 12 weeks to bloom in a warm summer. You might try annual aster, sweet alyssum, *Portulaca*, zinnia, *Sanvitalia*, *Convolvulus* and California poppy. If you can warm the soil in the containers in advance, perhaps by covering it with black plastic for several weeks, the seeds will germinate faster. Make sure that the soil is rich and moist, yet well-drained; also, fertilise the plants regularly with a soluble fertiliser or compost tea to ensure vigorous growth.

In favourable conditions, many annuals will bloom just 12 weeks after being planted and provide months of colour.

306. Can I plant white *Cosmos* near pink ones or will they cross-pollinate?

It should be fine to plant a drift of white seeds near to a drift of pink ones. The only time you'll get a mix of cosmos flower colours is next year, and that would only be if the white cosmos cross-pollinate with the other colours, set seeds and the seeds fall to the ground over winter and come up next spring. Cosmos can self-seed, but you can control this by removing any new seedlings that come up in spring as soon as you notice them. Then, after a few weeks, plant your desired mix of cosmos colours and the bed should be true to colour. A mixture of colours can also be very effective.

307. I'm planting annuals for the first time. Which ones are easy to grow from seed?

Lots of different annuals are very easy, and they are the perfect introduction to propagating plants from seed. You can buy heated propagators or special seedling heat mats from garden centres to help keep seeds warm, but a sunny windowsill is also fine. Ideally, the air temperature shouldn't fall below 10°C (50°F) at night.

> You can buy heated propagators or special seedling heat mats from garden centres to help keep seeds warm . . .

There are plenty of options for long-blooming, sun-loving annuals that you can grow from seed, including zinnias, marigolds, alyssum, nasturtium, California poppies, cosmos, *Celosia*, salvia, cleome, *Portulaca* and nicotiana. You can start these as late as six weeks before your final expected frost date and still get a very good show all summer long.

Annuals are very easy to grow from seed. To get the earliest blooms in spring, you can start them off indoors before the frosts. Alternatively, plant seeds directly in the soil once it warms up.

Preventing Overcrowding

It's important to sow seeds thinly so each seedling has plenty of space to grow. If not, overcrowding can lead to damping off, a fungal infection that can kill young plants overnight. It's exacerbated by high humidity and poor air circulation, so if you're growing seeds in a propagator, remember to keep the vents open. Overcrowded seedlings will also be difficult to transplant, as lifting them out is very tricky without damaging their stems or roots. When your annuals have four 'true' leaves (these will look like the adult leaves rather than the first two more rounded seed leaves), they are ready to be pricked out. Holding the seedling by a leaf (not the fragile stem), use a dibber to ease it up out of the soil and pop into a new pot.

308. Will my annuals survive if I take them indoors over winter?

When they grow in their native climates, there are some plants which we grow as annuals that are in fact perennials. Others, such as coleus, are not terribly long-lived no matter where they grow. Depending on the plants in question, you can try digging them up, potting them and cutting them back, and they will probably survive the winter for you. However, by next spring the plants may be very rangy and nearing exhaustion. For this reason, many gardeners will take cuttings of their favourite plants, such as geraniums, and keep them over the winter. Then, in spring, they will plant these replacements outside again. This way there are always newer and more vigorous plants and an insurance policy against loss.

Direct Sowing

Many annual seeds can simply be sown outdoors in spring, and this is ideal for flowers such as nasturtiums that have high germination rates. Direct sowing is when single seeds are planted at their final spacings. It's the best option for flowers such as poppies that don't take well to being transplanted. If you're sowing extremely fine seeds in drills, mixing them up with a little horticultural sand could help, as you will be able to see exactly where and how much you're sowing, helping you to do so evenly. Also, remember that such tiny seeds are unlikely to need much compost sprinkled over them. When sowing tiny seeds, it can be best to water the ground first, then sprinkle the seeds, so they aren't washed away.

The leaves, flowers and buds of nasturtiums are edible and they make a lovely addition to salads, so why not grow them around the edges of your vegetable garden?

309. What's the best spot for nasturtiums?

Nasturtiums grow best in full sun, perhaps with afternoon shade, where summers are hot. They will grow in poor-to-average, moist, well-drained, slightly acid soil. Avoid feeding them, as it will cause weak, sappy growth and you may get lots of leaves at the expense of the flowers. Make sure you water them regularly in dry spells, as they can bloom less if they dry out.

310. Any tips on growing *Portulaca* from seed?

Plants can be tricky to grow from seed as they are very sensitive to overwatering, especially if temperatures are low or they are stressed for light. In a way, this makes sense when you consider that they like it hot, relatively dry, and very sunny in the garden. You might try adding a bit of extra perlite to their potting mix to improve drainage, and take care not to overwater them.

311. How often should I water my annuals?

This depends on a number of factors, including how often it rains, how long your soil retains moisture, and how fast water evaporates in your climate. Soil type is another important consideration. Clay soils hold water very well – in fact, sometimes too well. Sandy soils are like a sieve, letting the water run right through. Both kinds of

> Generally, garden plants need a few centimetres of water a week. Plants in containers need to be watered more frequently because they dry out quickly . . .

soil can be improved with the addition of organic matter. Organic matter gives clay soils lightness and air, and gives sandy soils something to hold the water. So much depends on climate and the ability of different soil types to hold moisture that it's difficult to give specific directions for watering your garden. Generally, however, garden plants need about 2.5 cm (1 in) of water a week. Plants in containers need to be watered more frequently because they dry out quickly, especially in hot weather. You may need to water every day. Try watering your plants then lifting the pot to see how heavy it is when the soil is moist. Then just pick up the containers during the week. When they begin to feel lightweight, it's time to water.

312. How do I start poppy seeds in my garden?

Poppy (*Papaver*) seeds will germinate in soil that's barely warm (15°C, or 55°F), so prepare the garden soil by digging and amending with organic material and then sowing the seeds. They'll sprout in ten to 30 days, depending upon the outdoor temperature. Start them in the spring, cover the seedbed with a very thin layer of peat moss, and keep the bed well watered. After the seeds sprout, thin carefully by cutting the extra sprouts off with scissors. Poppies don't like to be transplanted, so take care when sowing the seeds that the plants won't be too crowded.

It's vital to ensure poppies are sown in the position where you want them to grow as it's almost impossible to move seedlings once they're growing as they rarely survive any damage to their roots.

313. Do morning glories come back from year to year?

Morning glories are annuals, meaning they need to be planted from seed each spring. If you grow them one year, your plants may well self-seed the following year, but as insurance (and to maintain purity if you grow a mixture of colours) you may want to plant new seeds each year. Since frost kills the vines outright there is no harm in cleaning them up and removing them.

Fast-growing morning glories can cover a large area in a short time. These annual plants die at the end of each year, so you'll need to plant new seeds every spring.

314. Can I take cuttings of pansies?

Most biennials (plants that germinate and grow for one season, winter over, then bloom, set seed and die in the second year) do not propagate well from cuttings. It is possible to have some luck growing second-year divisions of some biennials such as foxgloves, but they tend to stay in the behaviour mode of second-year plants, and die the same year. Annuals, (plants that germinate, bloom and set seed and die all in one year) certainly do not propagate well by cuttings. If nothing else, their life span is too short to make it worth the effort. Pansies are generally considered as annual-type bedding plants because they exhaust themselves after a full season of blooming. For that reason alone it probably wouldn't be worth trying, but you could always experiment!

315. Any tips on planting root-bound annuals?

In some cases, severely root-bound plants have already become so stressed that they will fail no matter what you do. But in general, moderately root-bound transplants do just fine. In fact, a strong root system will make a strong plant. The best thing to do is to try to loosen the roots somewhat so that they are directed outwards, and loosen the soil around the planting hole so that the roots can move into it easily. You might also pay special attention to those plants at watering time since they will have suffered some root damage in the process. Finally, they will establish fastest in moist but well-drained soil with a high level of organic matter and adequate fertility.

316. How do I grow really tall sunflowers?

The best indicator of height would be to select a tall-growing variety. Overall, health is also very important, so incorporate lots of organic matter, such as compost and possibly well-aged stable manure into the planting hole. Be sure to prepare the planting area deeply and allow plenty of room for the plant to develop. Full sun and even moisture are also important for fast and sturdy growth. Get all this right and you might need a ladder to pick them! Save a few seeds to plant for next year.

Choose the right variety and prepare the soil well and you can grow enormous sunflowers. As well as the cheerful blooms, you'll get huge heads of seeds which are a great favourite of wild birds.

317. How can I get my annuals to grow well?

Start by adding organic matter to the soil to help enrich and loosen it so the roots can penetrate deeply. Spread 10–13 cm (4–5 in) of aged manure or compost over the entire bed and dig it in to a depth of 20–25 cm (8–10 in). Then level the bed and start planting. After you've finished planting, spread an additional 5–8 cm (2–3 in) of organic matter over the bare soil to help suppress weeds and slow water evaporation. The other consideration is to make sure your annuals are getting the sun or shade they crave. If you plant a sun-lover in the shade, it simply won't grow well. Be sure to check the tags on the plants to see what they prefer. Watering deeply once or twice a week and feeding with a slow-release fertiliser in the spring should help your new plants grow well.

Station Sowing

A method that is often used for larger seeds is 'station' sowing. Two or three seeds are sown together in one hole at their final spacings. More than one may germinate, but these will later be thinned to a single plant. This method is ideal for plants such as sunflowers that you want to grow quite far apart in neat rows, and it means you have an insurance policy in place. Even if one seed fails to germinate or gets eaten by a bird, you will still have others at that 'station' so you won't have any gaps in your row. Another option is to plant a few 'spare' seeds at the end of the row, and transplant these seedlings into any gaps that may appear! This latter option is not ideal for sunflowers, however, as they don't like to be moved.

318. Can I plant cleome seeds on a slope?

You can start cleomes indoors so you'll have an earlier bloom, but this plant seems to do better if direct sown once the ground has warmed up. You might try starting a few indoors, and the rest outdoors, and see what works for you. Grow the plants about 1 m (3 ft) apart as they can get quite large. They like full sun and rich, moist, well-drained soil. The plant reaches a height of 1–1.2 m (3–4 ft), with delicate, spidery flowers. They make long-lasting cut flowers that look beautiful in a mass planting, though not so far away that you can't appreciate their delicacy. If your slope is in a sunny spot it could be ideal, just keep them well watered. The problem with slopes is that water can run off before it has soaked into the soil, so consider creating a terraced effect.

Choosing Annuals

The key to success when planning a mixed bed of annual flowers is choosing plants that do not overpower each other in terms of size or colour. Place large specimens such as larkspur towards the back of the bed, and choose smaller options as you work to the front. If your border is against a warm wall, try a climber such as a sweet pea to create a colourful backdrop to your planting. For the middle of the border, you could choose cleome or godetia. Easy to grow, either of these will attract a range of beneficial insects. Shorter varieties, such as violas, are ideal for the front of your planting scheme. Then you can have an option like sweet-smelling alyssum cascade down from your beds and onto the edges of your paths to blend into an informal display.

Bees are vital to our gardens, and their hard work pollinating fruit and vegetables can help you to get bumper crops. Attract more to your plot by choosing bee-friendly plants and avoiding pesticides.

319. What annuals can I plant to attract bees?

To attract these helpful insects, and keep them around to pollinate your fruit and vegetable crops, try to have something blooming at all times, and avoid using pesticides on your plants. *Monarda*, *Agastache*, borage and Viper's Bugloss are all very decorative plants that are easy to grow and can be cultivated alongside your kitchen garden.

320. What flower seeds can I plant at the end of summer?

There are lots of ornamentals you can start from seed the year before you want them to bloom. In early autumn, sow seeds of larkspur, foxglove, *Delphinium*, rose campion and pansies. Right before hard frost you can sow calendula and annual dianthus.

321. Slugs have eaten my annuals. Can I plant fast-growing ones in pots?

Varieties such as cosmos, cleome and sunflower can be planted later in the season, and you can still get a good show by the end of the summer, although these would need a fairly large container to do well. Slugs can be an ongoing problem, so you will need to keep working at controlling them. Methods to try include the beer-baited traps, sprinkling diatomaceous earth (horticulture grade powder) on the soil surface around the plants, and picking them by hand in the late evening or at night (drop them into soapy or salty water). Finally, avoid watering in the evening as the moisture attracts them, unless you are going to go round afterwards with a torch to collect them (which can be a very effective way of keeping their numbers under control).

322. Should I deadhead my *Oenothera speciosa* 'Siskiyou' or trim off whole stems?

Your Mexican evening primrose is a perennial plant that will bloom from spring until autumn. When it's finished blooming and the stems die back to the ground, you can cut them away. Don't prune out any live stems, though – your plant will need the leaves to produce energy for the roots. Once the stems have died down on their own, it's safe to prune them off. The more commonly grown options are annual plants but they often self-seed and so may pop up again.

323. Any tips on growing annual *Vinca*? I want lots of plants for edging a path.

Vinca seeds take 15 to 30 days to germinate at 20–24°C (70–75°F). They won't germinate in light, so make sure the seeds are covered. If you have a seed-starting heat pad, place the tray of seeds on the heat source, but don't supply any additional light until the seeds have germinated. Once they've sprouted, turn off the heat source and place the seedlings under a source of artificial light or on a sunny windowsill. Some seeds take longer to germinate than others, so be patient and they'll come up eventually!

Evening primrose is an undemanding plant that fills the night air with fabulous scent and can make sitting outside a real pleasure.

324. When and how do I plant sweet peas?

Sweet peas can be planted about two weeks before your last frost date, which means you can put them in the ground in mid-April. If you soak the seeds in warm water for 24 hours before planting, the seeds will germinate faster. Set up your trellis for the peas to climb on before you plant. Sweet peas send out tendrils that need narrow horizontal wires or wood strips for support so you may need to add some horizontal string or wire to your trellis if it consists of mostly vertical strips. Plant the seeds about 0.5 cm (¼ in) deep and lightly firm the soil on top. Water well and keep the soil moist. When the seedlings emerge, mulch the soil to keep it cool and moist.

As long as you remove the seed pods regularly, sweet peas can bloom for months on end, providing fragrant cut flowers for the home as well as an attractive display for the garden. Bees love them too.

325. Can I grow annuals in shade?

A tender bulb that is often treated like an annual is tuberous begonia (*Begonia x tuberhybrida*). The stunning rose or camellia-like flowers are available in pink, red, orange, lavender, yellow or white. Leaves are thick, heart-shaped and sometimes variegated. Plants are commonly grown in containers or hanging baskets. The tubers should be dug up in autumn and stored indoors over the winter, to be planted out again in spring. A few other annuals that tolerate shade or partial shade are nasturtium (*Tropaeolum*), flowering tobacco (*Nicotiana*), pansy (*Viola*), lobelia (*Lobelia*), button bachelor (*Centaurea*), pinks (*Dianthus*), bells of Ireland (*Moluccella*), forget-me-not (*Myosotis*), baby blue eyes (*Nemophila*), perilla and fuchsia. Shady spots under trees and shrubs or near walls are often quite dry, so ensure you water your flowers regularly.

326. How do I keep forget-me-nots from one year to the next?

Forget-me-nots are annual plants so they die back every year but fortunately they self-seed with great abandon. In some areas of Australia these plants are considered a weed; be sure to check with your local council to see if it is appropriate to grow these plants in your area. Once forget-me-nots have finished flowering and set seed, you can trim the plants and tidy the brown foliage away. Late summer or early autumn is often a good time to do this. Next spring, you'll see healthy new plants emerging from your garden. If they happen to pop up in places where you'd rather not have them, simply pull up the seedlings – they are shallow-rooted, so it doesn't take long to remove any that you don't want.

Although they are annual plants and die at the end of each summer, forget-me-nots set seed very readily and tend to pop up again every spring.

327. Should I start my bells of Ireland seeds indoors?

The seeds of bells of Ireland (*Moluccella*), can be sown outdoors in early spring or started indoors eight to ten weeks before planting out. If you start your seeds indoors, sow them in individual peat pots. The seeds require a pre-chill period before they will germinate, so mix the seeds together with moist growing medium, seal in a plastic bag, and refrigerate for five days. Then sow on the surface of moistened seed-starting mix in individual pots. Seedlings will appear in eight to 35 days when kept at 10–16°C (50–60°F). When you're ready to plant outdoors, space the plants 30 cm (12 in) apart in ordinary soil in a sunny to partly shady garden spot. They make great cut flowers.

Using Seed Trays

When you need to germinate a large number of seedlings, perhaps for use as bedding plants, it can be helpful to use trays. Modular containers can be useful for varieties that do not like their roots disturbed when you transplant them, as you can lift them out in a block, roots and all, with the growing material. They also use a minimal amount of compost. Pots are useful for when you only need to propagate a small number of seedlings. Biodegradable options are best used for plants such as sunflowers that don't react well to transplanting, since you can plant the container, too. If you use them for plants that have large seeds then you can avoid the bother of pricking out. These pots are often made of recycled organic fibres and they are a boon for busy gardeners as instead of storing over winter, just buy new ones every spring.

328 What kind of plants can I grow to attract more butterflies to my garden?

Lismanthes or poached egg plant is very easy to grow, just prepare the soil, scatter the seeds and water, and the seedling will soon emerge. The pretty little flowers are loved by butterflies and bees.

Butterflies are attracted to almost everything in bloom, but especially things planted in large swathes or drifts of all one plant. For butterflies, it can also be important to plant larval feed sources as well as nectar plants. Some particu- larly useful plants include annuals such as borage, calendula, catnip, hyssop and *Lisianthus*. Additional options include parsley, dill, Virginia creeper, *Asclepias*, *Buddleja*, purple coneflower and *Verbena bonariensis*.

Fast-Growing Annuals

If you don't have time to choose lots of different annuals and you have lots of beds to fill, look out for packets of mixed seeds. These mixes are often colour-themed. Other options include annuals for butterflies, birds or bees. All these tend to include fast-growing annuals in bold colours that are ideal for filling large spaces with the minimum of fuss. You can simply prepare the ground by weeding it, then rake it over, scatter the seeds thinly in drifts, and sprinkle with water. Once the seedlings emerge water regularly and remove any weeds that pop up. Fast-growing annuals are also useful for filling gaps in the border if a larger plant has finished for the season. Mark rows with the tip of a hand trowel and water well, then sprinkle seeds along the rows. When the seedlings pop up you'll be able to spot any weeds, and it will be easier to weed between each row.

329. Should I cut my godetia back to get more blooms?

Godetia, also known as *Clarkia*, is a very pretty annual that deserves to be more widely grown. Cutting them back isn't recommended; just keep them staked and don't overfeed them. These plants actually bloom best when they are a little crowded together. Their blooming slows during hot weather. Water them regularly and they should provide a good show for weeks.

330. When should I start planting my annuals indoors?

The length of time depends on what you are trying to grow, but a typical time frame might be eight weeks prior to the last average frost date for your area. The seed packets often include an indication of weeks for the specific plant in question. Unless you have a very sunny window-sill, you may find it necessary to add supplemental lighting on a timer for about sixteen hours a day in order to produce good quality, healthy seedlings indoors. You might keep an eye on your plants and consider doing that if they seem to be 'leggy' (taller and thinner than average!).

331. Is Sweet William a perennial?

Sweet William (*Dianthus barbatus*) is a biennial, meaning that the plant starts to grow one year, and flowers the next. There is a new variety of Sweet William called 'New Era' that blooms both years if planted early. There are other *Dianthus* species that are annuals (*D. chinensis*, *D. caryophyllus*), while the ones commonly known as pinks are perennial and come back every year.

With their heady, almost clove-like scent, Sweet Williams are ideal for planting along pathways and patio areas so they can be enjoyed at their full.

Roses

With their large, distinctive blooms and heady fragrance, it's hardly surprising that roses are so widely popular. They can be easy to look after and provide pleasure year after year.

332. How can I prevent weak-stemmed roses?

What you describe is often called 'weak neck' and is the inability of the stem to support the flower in an upright position. If this is not an inherent characteristic of the particular variety you're growing, the addition of phosphorus to the soil can aid in strengthening the stems. Also make certain that the roses are receiving sufficient sunlight, as shade can also cause weak stems. Roses prefer full sun.

Rose Sickness

It's not advisable to plant new bushes where other roses have grown in the last three years, as this will greatly increase the risk of 'rose sickness'. This occurs when fungi that grew around the roots and soil of the old plant start to attack the new one. In this situation, it's best to grow a different type of plant altogether. In terms of what to plant where, bush roses look great in island beds mixed with perennials, while miniature varieties make excellent edging plants in front of the taller varieties. Shrub roses, on the other hand, planted singly, can make excellent specimen plants, and you can also try clustering shrub varieties to make a decorative and secure flowering hedge.

333. What are the advantages of 'own-root' roses?

Own-root roses are ideal for gardeners living in cooler areas, as the roses are not grafted onto a rootstock from a different rose. They are very hardy, and they don't produce suckers. If the rose dies back to the ground in a hard winter, it will come back true-to-type when it re-sprouts. A rose grafted onto a rootstock will often sprout from only the rootstock if it dies back in the winter, and rootstocks are not usually desirable roses. Also, keep in mind that hybrid tea roses aren't typically available on their own roots. If you have a grafted rose, remove any suckers as soon as you see them.

334. How do I prepare rock roses for winter?

These pretty little perennial shrubs are from a different family of shrubs known as *Helianthemum*. They have a short blooming period (late spring to early summer) and are often used as a ground cover, in a rock garden, or tumbling over a rock wall. Rock roses grow well on dry, sunny slopes and tolerate heat and drought. They thrive in well-draining sandy soils, performing poorly in rich, loamy soil or acid soil. Prune the plants after flowering and mulch over the crowns of the plants to provide winter protection. When plants are a few years old, you may need to divide the clump.

335. What are the advantages of deadheading rose bushes?

Roses look beautiful when planted with lavender and it's even said that the latter helps to keep aphids away from the blooms.

If you let your rose bush develop hips then it is going to 'seed'. If you want it to keep blooming, you should deadhead the flowers before they form rosehips so the plant isn't putting its energy into seeds rather than flowers. However, some roses are grown specifically for their decorative hips, which can provide weeks of brilliant colour as the weather cools and the winter months draw closer.

If you want your roses to keep blooming, you should deadhead the flowers before they form rosehips, so the plant isn't putting its energy into seed rather than flowers.

336. What kind of plants and flowers grow well with roses?

Quite understandably, roses like to be the centre of attention, so whatever you plant should grow lower, and be of a complimentary colour. A general rule to follow is to choose annuals and perennials that have the same sun and water requirements as your roses. How about lavender, *Gallardia*, coreopsis, aster, *Centaurea* and campanula? For a blanket of colour, try thyme, California poppy or ice plant (*Sedum*).

Different varieties of rose have varying needs in terms of their winter care, and the local weather conditions are also a key factor.

337. What is the best way to prepare my rose bushes for the winter?

There are different classes of roses and they are treated differently for pruning and for winter care. In addition, some roses bloom only once in spring while others cycle in and out of bloom all summer. To remove spent roses, cut back the flower stem to just above the first leaf with five leaflets that is facing away from the centre of the plant. This will make the bush look neater, and encourage it to re-bloom sooner if it is a re-blooming type of rose. An annual mulch of well-rotted manure is also wise.

338. Any ideas for growing my own roses rather than buying them?

You can propagate roses from cuttings but there are two things for you to consider: most roses are grafted onto a hardy rootstock rather than grown on their own roots, and roses still under patent cannot be legally propagated without paying a royalty to the breeder. With this in mind, here's what you'll need: pruning shears, garden gloves, a sharp knife, peat pots or small plastic pots (8–9 cm, or 3–3½ in), sterile potting soil, rooting hormone, plastic bags and twist ties.

The easiest part of the rose to root is the tip of a stem that has recently bloomed. Ideally, the stems should have withered flowers or hips beginning to form. The flower heads or hips should be removed down to the first set of healthy leaves. Propagation cuttings should be 15–20 cm (6–8 in) long, and should be cut from the rose bush with a sharp knife or pruning shears, at an angle of about 45 degrees. Press your gloved thumb against each thorn to remove it (if the thorns don't pop off easily, the cane wood probably isn't ripe enough). Remove all but the topmost one or two leaves; be careful not to damage any of the buds. Scrape off the bark at the bottom of the cutting, making a narrow 2-cm-long wound, one on each side.

Once you've taken your cuttings, fill a round, 8-cm (3-in) peat pot with sterile potting medium. Soak the pot in warm water, and allow it to drain. Peat pots are good, because they allow you to see the roots as they push through the pots. That's the sign it's time to repot. You can transplant a rooted cutting, peat pot and all, to a larger container without disturbing the young, fragile root system Punch a hole in the centre of the potting medium in the peat pot. Insert the cutting in the hole and gently firm the soil. Punch holes through the bottom of a plastic cup. Label it with the rose's name, the date and the source.

Rose cuttings need constant moisture and humidity. Cover each pot with a plastic bag, making sure there's plenty of space between the cutting and the bag. Place the cuttings in a warm place with bright light but not in direct sunlight. Each cutting will develop differently. You may notice a flush of new growth as the first sign that roots are forming. Or you may see roots push through the sides or bottom of the peat pot. It may take as little as two weeks or as much as six months for roots to develop. Transfer the rooted cutting to an 20-cm (8-in) pot or larger. Add organic potting soil, completely burying the peat pot. Do not expose any part of the peat pot; it must be totally buried. Sprinkle a teaspoon of a slow-release, balanced fertiliser with trace elements over the soil. Place the container in cool

shade, and keep it well watered. Over the next ten days to two weeks, gradually move it until it gets direct sunshine for at least six hours a day. Transplant vigorous cuttings into the garden during the first autumn in milder climates, and mound soil 10–15 cm (4–6 in) high around the canes. After the ground freezes, surround the plant with wire mesh, and fill it with mulch. This will provide all the winter protection your new roses need.

339. I used bone meal when planting my roses and now the dog keeps digging it up. Any ideas?

When you apply bone meal, try digging it deep into the soil so the smell won't be so obvious to your dog. Or you could temporarily put a screening barrier over the soil. You may be able to use chicken wire if that's readily available. Use garden stakes to anchor it down.

Positioning Your Rose

One of the most important rules of growing roses is to plant the rose bush in an area that receives at least six hours of sunshine every day, although there are some varieties that fare well in shade, so seek advice from a specialist if your plot is overshadowed. The best soil for planting roses should be free-draining, slightly acid and medium in texture – neither sandy nor clayey. If your soil type differs from this, you can improve it by digging in lots of organic material – a few minutes of extra effort at this stage can lead to a healthy plant that gives you years of good service.

As well as having beautiful, multi-petalled blooms, many old roses have a heady aroma. They tend to only bloom once in the season, but they are often very disease resistant.

The Old English Rose

Old English roses are the true old roses of early European origin. They flower only once in the summer, but when they do they provide a magnificent display. They are extremely tough and have wonderful fragrances. Old roses require little pruning, merely thinning out of weak and old growth. If you want to get really large blooms, the remaining growth may be reduced by a third. Old English roses make excellent garden shrubs that mingle well with other plants. They can be cut down by between one- and two-thirds of their size, but should only be thinned a little. English roses, by contrast, combine the forms and scents of old roses with the repeat flowering of modern roses. They are also often disease resistant.

340. Are old roses more hardy?

There are many varieties of old roses or old garden roses or old shrub roses, and now there are modern roses such as the David Austin English roses that have been bred to include some of the hardiness, disease resistance and fragrance of the older varieties. Many of them also repeat flower. It is a complex subject; one good idea is to look at the websites of some of the famous rose breeders to find discussions of the many types of roses, suggestions for selecting roses that will do well in the growing conditions you have to offer, instructions for planting the roses, and step-by-step care information, including winter protection, pruning and trouble shooting. There are also specific plant lists of roses with particular attributes. In the meantime, why not start with a rugosa rose, either the species or a named variety. These are tough, cold hardy, require minimal pruning and produce beautiful flowers. They also have very few pest or disease problems.

341. Can I plant roses near a tree?

Roses need full sun to perform at their best, so avoid planting them closer than the outer branch spread of the tree for the sake of keeping them in bright sunlight. Otherwise, their blooming will be dramatically reduced. The roots of the tree are a secondary concern. Whether you plant roses 3 m (10 ft) from the trunk or just past the drip line, the tree roots will find and proliferate in the rose bed. Yearly root cutting by trenching or use of a sharp shovel to vertically cut down into the soil to sever the encroaching tree roots will help reduce the competition for the roses. These cuts should go down 25–30 cm (10–12 in) deep to be most effective.

342. I'd like to add longer-blooming plants to my beds. What would you recommend?

Bush roses are the most popular option for growing in beds and borders. They form compact bushes and give you lots of blooms throughout the summer. They generally have two flushes of flower – the first around midsummer, and the second from late summer until the autumn. Bush roses generally fall into two broad categories: large flowered or hybrid teas and cluster flowered, or floribundas. The only difference between them is the number and shape of the flowers. Large flowered roses have a single bloom on each stem. They are usually very well shaped, making them a classic rose for cutting. Cluster flowered roses by contrast have several blooms on each stem. They are cared for in much the same way as shrub varieties.

343. Any tips on revitalising scrawny roses?

These flowers have very particular needs. Roses need a minimum of six hours of sunshine per day. They also like light, well-drained soil. The soil around their roots should be kept loose by cultivating often. This brings necessary oxygen to the roots of the plants. They also like to be fed a good organic fertiliser regularly and mulched around the bottom of the plant to help keep the roots cool in the heat of summer and warm in winter. Roses also need regular care to keep insects and disease at bay. An organic fungicide spray will keep away Black spot, a disease very common to roses. Watering the soil around the rose rather than the foliage is also a good prevention against black spot. If you have an irrigation system, try to keep the direct spray away from your roses as they do not like wet leaves and will also not flower as well. The old adage, 'an ounce of prevention is worth a pound of cure' definitely applies. When pruning your roses, or simply clipping some for a vase, be sure to use good, sharp pruning shears. Dull shears can tear the stems, leaving ugly dark marks. This also leaves a larger open wound for disease and insects to feast on, and can even inhibit new growth. When pruning a rose, prune just above a leaf node. This will encourage the plant to grow bushy and thick. Leaving long stems will make the plant lanky. It is also important to prune out any old or dead canes.

Roses need a minimum of six hours a day of full sunlight to bloom at their best. They also benefit from a generous layer of organic mulch placed around the bottom of the plant but not too near the stems.

You can grow roses in a variety of different ways, depending on the look you want to achieve. Older varieties can be pegged along the ground to form very decorative ground cover.

344. I've heard you can peg roses. How do I do this?

Some of the vigorous, older varieties of roses can make very effective ground cover. This is accomplished by securing the ends of the canes to the ground with U-shaped wire stakes or pegs, hence the term 'pegging'. The canes will form gentle arches and should bloom along their entire length.

345. What's the best way to prune wild roses?

Rosa rugosa is a wild rose that grows almost anywhere, so this is probably the variety you have. The plants will grow up to 2.4 m (8 ft) tall and wide, but mostly they just trail on the ground. These are very tough and hardy roses; you can prune at any time of the year without harming them. Cut out some of the oldest stems and cut the remaining stems back by about one-third. If you need to reduce the plant size by more than that, plan on pruning it back again the following year, in the early springtime.

346. Can I plant roses near the roots of a tree that has been cut down?

It's fine to plant roses near the tree roots but you need to be aware that the tree roots may send up suckers if you water the area after planting your roses. If you know the tree roots are dead, water won't be a problem, but if you've only recently removed the tree, the roots may still be alive and may send up suckering growth. If so, keep pruning it and eventually it should die, or you can have the stump ground out.

347. When and how should you trim roses?

Pruning roses is really quite simple. Wait until your roses begin to show some signs of waking up from their dormant period. Just watch for swellings on the canes indicating new leaves are about to emerge. Then prune everything down to 38–45 cm (15–18 in) tall. Remove any obviously diseased or dead canes, and any old, non-productive canes. Save between three and five of the healthiest canes and remove all others. The ideal result is a V-shape with a relatively open centre. If any suckers are growing from below the grafted part of the rose, pull them off with a downward motion, to help remove any growth buds that might result in additional sucker growth. Finally, cut the remaining canes to an outward-facing bud in the direction you want the growth to take. It's okay to leave the last of the season's flowers on the bush – they develop into rose hips. When that happens, the plant stops growing new shoots to prepare for winter. Many rose hips can also be very decorative in their own right.

348. How do I take care of bare-root roses until it's time to plant them?

If you're unable to plant because of frozen soil, simply store the roses in a protected area such as an unheated garage. Most bare-root roses have moist sawdust sprinkled around the roots and the lower half of the plant is bagged in plastic or covered with a lightweight cardboard container. Keep the plants cool, but above freezing, and they should be just fine in their containers. Plant as soon as practical in your area. If there's no snow cover and your soil isn't frozen, you can plant your bare-root roses straight away. The plants are dormant and won't wake up and grow until the air temperature is just right. Planting while they're dormant is a perfectly acceptable practice.

Ground Cover Roses

Also known as carpet roses, ground cover varieties are low growing and form a dense bush that is very striking when in bloom. There are also options that arch up to 0.6–0.9 m (2–3 ft) and then spread along the ground, which are ideal for tumbling over walls. Ground cover roses are popular due to their long flowering period, their resistance to disease, and the fact that they require little maintenance. The main requirement is that, in the spring, you cut out some of the old flowering wood from the previous year. Remove about 25 percent of the old shoots (cut to about 15 cm [6 in] from the ground). This will encourage fresh new shoots to grow and flower in the summer. Fertilise and mulch immediately after pruning.

349. How can I encourage my climbing roses to bloom more freely?

You can get more blooms on your roses if you give them a specialist fertiliser that is high in phosphorous. Avoid plant foods that are too high in nitrogen, or you'll get lots of leaves at the expense of flowers.

The non-blooming of roses could be due to lack of sufficient sunshine or to lack of pruning. Climbing roses bloom on new stems that grow on old wood. Pruning them back in late winter or early spring will encourage new, flowering stems. If you do not prune, most of the new growth will be at the ends of the main canes instead of lateral stems that produce flowers. Roses need two other things for blooms: sun and nutrients. Are your plants receiving at least six to eight hours of sun daily? If so, they might be missing essential nutrients. Nitrogen, phosphorous and potassium are the major nutrients for all plants. (They correspond to the numbers on fertiliser packages.) Nitrogen promotes growth of green leaves. Phosphorous is essential for blooms. Roses are heavy 'feeders' during their bloom period so it's a good idea to apply a rose fertiliser. The second and third numbers on the package should be higher than the first. The thing to avoid is giving them high-nitrogen fertiliser that will encourage foliage growth at the expense of flowers. Keep them consistently moist and mulch with 5–8 cm (2–3 in) of potting soil to help maintain soil moisture.

Climbing Roses

As the name suggests, climbing roses are ideal for growing on walls, fences, pergolas and trees. Within this category are ramblers, which are very vigorous and can grow up to 50 cm (20 in) in one season. The key to success with climbers is to train the main shoots horizontally as this will encourage side shoots to grow and give you more flowers. The flowers of climbing roses appear at the tips of the shoots. Consequently, if you let the shoots grow straight up, you will only get flowers right at the top of them with the rest of the plant left bare. Ensure that the main shoots grow horizontally by fanning them on a wall or twisting them around an arch. This will encourage small side shoots to grow from the main shoots and each one of these will produce flowers.

350. What's the best way to keep powdery mildew off roses?

Roses need lots of sunshine and good air circulation all around to help them avoid powdery mildew. While some plants are more prone to it than others, improving the sunlight exposure and air circulation will certainly help. Once you notice the powdery mildew, the plant is already infected, so you may have to resort to sprays. To control this disease, you must treat over a ten-day to two-week period. Sodium bicarbonate, commonly known as baking soda, has been found to posses fungicidal properties. It is recommended for plants that already have powdery mildew to hose down all the infected leaves prior to treatment. This helps to dislodge as many of the spores as possible to help you get better results. Use as a prevention or as treatment at the first signs of the disease. To make, mix 1 tablespoon baking soda and 2½ tablespoons of vegetable oil with one gallon of water. Shake this up very thoroughly. To this mix add ½ teaspoon of pure castile soap and spray on your plants. Be sure to agitate your sprayer while you work to keep the ingredients from separating. Cover upper and lower leaf surfaces and spray some on the soil. Repeat every five to seven days as needed.

It's a good idea to deadhead your roses during summer by snipping off the spent blooms. Stop doing this around six to eight weeks before you expect the first frosts and leave the roses to form hips.

351. Should I continue to deadhead my roses until the frost hits?

It's a good idea to stop deadheading at least six weeks before the first frost in your area and let the spent blooms turn into hips (seed pods). When this occurs, it triggers the rose to begin going into dormancy. The hips are decorative in their own right and provide food for wild birds. If you regularly fertilise your roses, make sure you stop around this time too. If you apply fertiliser later than that, you can get a flush of new growth that will be quickly destroyed when the cold weather hits. Other than that, you should remove any damaged or diseased canes before winter. To help minimise disease problems, be sure to clean up any leaf litter or plant debris from around the roses as pests can overwinter on this material.

352. I'm moving house and want to take my favourite rose bush with me. Any tips?

You can cut back your roses to make digging them up and moving them a little easier. You might also want to take cuttings as a back-up plan. There's no guarantee that they will root but you can try. Cut stem tips (10–15 cm [4–6 in] in length), dip the cut ends in rooting hormone and place them in a container filled with moistened

Pruning climbing roses regularly encourages them to produce more blooms. Ensure the blades are sharp and clean and wipe your tools before storage.

potting soil. You can set many cuttings in a single 15-cm (6-in) pot; just place them about 5 cm (2 in) apart. Once the container is filled with rose cuttings place three or four bamboo skewers or sticks in the pot evenly spaced near the pot edge. Drape plastic wrap over them to make a mini-greenhouse. The plastic will help slow water evaporation. Set the pot outdoors in a shady spot in your new garden. If the cuttings root you'll see new leaves develop on the stems. When that happens, remove the plastic wrap. In about a month the root systems will be strong enough that you can repot each of the cuttings into a pot of its own where it can grow until planting out in the garden next spring. Good luck with the move and with your rose cuttings!

353. What are your tips for success with roses?

Roses need full sun all day long (or a minimum of half a day of direct sun including the hour of noon) and soil that is evenly moist (not soggy or saturated). They also benefit from good air circulation during the summer, but most need a certain amount of protection from cold winter winds. If you use roses grown on their own roots instead of grafted, they will be able to come back each year even if there is substantial winter damage. Many roses need only a heavy winter mulch to survive and do not need specialised care.

354. Should I use bypass or anvil secateurs for my roses?

As a general rule, when it comes to different types of roses, bypass secateurs are preferable because the anvil type tends to crush the stem rather than slice it clean.

355. What is the best time of year to plant roses?

It is possible to plant container-grown roses at any time of year (unless of course the ground is frozen). However, autumn is the best time to plant roses, or any shrubs for that matter, as roses can dry out very quickly and the roots can struggle if they are planted in a dry spring or summer. The extra rainfall after summer is finished provides the perfect conditions for roses to establish.

356. Do deer eat roses or will the thorns put them off?

Sadly, deer will eat roses, especially the more modern hybrids, despite the thorns. You could try growing the old fashioned 'crinkly'-leaved varieties of roses such as *Rosa rugosa* as the deer may not like these as much. You may also have success with growing climbers and ramblers, and simply using protection such as heavy-duty mesh around the lower part of the roses.

If possible, wait until the very end of summer before you start to plant roses as this gives them cooler weather in which to get established before winter sets in.

Mail-Order Varieties

Bare-rooted roses will be available from most mail-order nurseries. The roots are wrapped in lightweight material to reduce packaging and postage costs. Buying in this way usually means you have the largest possible choice of variety. However, if you're buying container roses, which are a better choice for later spring and summer, make sure you follow these simple rules. Examine the root ball: avoid plants where the roots have grown through the container into the soil below. Then ensure that leaves look healthy and have no black blotches, aphids and white fly. Make sure that the plant is no bigger than roughly one and a half to two times the height of the pot. Any larger, and the plant may be rootbound. If in doubt, lift the pot up and have a look at the holes in the bottom.

Roses benefit from good air circulation in summer, but in exposed areas they may need protection from cold winter winds.

Transplanting Roses

To plant container-grown roses, simply dig out a hole a little wider than the root ball, remove the plant from the container, and place it into the hole, ensuring that the surrounding soil is level with the top of the container soil. Fill in around the plant with soil and gently firm it down. If conditions are dry, water the area well. When it comes to bare-root roses, spread the roots out and place them in the planting hole with the bud union about 2.5 cm (1 in) below the surface of the soil. Now fill in with soil and gently firm it down. Again, water well if the conditions are dry. The planting method for climbers and rambling roses is the same as above, except the planting hole should be at least 40 cm (15 in) away from the wall or fence in order to let rain get to the roots.

357. I'd like to add shrub roses to our garden. Any advice on how best to prune them?

There are lots of different shrub roses, and the thing that links them all is that they grow into bushy, less formal plants. Some can get very big (over 15 cm, or 6 in) while others stay small and compact. You can grow these roses in among shrubs and plants or as single specimens on their own. Some only have a short flowering period, while others will bloom through to the autumn. In spring, cut out some of the old flowering wood from last year. Take out any dead or weak shoots and remove any that are growing into the middle or rubbing against other shoots. Then remove about 25 percent of the old shoots (cut to about 15 cm from the ground). Always try to cut just above an outward-pointing bud. Fertilise and mulch immediately after pruning.

358. What angle should I prune roses at?

When you prune roses (or anything for that matter) try to prune just above a leaf node that is pointing in the direction you want the new growth to take. With roses you will want the new growth to be from an outward-facing bud. This will keep the centre of the plant more open, which will promote good air circulation and provide more sunshine for the flowers. With roses, if you prune the stem down to just above a five-leaflet leaf, you'll certainly notice more blooms.

359. I forgot to prune my roses and now they are in leaf. Is it too late to cut them back now?

Better late than never in terms of pruning your roses. If you do not prune them, they will grow quite large this year. If you do prune them, you will be able to control their size, and they will bloom more freely because pruning encourages lots of new growth. Go ahead and prune them back now. It won't hurt the plants and you'll end up with more flowers later in the season.

It is possible to grow roses in large containers, but it is vital to keep them well watered and ensure they don't get too hot in warm weather.

360. Any tips on growing roses in containers?

Plants in containers have a whole new set of circumstances with which to deal. First, potting mix can dry out quickly so containerised roses will need to be checked often to make sure the soil does not get too dry (or remain too wet). Also, roots in containers that are sitting directly in the sun can bake when the sunshine falls on the pot during hot afternoons. You can either group pots together so they can provide some shade to each other, or set the containers in the shade of a decorative stone or small shrub, or use a double layer of containers by planting in one and then sinking that pot into a slightly larger pot. You can stuff insulating material between the pots to help keep the root systems from overheating.

Bulbs

It doesn't take long to plant bulbs – in fact, you can literally get hundreds in the ground in just one evening, and the results are spectacular, so do your research and choose all your favourites.

361. Can I plant striped squill and grape hyacinth together?

Unfortunately, grape hyacinth usually spreads more rapidly and may crowd out the squill. The hyacinth also produces abundant foliage which may hide some of the squill. Try planting drifts of them in adjacent areas rather than intermingling the two, so you get the best of them both.

Planting Bulbs

Check the packaging to see how deep the bulbs should be planted; generally it should be around two or three times their width. When you're planting large bulbs such as lilies, it tends to be easier to dig individual holes with a hand-trowel. Or you can use a bulb planter to create a hole for each one. But you can save a lot of time when planting smaller varieties by simply digging a trench to the right depth, spacing the bulbs at the correct intervals along it and back-filling with soil. You may want to create a few rows of short trenches together to achieve a bold display – planting in groups of five or seven works well for larger flowers. Mix some grit into the planting hole if your soil is very heavy. Always use a label to mark where you've planted as it's easy to forget.

362 How deep should I plant bulbs?

A good way to gauge the depth is to plant a bulb twice as deep as it is high. If you're following the exact instructions on the packaging, 15 cm (6 in) deep means the bottom of the hole should be 15 cm from the soil level, regardless of the size of the bulb. If you plant bulbs too deeply, they can run out of stored energy before the stems can reach the soil surface, but if they're too shallow, they may not survive the winter.

363. My European wood anemones seem to be crowded. When and how can I divide them?

Wood anemones (*Anemone nemorosa*) are very easy to grow and can be propagated by division every three to four years. Wait until just before the foliage has completely died back – usually mid- to late summer – before digging and dividing them. Using a sharp blade, slice into a section of soil that contains an abundance of roots. The roots look like brown worm-sized sticks and are only a few centimetres beneath the surface. Dig up a section of roots and wash them carefully in warm water, making sure to remove all the soil. Untangle the roots by hand and carefully cut them so that each

Dahlias grow from tubers and they can easily freeze in a cold winter, or rot in damp soil, so it is safest to lift and store them right after the first frost.

division has at least one eye. To replant, choose a location that is protected from winds and gets only dappled sunlight in summer. The location should also have loose-textured, damp soil containing a high amount of leaf mould. Wood anemones do best planted around deciduous trees and shrubs. Dig a shallow trench and amend the soil with a 1-cm (½-in) layer of compost and a handful of bonemeal. Plant the divisions horizontally, and keep the soil moist. Wood anemones are such vigorous growers that first-year divisions will flower the following spring. If you can't replant immediately, place the roots in a plastic bag filled with moist vermiculite and store in your refrigerator until the bed is ready.

364. Any tips on storing dahlia tubers over the winter?

Dig the tubers up before or just after the first mild frost. Gently shake the soil from the tubers, air dry in a cool (2–4°C, or 35–40°F), dry location for a few days, and then store them in dry peat moss in the same type of dry, cool environment. Cool garages and attics generally work well for storage but watch out for mice and squirrels – they love to snack on tubers, bulbs and rhizomes.

Cool garages and attics generally work well for storage but watch out for. mice and squirrels – they love to snack on tubers, bulbs and rhizomes.

365. Any tips on planting alliums? Are they hard to grow?

Ornamental alliums can be planted at the very end of summer. After being established for a few years they become crowded and may need to be divided. Autumn is the best time to do this. The bulbs do not need to be soaked overnight, but be sure to water the garden well after you plant them. Giant alliums generally bloom in July. Look for spectacular clusters of bright lilac colours on tall stems. The pink options are lovely too.

There are various different alliums that are very easy to grow and perfect for making a bold statement in pots or flower beds.

366. How soon after flowering can I move tulips?

As long as the foliage is green it is manufacturing and transporting energy back into the bulbs. If you interrupt this process by moving them or cutting off the leaves, your bulbs won't flower next year. Ideally, you should let the leaves die down on their own before digging and storing the bulbs.

Selecting the Best Bulbs

Always choose bulbs that feel firm to the touch and heavy for their size. You tend to find that the larger the bulb, the more blooms you'll get. Avoid any bulbs that look old, dried-up or damaged. If they've gone soft around the bottom, they are splitting up, or shoots are already sprouting then they won't do as well as fresher options. Look closely for any signs of mould — this can often be a problem if bulbs are stored in polythene. Most bulbs, including alliums and gladiolus prefer a sunny spot with well-drained soil, but there are plenty of options, such as cyclamen, which are perfectly happy in shade. If you have a damp spot in your garden that could do with cheering up then woodland bulbs like *Erythronium* and *Galanthus* are ideal.

367. Any tips on growing tuberous begonias? I'm having no luck.

If you receive them by mail order, tuberous begonias should be stored dry until about two months before the expected arrival of warmer nights (10°C, 50°F). Press them, hollow side up, into trays filled with damp potting soil but do not cover them. When growth starts, pot in 13–15 cm (5–6 in) pots of a suitable growing medium. When night temperatures rise above 10°C (50°F) set the plants outdoors. Feed with a weak, all-purpose fertiliser every two to three weeks from the time the first shoot appears until the foliage starts to wither. When the plants have died back to the ground, dig up the tubers, allowing some soil to cling to them; place the tubers in a sheltered frost-free spot for a few weeks until they are so dry that their stems and the soil around them break away easily. Store the tubers over the winter in bags of dry vermiculite.

368. Our tulips are growing leaves but no flowers. What's wrong?

This can happen for several reasons. First, the bulbs must be large enough and strong enough to bloom. They build their strength through their foliage, so it must be allowed to grow, mature and ripen naturally in order to restore the bulb each year. They should be planted in full sun and in soil that is of at least average fertility. You might give them a top dressing of compost and/ or complete fertiliser in early spring as they begin to show, in mid-spring after they bloom, and again in early autumn when they will be beginning to grow again. This should help them gain some size and strength from year to year. Next, large bulbs tend to divide into smaller bulbs and these smaller bulbs may take a few years to reach blooming size. If you planted top size bulbs, they may have divided quickly. Next, tulips that are planted very shallow tend to divide more often than those planted at a deeper level. Finally, some tulips perform better over time in the garden than others – experiment with different varieties.

There are a number of reasons why bulbs can grow foliage but no flowers. They may have been planted too late or at the wrong depth. However, if you leave them to build up their strength, they may flower next year.

369. Is there a crocus that flowers at the end of summer?

Autumn crocus produces leaves in the spring and flowers in the autumn. The plants prefer semi-shade but take full sun if watered well. Plant in moist soil containing lots of organic matter. Unless the plants show signs of overcrowding leave them alone. A bulb, set in a sunny window, blooms without soil or water. Once a bulb is forced in this manner, plant it. Give it plenty of room as the leaves take up a lot of space in the spring. The bulbs are divided when the foliage matures and are replanted immediately. Plant them 5 cm (2 in) deep and 15 cm (6 in) apart. The plants reach a height of 25–30 cm (10–12 in).

370. What is the best way to naturalise crocus bulbs in a lawn?

The planting depth depends upon the size of the bulbs, so a general rule of thumb is to plant your bulbs at least twice the diameter of the bulb. For crocus, that equates to 5–8 cm (2–3 in) deep. If you want a naturalised effect, scatter the bulbs by tossing them by the handful. Then plant each one where it lands. For a massed effect, plant close together, but to allow space for the foliage, don't plant any closer than about 10 cm (4 in).

You can plant crocus bulbs in drifts in your lawn for a natural effect. Don't be too keen to mow your lawn in spring – it's best to wait until the foliage has died down naturally.

371. How do you grow lily-of-the-valley? Are they as tender as they look?

Although it looks delicate, lily-of-the-valley is a strong grower that needs only minimal care once established. In fact, it can almost be invasive in a spot where it is happy. It does best in a moist, rich soil in a shady or partly shady spot. It is usually planted as bare bulbs or as a container plant or division from another garden. Water well until it becomes established and as needed to supplement rain and keep the soil moist. If the soil is not naturally rich, apply compost and or a complete fertiliser according to the label in early spring. You can pot up extra plants for friends.

372. How hardy is eucomis or pineapple lily?

This plant is a tender perennial in that it is only hardy in warmer areas. You could grow it in a container year round (place several in a good-sized pot, plant so barely covered or the neck is at the surface) or you could plant it in the garden each spring (plant about 15 cm [6 in] deep and 30 cm [12 in] apart) and then dig and store it for the winter. These bulbs need a rich, organic, yet well-drained soil. They need ample moisture when

These sweetly-scented plants thrive in a moist, shady spot and if they are happy in their growing conditions, you'll have plenty to pick for use in vases in your home too.

growing and then a dry period when dormant. Eucomis will increase slowly by offsets and these can be easily separated each spring if grown in a container. In the ground it may eventually over the years spread to form a small colony but it is a slow grower and may even take several years to bloom.

Protecting Bulbs from the Winter Cold

Many bulbs, such as crocosmia, lilies and alliums are generally quite hardy and will come back every year. Before winter, treat them to a deep mulch of bark or well-rotted manure, or compost if they're in a cooler spot. Some of the more unusual bulbs, such as spider lilies, eucomis and glory lilies are far too delicate for this treatment and the bulbs will need to be carefully unearthed in late summer and stored in trays of dry potting soil in a frost-free place. Unless you live in a warmer spot, dahlia tubers will also need this extra attention. Keep them cool and dry over winter and then plant them out again the following spring.

Jonquils have an elegant beauty and are very easy to grow, so why not put some bulbs in pots so you can enjoy them indoors too?

373. Can I separate bulbs if they're grouped into one larger bulb?

You can separate the bulbs and you can either store them in a cool, dark place where there's good air circulation or you can separate them and plant them in your garden immediately. Many bulbs will multiply (as you have seen) if they are left in the ground for years and years. They are obviously growing well in the conditions that you are growing them in so it won't hurt them to replant them right away.

374. Can I plant spring-flowering bulbs in pots?

Many gardeners do exactly what you describe as you can rearrange the pots when the flowers are spent, which means you can allow the foliage to yellow and wither on its own without having the process detract from other blooming plants. You can even bury the pots in the ground, so the bulbs won't need any other special care. If, however, you plan to put your bulbs into above-ground containers, keep the

You can separate the bulbs and you can either store them in a cool, dark place where there's good air circulation or you can separate them and plant them in your garden now.

following information in mind: in cold climates, bulbs planted in containers often don't overwinter well. Containers are exposed to repeated freezing and thawing during the winter, and this can damage the bulbs. Your best bet is to bring the containers to a protected spot, ideally one where the temperature will stay around 4°C (40°F) throughout the winter. This temperature will satisfy the bulbs' chilling requirement. The bulbs should be kept moist, but not waterlogged. Kept in a cool spot, they shouldn't need watering very often during the winter. Check them regularly, and water them if the soil is dry at a depth of 2.5 cm (1 in) or so. If you can't move your containers to a protected spot, huddle them together in a group and mulch with a thick layer of chipped bark.

375. What will look good planted next to crocosmia flowers?

You might try early spring bulbs, a perennial geranium such as 'Johnson's Blue', a late bloomer such as *Boltonia* 'Snowbank', and possibly a dark-leafed heuchera such as 'Palace Purple' for foliar contrast. There are many other plants that would do nicely depending on your colour preferences. Ask at your local garden centre or look online for inspiration.

Often found in intense shades of red or orange, crocosmia also has bright green strappy leaves that are attractive in their own right during the warmer months of the year.

376. What bulbs have instant impact?

If you like bold colours, then you could try dahlias, lilies, tuberous begonias and gladiolus. These all have beautiful large flowers in bold colours and you could pick a fiery colour theme such as reds and oranges, or choose a profusion of reds, pinks and purples for a more tropical look. Just remember, the more you plant, the more there are to take care of!

377. How do I grow my own saffron?

Saffron comes from the dried stigmas (yellow threads in the centre of the flower) of *Crocus sativus*. However, it takes 100,000 blossoms to produce one pound of saffron. The stigmas are collected at maturity and air dried, then stored in an airtight container to be used as a flavouring in foods. If your crocus are the sativus type, you can harvest your own saffron!

378. What summer blooming bulbs can I grow in a windowbox?

You might try tuberous begonias, *Sprekelia*, or perhaps just a few tuberoses per windowbox. Scarborough lily would be another possibility. Alternatively, you might also have luck with the dwarf oriental lilies. Another excellent performer is the calla lily, although it will need to be kept well watered.

379. Why won't my nerine lilies bloom?

These flowers usually bloom in August, September or October. The bulbs don't like to be moved or disturbed, so if you live in a very cold area, rather than planting and digging in the autumn, it might be better to grow them in pots. Bulbs should be planted in spring in a sunny site.

With their tall spikes of vivid, blowsy blooms, gladiolus will bring vibrant interest to the back of a border. They also make good cut flowers.

Also known as the Guernsey lily, *Nerine bowdenii* is actually a South African plant and does best in milder spots.

They like a well-drained soil with plenty of organic matter. They are usually dormant during the summer and do better if kept somewhat dry. They do need warm summer temperatures during their dormancy to flower at their best. Bulbs should be planted about 8 cm (3 in) deep, with about one-third of the bulb showing above ground. Water and fertilise only when leaves are actively growing, usually in winter and spring. Reduce watering when leaves start yellowing, which means dormancy is approaching. For *Nerine bowdenii*, gradually dry off in early summer and let it go completely dry from summer until it blooms. If you have not already done so, try using a fertiliser that is only phosphorous, such as rock phospate, or 0–45–0. Phosphorous promotes bloom over foliage. If overly fertilised with nitrogen, nerine has a tendency to produce lots of strappy leaves.

A Summer Bloom

Bulbs to flower in the spring are planted before winter, but spring is the best time to prepare for a vibrant show of summer blooms. You can plant a host of summer-flowering bulbs, corms and tubers and many of them are far easier to grow than their exotic looks suggest. It's important to remember that these bulbs can quickly dry out or rot if not stored in the right conditions, so if you want the best possible results, try to plant your bulbs as soon as possible after buying them. This is reasonably straightforward if you do some planning in advance so you have an idea of what you want to grow and the different spots that you have available in your garden. If you're not able to plant your bulbs right away, store them in a cool, dark, airy place, such as in a garage. Never leave them in a warm room or in direct sunlight.

380. Why won't my crown imperial bloom? I planted it two years ago.

Crown imperial is a fritillaria and needs both a heavy mulch in winter and a very well-drained location, although it appreciates some soil moisture when it is growing. It does best in a rich, friable soil and should be planted where it will not be crowded by other plants. The foliage should be allowed to ripen naturally each year so that it can replenish the bulb and build its strength to bloom; be sure you don't remove the foliage until it has completely withered. The bulb should only be transplanted when dormant, right after the foliage dies back. If the foliage seems healthy, it may simply be a matter of time. Perhaps your bulb has taken some time to settle in after transplanting and is not yet of blooming size. It might also need a richer soil. Another possibility is that it needs to be planted deeper – they should be about 20–30 cm (8–12 in) down!

The tall, stately blooms of crown imperials may take a while to appear after planting the large bulbs as they can take a little while to settle in. However, they are well worth the wait.

> Crown imperial is a fritillaria . . . whose foliage should be allowed to ripen naturally each year so that it can replenish the bulb and build its strength to bloom.

Noting the Fragrance of Your Bulbs

Summer bulbs such as freesias offer some of the loveliest perfumes in the garden, but be careful when it comes to the perfume of certain bulbs! While lilies can also often smell wonderful, when planted *en masse* the perfume can be overpowering, so it may be best not to have too many under the kitchen window or next to your favourite garden seat. The eucomis, or pineapple lily, has very eye-catching blooms, but avoid planting them around a patio or seating area as the smell is thought by some people to be vaguely reminiscent of a dead mouse. Crown imperials also look stunning, but they have a very strange smell that may be far too strong for a small garden! They are beautiful, nicely structured plants, although they certainly won't be to everyone's taste.

381. Are there any dahlias that don't have to be dug up in the autumn?

The general advice for dahlias is to dig and store them over the winter months because they are susceptible to rot if left in the ground and are also susceptible to freezing because they are tender-skinned tubers (as opposed to thick-skinned bulbs or corms). In mild climates, you can certainly improve their chances of survival in the ground over the winter months by enhancing the planting soil with grit and planting them at the correct depth. Wait until frost kills the tops back and then cut off all the dead foliage and remove it from the garden. Cover over the area with a thick mulch such as straw or pine boughs to keep the soil from heaving in the thaw and freeze cycle of early spring. With any luck at all your dahlia tubers will survive and sprout when the weather warms.

382. Can I trim back my lilies now they've bloomed? They look floppy.

To make sure they continue producing flowers, it's best to stake them up rather than cut them back. If you remove the foliage the bulbs won't be able to collect and store carbohydrates and they won't bloom for you next year. Just stake them up to keep them from flopping into your beds. The foliage and stems will die down soon. When that happens it means the bulbs are dormant and can be safely trimmed back or carefully dug up and transplanted if you prefer.

383. How do I grow *Scilla*? I think they are the loveliest spring flower of all.

You could be talking about a few different flowers as this name is commonly used for lots of different bulbs. Three that come to mind are English bluebells (*Scilla nutans*), spring beauty (*Scilla siberica*) and grape hyacinths (*Muscari armeniacum*). Look online to see the ones you like best, or perhaps grow them all – each one is lovely in a different way!

Lots of spring bulbs bear the name *Scilla*, but *Scilla* 'Siberian Squill' is one of the daintiest forms and has very vivid blue blooms.

384. If I store ranunculus corms over winter, can I replant them?

Yes, you can dig and store the corms for replanting next spring. After the foliage has died down but before a heavy frost, dig the corms and store them in a cool, dry place. You can replant in the spring, after the soil has warmed. It won't take long for green shoots to emerge.

Mixing summer bulbs such as lilies, gladiolus and dahlias with annual flowering plants is an effective way to add impact and fragrance to a border.

385. When should I plant corms of *Anemone* 'St. Brigid' and *Anemone* 'De Caen'?

Poppy-flowered anemones have finely divided leaves and flowers that are around 5 cm (2 in) across. 'De Caen' produces single flowers and 'St. Brigid' produces semi-double to double flowers. You can plant them at different times of the year, but they are often planted in spring , 2–5 cm (1–2 in) deep in rich, light, well-draining soil, then mulched with peat or leaf mould. (Excess soil moisture will rot the bulbs.) Carefully inspect the bulbs (tubers) to find the scar from last year's stem and plant that side up. They will grow best in partial afternoon shade.

Lots of bulbs make very good cut flowers and anemones are no exception. The velvety petals in rich shades are lovely in the garden or in a vase.

386. How long should my summer bulbs take to bloom in a container?

Summer flowering bulbs such as lilies generally sprout just a few weeks after planting, providing the soil is warm enough. If you've planted some that are taking longer than this to show signs of life then just out of curiosity, empty the container and inspect the bulbs. If they dried out, or if they were kept too wet, the bulbs may have died. Sometimes, if bulbs are planted too deeply, they will run out of stored energy before the sprouts can reach the soil surface. If, after inspecting the bulbs, they still look healthy, replant them about 5 cm (2 in) below the soil surface.

With their jewel-like colours and velvety centres, anemones deserve to be enjoyed at close range, so buy extra bulbs and plant some where you can cut them to enjoy in a vase in the house.

387. Any tips on planting Angelique tulips and *Anemone blanda*?

Tulips are best planted in a sunny location in soil that is well-drained (meaning not soggy) with about 15 cm (6 in) of soil above the bulbs. Plant them pointy end up. Water and cover with a few centimetres of organic mulch. Grecian windflowers (*Anemone blanda*) are best planted in a lightly shaded area about 13 cm (5 in) down. It can be hard to tell which end goes up so don't worry about it and plant it sideways. Prior to planting, the anemones should be rehydrated a bit. One way to do this is to wrap them in damp paper towels overnight (loosely wrapped in plastic) so they can absorb the water and plump up. Then plant them right away the next day. Again, water and cover with a few centimetres of organic mulch.

Cultivating Lilies

Lilies have been cultivated for 3,500 years. There are many reasons for the enduring popularity of this flower – they often have a lovely perfume, they are surprisingly easy to grow and there is a huge variety of shapes, forms and colours to choose from. If you're new to growing lilies, there are a couple of things to bear in mind however: the pollen can be poisonous to pets, so grow pollen-free hybrids if this could affect you. Also, the pesky lily beetle is on the rise. While the adults look quite striking with their red bodies and graceful antennae, both the adults and their grubs eat the flowers, buds and leaves. The best way to deal with these beetles is to go on regular patrols to catch them. They will cunningly drop to the ground if you tap the stems of the plant, so put one hand underneath to catch them. Repeat this every day until they are all gone.

Food
Gardening

Few things in life beat the satisfaction you can get from tucking into your own delicious fresh produce. You don't need a big space to enjoy the benefits of eating fruit and veggies straight from your plot. In this chapter, we guide you through all the different options and reveal the potential pitfalls, whether you're growing in a few pots on a balcony or you have room for an orchard and a formal kitchen garden with raised beds. From succulent strawberries to fragrant herbs, you could be enjoying that just-picked taste in no time.

Vegetables

Nothing beats the flavour of home-grown vegetables, nor the satisfaction of sitting down to food that you have raised from seed. Growing your own can also help you to save a small fortune, so if you haven't already got a vegetable plot, why not make room for one this weekend?

388. I'm new to gardening but have lots of space – any tips?

For gardeners starting out, the temptation always seems to be to make the first garden too big. This results in too much work and not enough fun. For example, unless you plan on canning tomatoes, just a handful of plants will keep you well supplied. You can always make it bigger the next year! So plant a small garden full of things you like to eat. In other words, if nobody likes radishes, skip them. Use graph paper to estimate the area each 'crop' will need and allow for a minimum of four growing areas. The four areas are needed so that you can rotate your tomatoes (and others) from spot to spot each year. Rotation helps cut down on disease problems. To help keep track of this (and other things like which varieties do best for you), start a garden journal. Soil preparation is very important; in fact, it's the most important thing you can do to ensure success. You will need to start with a soil test and add amendments as indicated by the results. Finally, I like to grow cutting flowers in the vegetable garden, because they're cheerful and attract useful insects. You may also want to grow a few annual herbs such as parsley, dill and basil, because they're great to add to your cooking.

Rotating Your Crops

Crop rotation is especially important with vegetables like cabbages and broccoli as many of them are slow-growing and can be in the soil for many months, which means they deplete it of the particular nutrients they like. It also allows pests and diseases to build up, which means if you try to grow another plant from the same family in that spot, it will be vulnerable. For crop rotation, simply divide your growing space into four and keep each family of vegetables restricted to one quarter. With each new growing season you circulate the crops, so that each quarter of the plot hosts the next family on the list. The correct order of rotation is disputed; the most important thing is to choose a sequence and stick to it.

389. When is the best time to plant broccoli?

Broccoli is a cool-season plant and can go outdoors much earlier than many other vegetables. You can plant it in early spring, and if temperatures threaten to dip below about 4°C (40°F), place temporary frost protection over the plants. It's also worth covering plants to prevent them from being eaten by caterpillars.

390. Can I grow vegetables and butterfly-friendly plants in a small space, or is that asking for trouble?

If you're short on space, one option is to grow crops slightly closer together than normal and harvest them at the tender 'baby vegetable' stage.

Many gardeners successfully grow a very wide variety of plants in close proximity. If you want to attract butterflies then, as well as including plants to serve as nectar sources for the butterflies themselves, you may want to grow some extra plants that their caterpillars like to eat, such as parsley, fennel and dill. You can protect vulnerable vegetables such as cabbages by covering them with lightweight row covers. Butterflies are very specific in terms of where they lay their eggs, and luckily not that many of them have larvae that eat vegetables on a regular basis. As you research the butterflies in your area and look into butterfly garden plants,

> If you want to attract butterflies you could grow some extra plants that their caterpillars like to eat . . .

you will find that a wide variety of plants can be grown in a small kitchen garden. Experiment and see what works best.

391. How do I deal with aphids on my beans?

There is no need to be apprehensive about removing aphids from your beans – this is much easier to take care of than you might imagine. A good blast from the garden hose will get rid of most of them – it washes them off and kills them all in one. Do it every day or two for a week or so and you will be amazed at the difference. What's more, you'll be able to eat your beans without worrying about harmful pesticide residues.

392. When is the best month to start planting carrots and other vegetables that take a long time to grow?

It is possible to start warm-season plants, such as tomatoes and pumpkins, indoors ahead of time to try to harvest earlier. Counting back from the average last spring frost date I would allow about six to eight weeks for tomatoes and peppers and only about two weeks for squash because the plants get big so fast. You can plant them outdoors once the weather has settled and the soil has warmed. You can also start both of these outdoors after frost and once the soil has warmed (to around 21°C (70°F). Carrots, however, are best planted in the garden where they are to grow. They can be planted outside from early spring to mid-summer. If you are wondering about late-summer crops, check the 'days to maturity' for the variety you are growing and see if you can plant successively for more than one crop, or plant both an early and a late-maturing variety of the same crop. This is commonly done with beans, and many gardeners plant both an early and a late tomato. Planning for an autumn garden is a bit tricky. For some plantings, such as peas and beans, you need to calculate backwards from an average date of the first autumn frost and add about a

Broad beans can be a magnet for aphids but they are very simple to deal with. Wash them off with a fine jet of water from your hose and you'll soon have the situation under control.

week or so (to allow for the slowing of growth as the season progresses) to the maturity date. In addition, the more cold-tolerant vegetables such as cole crops, carrots, greens and radishes can sometimes be kept going long after frost by use of a cold frame or other form of protection.

393. When do I harvest my marrow?

Marrow will taste watery unless allowed to mature fully on the vine. Wait until the vines die before harvesting your marrow, but plan to cut them from the vines before the first frost of the season. Choose a dry day and cut the fruits from the vine, leaving a 8- to 10-cm (3- to 4-in) stem. Allow them to cure in the sun until the stems dry, then wipe the dirt off the marrow and store them in a cool, dry area, such as a garage. They should store well for months.

394. How do I start a vegetable garden?

First, choose the sunniest part of your property for the garden. Vegetables will produce best in full sun, but will produce some yields if you get at least six hours of sun. Good drainage is also essential. Next, dig up the sod and shake as much soil from it as you can. It's easier to do this if you moisten the area first and let it sit overnight. If you have access to potting soil, spread it 2.5 cm (1 in) thick over the area and mix it in. Correct soil acidity is crucial for good plant growth – you can purchase a home pH test to see where yours stands. Buy young plants and sow seeds according to the directions on the seed packets. Lay mulch between rows and between plants to keep weeds under control. For a simple, inexpensive mulch,

A Rotation Plan

Following a crop rotation plan is an easy way to maximise your harvests. The main groups of vegetables are as follows:

- **Legumes:** An important family in the crop rotation cycle, they include all sorts of podded vegetables from broad, runner and French beans to peas and green manures like clover or alfalfa.

- **Onion family:** Bulb and salad onions are included here, as well as shallots and garlic. Don't forget leeks, which are obviously related when you consider their habit.

- **Carrot and tomato families:** Carrots, parsnips, celery, peppers, aubergine, tomatoes and spuds make up this diverse, but very useful, group. Many of these are particularly prone to soil-borne pests.

- **Brassicas:** Cabbages, Brussels sprouts and cauliflower are obviously close relatives, but also covered here are rutabagas, turnips and radishes.

use newspaper covered with straw, grass clippings and shredded leaves. Moisten the soil well before planting, and keep it evenly moist with frequent watering. Soaker hoses are an easy way to provide needed moisture to your garden, are easy to install and save a lot of time and effort. You can fertilise the garden with a balanced fertiliser applied at the rate suggested on the label. Be careful not to over-fertilise as it can cause just as many problems as not adding enough. Follow a crop rotation plan (where you grow a different family of vegetables in each area) every year for best results.

395. What's the best way to grow artichokes? Do they need lots of care?

Artichokes will develop more and more edible flower buds as the plant matures. On a young plant, you may only get two or three but on a three to five-year-old plant you can get dozens and dozens. Lots of water is required, as well, so water deeply every two to three days as the buds begin to develop. You can dig and divide your plant when it is three to four years old. If left alone, an artichoke plant will generally slow or stop production when it is about seven years of age.

396. What is the best way to keep weeds down in a vegetable garden?

Mulch over the bare soil and between the plants. A solid 2.5-cm (1-in) layer of newspapers laid flat in the row, followed by a layer of straw mulch is ideal, and also has the advantage of keeping moisture in the soil so you need to water less. You could also use black plastic, landscape fabric or a very thick layer of grass clippings or straw. Plant seeds in rows, so you can easily hoe between the rows. As soon as seedlings are up, begin mulching around them; you can use grass clippings piled thickly between plants. You could even put a layer of landscape fabric down, with holes cut in it, and plant your seedlings in the holes. This is especially good for tomatoes and peppers, or any plants that need to be widely spaced. You may want to add a thick layer of straw mulch around each plant, so the soil doesn't heat up too much under the dark fabric. All these things take a little time in the spring, but they are well worth the effort, and will save lots of time later on in the season.

You can harvest artichoke buds when very young and eat them whole, or leave them to mature a bit longer and eat the stem and base, discarding the fibrous parts.

397. My runner beans are flowering profusely but not producing beans. Any tips?

Scarlet runners are beautiful additions to any garden. They love to climb a wall or run along a fence, and the blossoms are spectacular. Since yours are blooming, you must have them in full sunshine and you're probably giving them enough water. The only other thing that might be hampering the formation of bean pods is lack of insect activity to pollinate the flowers. Have you used any pesticides in the area? Do you have a huge population of hungry birds that might be eating flying insects? Last but not least, it's possible the flowers have been pollinated but it's too early in the season for the beans to form. I'd take a wait-and-see attitude. But, even if you don't get any beans, the plants are worth having in the garden!

398. Any tips on growing tasty peas?

Since peas are a cool-season crop, you'll have best results by planting them four to six weeks before your last frost or 10 weeks before your first frost. As long as the soil temperature is 4°C (40°F), you can plant the first crop in early to mid-February

Peas are well worth growing in the garden as the flavour of a just-picked pea is unforgettable. There are various heritage varieties that are well worth looking out for. Some grow extra tall, others have pretty flowers and blue pods.

easy on manure or other fertilisers. Peas manufacture their own nitrogen and do not require regular fertiliser applications. Mix compost or leaf mould into the bed, then sow your seeds. Applying just the right amount of water to peas can be tricky – too much water before the plants flower will reduce yields. On the other hand, dry soil when the seeds are germinating, or the plants are flowering and the pods swelling, will reduce the

> Go easy on manure or other fertilisers. Peas manufacture their own nitrogen and do not require regular fertiliser applications.

and your late crop in mid-August to early September. Peas grow best in a sunny spot, in well-amended and well-draining soil. Work some organic matter into the soil prior to sowing, but go

quality and quantity of harvest. Supply 1 cm (¹/₂ in) of water every week until the plants begin to bloom. Then increase their water supply to 2.5 cm (1 in) per week until the pods fill out.

399. What's the best way to avoid blossom-end rot on tomatoes?

Blossom-end rot is a physiological condition caused by a lack of calcium at the growing tip of the fruit. While your soil may have adequate calcium, fluctuations in soil moisture content from dry to wet really increase the incidence of blossom-end rot. It is especially bad on early fruit each summer and in sandy soils. The damage occurs as cells die at the tip of the fruit. In time (and as the fruit grows) the spots enlarge and turn black. So, by the time you see it, the damage actually has already been occurring for a while. Remedies include adding organic matter to a sandy soil to increase its moisture-holding capacity and keeping plants evenly moist, especially during the development of the first fruits (mulch helps maintain soil moisture). Affected tomatoes are still edible, just cut away the brown portion.

Watering regularly, but not too much, and not letting your plants dry out and wilt is the key to avoiding blossom-end rot.

400. Why are my root vegetables unsuccessful?

Root vegetables, like most crops, need rich, moist soil and plenty of sunshine to thrive. The problem may be poor soil, lack of nutrients, lack of water or inadequate sunshine. If your raised bed is in a sunny site, you can grow carrots, onions and beets. If it's shady most of the afternoon, you'd have better luck with shade-tolerant crops such as lettuce or spinach. Amend the soil by spreading 10–13 cm (4–5 in) of organic matter over the top and digging it in to a depth of 20–25 cm (8–10 in). Use aged compost, leaf mould, peat moss or aged manure. Based upon your description of the unsuccessful crops, I'd guess your soil has a high clay content. If that's the case, add even more organic material and some sand too. Do whatever you can to loosen the soil and make it easier for the roots to penetrate 20–25 cm. The organic matter will help the soil retain moisture and will release nutrients to the plant roots as it decomposes. After planting, keep the soil evenly moist by supplying water every week. Make sure you apply enough water to thoroughly wet the entire root area. To check, dig down after watering to see how far the moisture has penetrated.

> Do whatever you can to loosen the soil and make it easier for the roots to penetrate a good 20–25 cm.

401. Can I grow herbs and vegetables in containers on my patio?

As long as you have enough sunshine, you can grow almost any kind of vegetable or herb in pots. Most vegetables adapt well to containers. The size of the pot depends on the mature size of the vegetable. For tomatoes, you'll probably want a large container – at least 30–45 cm (12–18 in) is good. For smaller plants, like lettuce or radishes, a depth of 15–18 cm (6–8 in) will work. Experiment a little and you might be able to grow some annual flowers along with your vegetables, for a festive and functional patio garden. Remember that smaller containers dry out very quickly; it's much better to have a few large pots than lots of little ones as you can always grow more than one vegetable in any one pot.

402. What are the advantages of heirloom seeds?

Heirlooms are those old, open-pollinated varieties that have stood the test of time. The best of them are among the finest vegetables ever known. They would be well worth growing for their mouth-watering flavours alone, but they also have other important qualities. Heirlooms are living artefacts. Popular in living history exhibits, these old-time varieties offer a glimpse of life in earlier times. Heirlooms are also a reservoir of genetic diversity. Traits encoded in their DNA may someday prove critical to feeding the world. And there is more. Heirlooms invite passion. There is just something about all their wonderful shapes, sizes, colours and flavours that sparks a sense of wonder. Take heirloom tomatoes, for example. They can be big, small, fluted, smooth, red, orange, pink, purple, yellow, green, white, striped, round, pear-shaped, determinate, indeterminate, potato-leaved and more. They also vary in traits you can't see such as taste, hardiness and adaptability. While tomatoes may be the most popular heirloom, many other vegetables are just as diverse. Peppers come in all kinds of colours, sizes and shapes. So do corn, beans, kale, aubergine, squash, lettuce, potatoes, peas and nearly all the other crops. Today, seed companies and seed savers offer literally hundreds of heirlooms. Some are standard varieties that have never been superseded. Others were popular once, but disappeared from the seed trade. Many of these would have been lost, but seed-saving gardeners kept them alive. Still other heirlooms never made the big-time. They were regional or family favourites, passed down by generation after generation of gardeners rather than sold by seed companies.

Cultivating Tomatoes

Water your tomatoes on a regular basis, giving them a good drink and then allowing them to start to dry out before watering again. Avoid allowing them to completely dry out to the point of wilting, but also try to avoid keeping them constantly moist as this will cause them to grow quickly but the flavour won't be as intense. If in doubt, keep them on the dry side. Soon after planting into their final position, start a fertiliser regime. With the young plants, and before any flower is showing, use a good, balanced organic liquid fertiliser once a week, or alternatively twice a week at half-strength. As soon as the first flowers appear, switch over to a fertiliser higher in phosphorus and apply as per their recommendation.

403. What vegetables can I grow in partial shade?

As a general rule of thumb, any plants that do not flower will grow well in the shady area. Leaf lettuces, carrots, radishes and cabbage should produce well for you. A shady spot actually makes growing some vegetables, such as spinach, easier as they are less likely to run to seed if grown in these conditions.

Chard is a very decorative plant that can be grown in vegetable gardens or flower borders.

404. What exactly is an heirloom vegetable?

The term 'heirloom vegetables' is certainly open to interpretation. In general, it would be safe to say that these are seed strains and hybrids that come true from seed and have been cultivated as such for generations because they have been selected for outstanding characteristics. Originally, many were identified as superior plants by farmers and home gardeners who then saved seeds and culled through successive generations of plants to stabilise the desired characteristics. They will be heirlooms forever, as long as they are passed along from year to year and grown from seed descended from those original plants. With that definition, it is possible to identify a seed strain today that could become worthy of being passed along as an heirloom in the future.

405. Can you give me some tips on growing chard?

Swiss chard, like spinach, does well in a rich soil that is evenly moist but not soggy. A soil that is well prepared and deeply dug, with ample organic matter added (such as well rotted manure and compost), will give you a good start. You may want to have your soil tested; the results will provide recommendations for adjusting pH and nutrient levels. Based on test results, you may want to apply a balanced fertiliser such as 10–10–10, or an organic equivalent, according to the label instructions. Finally, occasional foliar feeds of compost tea or a seaweed-based fertiliser should do the trick for luxuriant growth that you can pick for weeks.

406. Do you have any advice on growing potatoes?

You can start your potatoes in early spring, depending on the weather in your area. Plant the seed pieces 15 cm (6 in) apart and cover them with 10–13 cm (4–5 in) of soil. As the vines grow, it's best to draw soil, leaves or potting soil over them to keep the developing tubers covered. This is known as 'earthing up'. Leave only a small portion of the foliage exposed to encourage additional root development. Once the plants blossom, stop adding compost to the hill. When the foliage begins to wither and die, the tubers will be fully grown and ready to harvest. Leave to dry in the sun for two days before storage.

407. How can I get kids interested in growing veggies?

One of the best ways is to get them planting their own food from seed. Some of the easiest summer vegetables for kids to grow include beans, New Zealand spinach, pumpkins, squash and tomatoes. You can also plant marigolds in among the vegetables to help confuse incoming potential pests. As the vegetables ripen, harvest them with the kids and use them to make some of their favourite foods such as pizza, so the whole experience is good fun. Kids love having their own patch of ground to tend too.

Children will particularly relish learning about growing vegetables if they get to grow foods they like eating. Cherry tomatoes are a good plant to start off with as kids can eat them like sweets.

As the vegetables ripen, harvest them with the kids and use them to make some of their favourite foods such as pizza, so the whole experience is good fun.

408. What can I do to help make my pumpkins enormous?

The most important factor is getting the soil right. Dig in a large quantity of homemade compost or aged manure. Start the seeds in pots early to provide the longest growing season for your area. Move seedlings outside when it is warm (around 18°C, or 65°F, is ideal) or provide a mini-greenhouse or cloche. Plant in a very sunny spot and water regularly, fortifying with liquid fertiliser. After the first pumpkins start growing, limit the number to just one or two per plant, so all the energy goes into making each pumpkin as huge as possible.

409. How far apart should we plant vegetables to avoid cross-pollination?

This depends on the plants you are growing and whether or not you plan to save seeds. If you do not plan to save seeds, then it is not a problem. Seed savers use many methods, such as hand pollinating the best plants and then covering those flowers to prevent subsequent possible pollination form other sources. This method assures you are saving seeds from the best plants.

To get the largest possible pumpkins, prepare early by enriching your soil with plenty of potting soil or aged manure. Limit the plant to just one or two fruits and water regularly.

410. I'm planning on having a vegetable garden next year. Should I prepare the bed in advance or just before planting?

You can start now and when spring weather arrives you'll be all ready to sow your seeds. Start by removing all vegetation from the area and spreading 10–13 cm (4–5 in) of organic matter over the vegetable bed. You can use compost, aged manure (fresh manure can be too hot and might still contain weed seeds), shredded leaves, or whatever organic matter is readily available in your local area. Dig or till this organic matter 20–25 cm (8–10 in) into the soil. You can actually plant cool-season veggies in mid-August. Plant leaf lettuces, radishes, spinach and peas. After planting (if you decide to do so) mulch over the bare soil between the plants with additional organic matter. A 5- to 8-cm (2- to 3-in) layer will help suppress weeds and slow water evaporation. At the end of the season dig the organic matter into the soil and add a fresh layer. Repeat this process annually and you'll end up with rich garden loam and a spectacular vegetable garden. If you choose not to plant in mid-August, just

> When choosing vegetables to grow in small spaces . . . make the most of all the vertical space you have and ensure that you have beans and peas climbing up all the walls.

spread the 5–8 cm of organic matter over the bed to help improve the soil. Next spring dig the mulch into the soil and plant as above.

Sewing Vegetable Seeds

It's easy to grow vegetables from seed but it's well worth sowing little and often to get the best possible results. When you plant seeds, your crops will all mature at roughly the same speed, so you can save yourself money and time by only sowing part of your packet of seeds at a time. Then wait a few weeks and sow some more. This is known as 'successional' sowing and means you never get a glut, and you've always got a supply of fresh young veggies when its at its prime. Most packets contain a huge number of seeds, and you may have enough in one packet to keep you in fresh vegetables for months on end! Store seeds in a cool, dry place, such as a garage.

411. What dwarf vegetables can I grow in my garden?

When choosing vegetables to grow in small spaces, look for words like 'bush' or 'container' varieties. Make the most of all the vertical space you have and ensure that you have beans and peas climbing up all the walls. You can also plant 'tumbler' tomatoes and strawberries in hanging baskets and pots. Use the spaces between large, slow-growing vegetables to get quick crops of salad leaves and ensure you sow 'little and often' so that you have a continuous supply of your favourite veggies. Also, make the most of every inch of patio space to grow veggies in containers.

412. Why should you plant sweet corn in blocks?

Planting corn in a block of short rows rather than one long row is preferable because it helps to facilitate pollination. This is all-important with any edible crop as it will give you much higher yields. You can use the spaces between your rows of corn to grow shade-loving crops, such as spinach.

413. How often should you use fertiliser on your vegetable garden?

Soluble fertiliser can be beneficial as plant leaves can absorb the fertiliser just as well as the roots can. So, you can fertilise with a diluted liquid food such as seaweed or you can use fertiliser on the soil. However, time spent enriching your soil with an organic medium such as aged manure is the wisest way to ensure your plants are getting what they need – always prioritise this first and consider fertilisers as an additional treatment. Fertiliser is a poor substitute for rich, loamy soil.

414. I'm a first timer. How should I design my small veggie patch?

A 2.5 x 4-m (8 x 12-ft) vegetable garden should provide plenty of wholesome food. Choose the sunniest spot available and work in lots of organic matter to enrich the soil and make moisture and nutrients readily available to the roots of your plants. Choose the vegetables you and your family like best. As you gain experience, you may want to try some of the more

In order to get the best possible crops of sweet corn, plant them in blocks of short rows, rather than one long row. This way they can pollinate one another.

exotic veggies. The layout is important, as whenever possible the rows in the vegetable garden should run north and south, for best sun exposure and air circulation. If the rows run east and west the first row tends to shade the second row, the second row the third and so on.

The tall crops such as peas, beans and corn, should be planted on the north side of the vegetable garden. In this way they will not shade the rest of the vegetable crops. In the centre of the vegetable garden area, plant the medium-sized crops, such as cabbage, cauliflower, broccoli, tomatoes, squash and pumpkins. At the southernmost end of the garden you can plant the low-growing crops like radishes, carrots, beets, lettuce, onions and other low growers. By taking a little time to plan the layout of your vegetable garden before planting, your chances of harvesting a more bountiful yield this year are greatly increased. After planting your veggies, place 5–8 cm (2–3 in) of organic matter over the bare soil to help suppress weeds, moderate soil temperatures and slow water evaporation.

When choosing what vegetables to plant where, bear in mind that taller-growing varieties such as sweetcorn will shade smaller plants, so choose vegetables that like shade.

Time spent enriching your soil with an organic medium such as aged manure is the wisest way to ensure your plants are getting what they need, so always prioritise this first.

415. Why do my courgette flowers fall off before they have a chance to grow?

Courgette vines develop both male and female flowers; the male blossoms dry up and fall off after a few days, whereas the female flowers will develop fruit if they have been pollinated. You can help things along by attracting more bees to your garden through planting bee-friendly plants like borage. Having lots of different kinds of flowers blooming all the time will help to ensure there are lots of pollinating insects nearby.

Alternatively, remove a male flower and 'visit' female flowers, dusting the pollen from the inside of the male to the inside of the female. Male flowers have a straight stem from the blossom to the vine and female flowers have a characteristic swelling just behind the blossom.

Attract more bees to your garden by planting bee-friendly plants . . . Having lots of different flowers blooming all the time will help to ensure there are lots of pollinating insects nearby.

416. How do I get rid of caterpillars in my vegetable garden?

A number of different pests can be controlled organically by spraying beneficial nematodes on the lawn and garden area. These microscopic worm-like creatures attack only the grubs in the soil and not plants, animals or humans. Spray them in spring when the soil temperatures are above 13°C (55°F) and you should see a difference this summer. It's important to maintain soil moisture to keep the nematodes viable, so that they can move easily through the soil. I suggest that you moisten soil well the day before you apply them, or wait until after it rains. After application, apply mulch to the soil to keep it moist. This is much better than using pesticide sprays, which can kill bees and other beneficial insects which could pollinate your crops.

Female courgette flowers need to be pollinated in order to produce fruits. If not they can turn brown and fall off the plant.

417. How can I tell when potatoes are ready to harvest?

This crop can be harvested when the tops die down, if you plan to store them over the winter months. This will generally occur with the first frost of the season. If you'd like to dig some small (or 'new' potatoes) you can harvest any time after the flowers appear on the tops of the plants.

418. I'm building raised vegetable gardens – what's a safe wood preservative?

Linseed oil is a natural preservative. It's extracted from flax seed and is used, among other things, as a preservative for wood. The only downside is that it takes a long time to dry. If you plan for that, you'll be more than happy with its preservative qualities!

No matter how long you've been growing vegetables, you'll still get a huge sense of satisfaction every time you fork through the soil to reveal a huge haul of perfect potatoes.

Preventing the Blight

Potato blight can devastate an entire crop of potatoes or cause the tubers to rot in storage. As with most problems, prevention is better than cure. Blight is a fungal condition that takes hold during warm and humid conditions. Plants that have succumbed will have brown, blotchy leaves. Tubers affected with blight have dark patchy skin and a rotten, spongy and often foul-smelling core. In storage, the fungus will spread easily from one potato to another. For the gardener, the cause is often spores arriving on the wind, infected tubers left from last year's crop or poor quality seed potatoes. The best course of action is to be extra vigilant in humid conditions, especially after rain. Immediately remove affected stems and leaves before burning them.

Herbs

Herbs can enliven your borders just as they can bring new life to your cooking. Many are very undemanding to grow, as long as you can offer them freely-draining soil and a sunny spot.

419. How do I prepare perennial herbs for the winter?

Most perennial herbs, such as sage, mint, oregano and fennel should be cut back before winter to around 10–15 cm (4–6 in) above the ground. It's a good idea to mulch them with a 5–8 cm (2- to 3-in) layer of bark mulch, especially if you live in a cooler area. That will help them make it through the freezing and thawing. Low-growing herbs, such as thyme, don't need to be cut back.

Maintaining Herbs

Most herbs are perennial so you only need to plant them once to benefit from a crop for many years. Chances are you'll give them a regular 'pruning' simply by snipping the leaves off to add to your saucepan, but over a period of time they can start to look straggly if left untended, and their growth is inclined to be less productive. Prevent this from happening by giving them a good trim in late summer or early autumn after they've finished flowering. If you find that any of your herbs are starting to outgrow their pots, take each one out and divide it to form two or three new plants and give your extras away to friends and family. With herbs such as mint, you may find you use so much of it that you need several pots growing at once.

420. What herbs can I grow indoors on a sunny windowsill?

Herbs grown indoors need plenty of bright light or sunlight, such as from a south-facing window, and soil that drains very well. Many herbs are native to the Mediterranean area, so think about recreating those conditions. Some herbs that normally do well indoors are basil, parsley and coriander (all these need slightly more moist soil); and thyme, oregano and rosemary (these can allow soil to dry out a bit more). Fertilise once a month with a standard houseplant fertiliser. Once the plants are growing vigorously, start harvesting the leaves and pinch back the stems regularly to keep the plants from getting too tall and straggly.

421. I bought lemon grass last year, but it seems to have died. Any tips?

Lemon grass is not a winter-hardy plant, so if you leave it outside over the winter, unfortunately it will not survive. Try growing it in a container inside; it can be trimmed off short, allowing you to harvest it for use one blade at a time or as a clump. It can be expensive to buy lemon grass, so it's well worth growing your own fresh supply.

422. Is it possible to sow dill seeds directly into the ground?

Dill seeds need light to germinate, so the trick is to make sure you don't sow them too deeply in the soil. You can start dill seeds any time from spring through mid-summer outdoors. Try raking the seedbed smooth, sprinkling a little finely sieved potting soil on the surface, then broadcasting the dill seeds on top. The potting soil will catch and hold the seeds, providing a light, moist place for them to germinate. You can expect the seeds to sprout in 21 to 25 days at temperatures of 16–24°C (60–75°F). Water the plants regularly.

Dill is quite easy to grow from seed as long as you ensure the seeds get the light they need to germinate. The tall plants are ideal at the back of a flower border.

423. How can I grow lemon basil?

Lemon basil is a variety of basil and is grown the same way as its more well-known cousin. It is an annual, but it readily self-seeds if left to flower and go to seed.

Try raking the seedbed smooth, sprinkling a little finely sieved potting soil on the surface, then broadcasting the dill seeds on top.

424. Is borage is a good companion plant in vegetable gardens and, if so, why?

Borage is a wonderful annual herb. It is highly attractive to bees and other beneficial insects, which is why it is such a good companion plant. It is also an edible herb and the leaves and flowers are often used to enhance the flavour of lemonade and other summer drinks. The flowers can be candied or used to make pretty ice cubes. An added bonus is deer and slugs don't seem to like it and what's more it tends to self-seed, so once you buy one plant you'll have plenty more each year.

425. How can I prevent pests from nibbling my herb plants?

Most plants can tolerate some insect feeding and the safest method of control is to simply hose off the pests with a fine jet of water from your hose. As well as being much safer to use than pesticide, this method doesn't leave a sticky mess of dead pests on your plants! If you want to resort to chemical controls, you can control persistent infestations with a solution of insecticidal soap or a pyrethrum-based insecticide, both of which are safe for food crops when used according to label directions.

426. Is there anything I can do to get rid of spider mites?

These tiny pests thrive in hot, dry locations so to deter them you can simply wash your plants off on a regular basis. You can use a spritzer, or water from the hose, to thoroughly rinse all parts of your plants every week or so. This will wash off any mites that may be present and will discourage more from making a home in the stems and foliage of your herbs. A regular routine of washing them away will soon clear up the problem without using pesticides.

Pretty enough to grow for its flowers alone, borage is also a useful companion plant as it attracts bees. It does tend to set seed freely, but the seedlings have shallow roots and are very easy to remove with a hoe if they pop up in places where you don't want them.

427. My new chive plants are drooping – what is wrong with them?

Chives are perennial plants that grow in clumps and may reach 0.6 m (2 ft) in height, although they are generally kept cut back so the grass-like leaves can be used in the kitchen. They prefer growing in cool weather so yours may be getting too much summer sunshine or they could be

If your plants become dormant, the roots will remain alive.

stressed by the heat. Try moving your chives to a partly sunny or lightly shaded garden site, in moist, fairly rich soil. Harvest by cutting the amount of foliage you need with a pair of scissors. The plants will remain evergreen in mild winter areas but will go dormant if winter weather is cold. If your plants become dormant, the roots will remain alive and will produce new foliage the following spring. Some gardeners allow the plants to develop flower stalks, which produce a globe-like cluster of purple flowers. The flowers can be eaten in salads or used to flavour vinegars and oils.

The flowers of chives are edible and can be added to salads, or alternatively you can use them to make your own pretty flavoured herb vinegars.

Planning Your Herb Garden

No garden should be without a few key herbs as these undemanding plants offer big rewards in return for the minimum of care. Most have very decorative foliage, many have pleasing flowers and they all smell lovely when you brush past them. One of the best jobs in the garden is weeding the herb bed as the sweet scents are so evocative. As if all that wasn't enough, many herbs have medicinal uses too. If you have the luxury of choosing where to build an herb garden, choose a site near to your kitchen door. This will help you to get in the habit of nipping out to pick a few suitable leaves every night when you're cooking. You can create a very respectable herb garden in just a 1.8 m² (6 sq ft) area, such as at the centre of a patio.

428. What's an easy, decorative herb to grow in a pot?

One of the most simple herbs to start from seed is basil and it grows well in a container. It reaches a nice mature size in about 10–12 weeks if planted in early summer. Be sure to pinch the plants back regularly (every third leaf pair) to keep them from bolting and repot them as needed into larger pots so that they are healthy and in vigorous growth. You can choose the very decorative smaller-leafed, dwarf 'Spicy Bush Basil' which grows to about 30 cm (12 in). Another possibility would be extra curly dwarf parsley which also looks very attractive and grows well in containers. Alternatively, look out for variegated herbs, such as oregano and thyme. These literally look good enough to eat.

429. When will my chives and garlic chives flower and how long will the blooms last?

Chives tend to flower very heavily in mid-spring, along with the tall bearded iris. If you trim them back they will repeat in mid-summer and, if you trim them back again, there may even be a final flush of blooms before winter. The quality of the later shows depends greatly on the available levels of water and nutrients, however. In contrast, garlic chives bloom only once a year, in late summer. The blooms usually make a show for several weeks each time, attracting lots of bees.

Even if you only have a patio or balcony, you can still enjoy the flavour of just-picked herbs by growing them in pots. A wide variety of herbs will be happy planted in a large container.

430. What is the best way to freeze herbs for use in the kitchen in winter?

Herbs can be frozen, but the process depends upon the herb, and what you'll be doing with it after it's frozen. Tough-stemmed herbs like basil, tarragon and sage should have their leaves removed prior to freezing. Just pack the clean leaves into plastic bags or into freezer containers and place them in the freezer. Basil should be blanched before freezing, or it will turn black. Simply put basil leaves into a strainer and pour boiling water over them. Drain and freeze in the size portions you think you'll need. Other herbs, such as dill or parsley, freeze well if they're separated into sprigs and frozen individually, then packed into one large container. You can also freeze chopped herbs in ice cube trays. Place a teaspoon of herb in each section, then fill with water. Once they're frozen, the herb cubes can be removed and stored in plastic freezer bags in the freezer. They're great for popping into winter soups and sauces! They also add a depth of flavour to pasta dishes, casseroles and omelettes.

431. How can I use my fresh mint leaves?

You can use mint in many ways. You can add a few sprigs to lemonade, iced tea or to fruit salad. Put a handful in cheesecloth and steep it in hot water to taste for hot tea, or add lots of fresh leaves to tea glasses and serve, Moroccan-style, with sugar. Dry it and use it for hot tea, or to flavour jelly, or even add it to potpourri. It is used in many Middle Eastern dishes for example and a quick internet search will yield lots of recipes. You can also cut it and add it to the compost pile.

With their glossy leaves, bay trees are very attractive and they can be grown in pots if space is short. This plant is an ideal candidate for topiary, and standard bays look lovely on either side of a doorway.

Drying Herbs

Although you can pick some herbs fresh from a bright windowsill in winter, it is well worth having a supply of dried ones on hand. It's very easy to air dry varieties such as rosemary, summer savoury, bay, thyme, dill, marjoram and oregano, so you should never go short. On a dry morning in late summer use sharp scissors to cut 10-cm (4-in) stems of your favourites — around five or six of each is ideal. Remove any leaves from the very bottom of the stem and tie each bundle together. Then hang them up in an airy place and leave for a couple of weeks to dry. They are ready when the leaves are brittle and crumble easily when rubbed between your fingers. Pop them into labelled jars and remember that their flavour is concentrated so use sparingly.

432. Should I let my oregano plant bloom?

Unless you want to leave the flowers to attract bees and butterflies, or in order to collect seeds for next year, it's best to pinch any flowering stems as they develop. If you allow your oregano to flower it will set seed and then the leaves can develop a more bitter flavour. It also dies back once it has set seed, so try to avoid this.

Although oregano has pretty flowers, once it sets seed the plant will die back, so nip off any buds you spot if they start to emerge during the summer months.

433. I grow several edible flowers in my garden – can I use them to make candied flowers?

Most people know about candied violets, but many other edible flowers, such as rose petals, borage and nasturtiums can also be candied. Recipes vary, but the key elements to creating candied flowers are egg white and superfine granulated sugar. Bear in mind that you are taking a chance with salmonella when eating any part of a raw egg. Knowing the risk involved, you can decide if you want to go ahead with making the candied flowers. Whichever recipe you use, paint the egg white mixture on the flower with a thin artist's paint brush, then gently sprinkle the flower with sugar and place on parchment paper to dry. It also goes without saying that you should only eat flowers that have not been treated with pesticides.

434. Why has my coriander plant wilted and turned yellow?

Coriander is one of those annual herbs that keeps growing as long as you keep cutting it back. If it's allowed to flower and go to seed, the plant will die and it will also bolt if it is allowed to dry out in warm weather. It's best to sow seeds at two-week intervals and keep the leaves cut back, (or regularly picked off the plant), to prolong the life of your coriander plants. You can sow seeds right up to autumn – new plants will produce leaves until frost nips them.

435. Are gold variegated sage and purple sage as hardy as the usual garden herb?

Garden sage is definitely a perennial and the other two can sometimes survive in mild winters with a good mulch. If your plants do survive the cooler months, wait until they begin to show new growth in spring and then cut them back by as much as two-thirds. This will help renew the plant and encourage the production of healthy new leaves. If sage is left to its own devices for too long, the plants can become too large for most herb beds!

436. Any suggestions for growing dill and parsley? My plants never last.

Both these culinary herbs can be grown indoors, but they do best outdoors in full sunshine. Dill plants can reach upwards of 0.9 m (3 ft) tall and wide and are best placed in the back of your herb bed where they can spread out and grow without crowding other plants. Dill prefers moderately rich, well-drained, moist soil with a slightly acid

Sage is very easy to grow and there are various forms with decorative leaves. Add it sparingly to your cooking however, as just a little of this strong herb goes a long way.

If you decide to grow your plants in containers rather than in the ground, use a good commercial grade of potting soil.

pH (pH 6.0). Parsley also likes a moderately rich, moist, well-draining soil with a pH of 6.0, and it will grow in full sun to partial shade. If you decide to grow your plants in containers rather than in the ground, use a good commercial grade of potting soil and water the plants thoroughly, then allow the soil to slightly dry out before watering thoroughly again. Sometimes plants in containers are not watered thoroughly enough to saturate the soil and drive out air pockets around the roots. You can help avoid this condition by immersing the pots in a larger container of water once every ten days to two weeks. Allow them to sit in the water until air bubbles no longer rise to the surface. Then remove them from the water bath and allow excess water to drain away.

437. How can I stop my spearmint taking over my whole herb bed?

Members of the mint family are often considered invasive because the plants will spread by roots, seeds and by fallen stems that come into contact with the soil. To completely eradicate spearmint, you must hand dig the roots plus remove the stems. Any plant part left in the soil can root and become a new plant. There's no easy way to get rid of mint, especially in established beds. Just begin digging, and don't give up until the last of the plants have been pulled! Another approach is to starve the plants out. If you can keep the plants cut down, especially keeping the flowers from developing, the roots will eventually run out of energy to produce stems and leaves and will die out. It will take a while, but keep cutting and digging and you'll get the upper hand!

Mint is an incredibly versatile herb, but it has a tendency to take over, so think very carefully about where you'll plant it.

Cultivating Mint

Spearmint and peppermint leaves are said to be good for digestion and they can be used to make delicious tea with boiling water and an optional spoon of honey. You can also make a quick mint sauce by adding finely chopped leaves to a little vinegar and sugar. For a real taste sensation, add a few sprigs to the water when boiling potatoes or peas. Mint is almost too easy to grow – once established it is inclined to take over, so keep it in a pot if space is an issue, or another good tip is to plant it in a bucket (with drainage holes drilled in to the bottom) that's been buried in the ground to restrict the rampant root growth.

438. Should I allow my chives to flower?

Some people enjoy the appearance of the chive flowers and, depending where it's planted, it can add visually to the garden. If you let it flower, you can collect seeds to plant next year, or to use in a seed exchange with friends. Some chives will flower again later in the season if you cut them off. Some greens taste bitter once they go to flower, but luckily this doesn't seem to affect the flavour of chives. What's more the flowers are edible and look great when tossed in a salad!

439. Which herbs won't grow together?

In general, plants that have the same growing requirements can be planted together. An exception in herbs is fennel – it is allelopathic and should be planted alone.

440. What is the herb lavender used for?

English lavender (*Lavandula angustifolia*, syn *L. officinalis*) is used for its essential oil and flowers. Fresh flowers are used in some culinary products; dried flowers are used in arrangements. The essential oil is used in perfumes and aromatherapy. It has a long history of herbal uses, including as a calmative and for its medicinal properties and if you are interested in these, I'd recommend consulting an herbal professional. French lavender (*Lavandula dentata*) is most commonly used as an aromatic or dried flowers. There are numerous lavender species and varieties, and many are very popular in herb gardens as well as flower gardens.

441. How should I prune rosemary?

This herb tends to become woody, almost like a shrub, with age. Usually it is better to pinch the tips or shear it while it is growing rather than to cut it back hard into old wood. Regular frequent trimming will result in a denser, bushier plant as each spot where you trim should develop additional branching. Some varieties of rosemary are naturally taller and more upright than others, so to some extent your results will depend on that as well as your pruning technique. Newer growth can be trimmed back fairly hard, but I would be very cautious about cutting into hard wood. Avoid fertilising these plants during the winter.

Although it is often grown in flower gardens, lavender is also an herb and has culinary and medicinal uses. It also attracts bees, making it a great option for growing near the vegetable garden.

442. I know that Russian Comfrey is used as a soil conditioner. Can I use common comfrey and borage too?

Comfrey (*Symphytum officinale*) and borage (*Borago officinalis*) are members of the same family. Comfrey (Russian or common) has a reputation for improving soil, thanks to its high mineral and protein content, but borage isn't regarded as highly, probably because it can self-seed and become invasive. The properties of both should be similar, making them desirable green manure crops. If you grow either, turn the plants under before they flower and set seed.

443. How should I take cuttings from my lemon thyme plant?

Fortunately, thyme is easily propagated by cuttings. Simply cut a 3- or 4-inch-long (8–10 cm) piece of stem, remove all but the top 2.5 cm (1 in) of leaves and 'plant' it in a plastic pot filled with moistened sterile seed-starting mix. Put a plastic bag over the top, tie loosely and set in a warm place. Check frequently to see that the soil doesn't dry out and try to keep it evenly moist. After about a month, gently tug on one of the stems, to see if roots have formed. A rooting powder may help speed up the root growth. Another way to multiply the plant is to dig it up carefully and simply divide the plant and rootball into several smaller plants, each with their own roots.

Thyme is very easy to grow from cuttings, so it's a good plant to use to edge the front of an herb garden, or even as ground cover on the edges of paths.

444. I used a weed killer to destroy the weeds around my herbs but now they're dead too. Did I kill them?

The weed killer is probably responsible for the death of your herbs. Most weed killers do not discriminate; they kill anything in their paths and the chemicals can go into the soil and leach into the root zones of all the plants you do want. Next time you plant herbs or flowers, one option

Most weed killers do not discriminate; they kill anything in their paths and the chemicals can go into the soil . . .

is to cover the bare soil with weed matting or even several thicknesses of newspaper covered by bark or other decorative material. This will keep weeds from sprouting and you won't have to resort to weed killers around your sensitive plants. Alternatively, remove weeds by hand using a hand trowel. This is far more visually appealing than having dead brown plants in your garden and is a much safer option, particularly around plants you are planning to eat!

445. Can basil, thyme, oregano and chives be planted in full sun?

Not only can they, they should be planted in full sunshine. They will grow best with at least eight hours of direct sunshine each day.

446. We are trying to add colour to our herb garden. What do you suggest?

Some of the more decorative, colourful herbs include basil 'Purple Ruffles', which has purple foliage. Basil 'Armenian' is another good option and has silvery green leaves that are tinged red. Wormwood or *Artemisia* has lovely silvery grey foliage as does lavender. Variegated forms of your favourite herbs always look lovely. Golden sage is also worth looking out for. It has greenish centres on leaves with yellow margins.

447. Which herbs can I plant together in one large pot?

There are basically two kinds of herbs: those that need a lot of moisture and those that don't, so group each kind in their own container and they will grow happily together. Herbs that prefer moisture-rich soil include basil, coriander, tarragon and parsley, while herbs that don't need as much water, or 'Mediterranean herbs', include oregano, sage, rosemary, thyme, bay, marjoram and lavender.

Create visual interest by looking out for herbs in interesting colours. You can also vary the types of growth habits in your herb garden so that some plants trail or creep, while others have a more upright habit.

Making the Most of Your Herbs

Many herbs can be planted individually in pots or simply popped in anywhere you have space in between the flowers in your beds and borders. Because many of our favourite varieties originate from warmer climates they'll do best in a sunny spot, with well-drained soil. Many of them are very decorative in their own right and worth growing even if you don't particularly like the flavour. Others are good companion plants and can attract beneficial insects, or their strong smells can help to deter pests. When you're adding large-leaved herbs such as basil to your dishes, bear in mind that they are quite delicate. Breaking them apart with your fingers rather than snipping them with scissors helps to preserve their flavour and aroma.

Tree Fruits and Nuts

Fruit trees offer huge harvests for very little effort and deserve to be more widely grown. What's more, there are options for every size of garden.

448. Why are the leaves on my apple tree turning brown and crunchy?

Wilting, curling leaves are a definite sign of stress – this could be caused by too little water perhaps (or possibly too much if you are using a sprinkler). Wilting leaves is also a sign of a common fungal disease called apple scab. Given that the leaves on your apple tree are already suf-fering, it will be too late to prevent the problem this year. Instead, you should rake and remove the fallen leaves to prevent reinfection. Next spring you could spray your apple tree with Bordeaux mixture (lime sulphur), beginning just as the leaf buds begin to swell, and again (usually three more times) as recommended on the label. These treatments will protect the leaves from scab.

Protecting Fruit Trees

It's surprising how often there can be a very dry period of weather, and if you don't keep on top of watering any newly planted fruit trees their development could suffer. Any weeds will be competing with them for moisture so try to hoe and hand-weed around them where necessary. Even grass that is seemingly harmless should be removed from 0.9 m (3 ft) all around your fruit trees as it will take food and water from the soil before it gets to your plants' roots. Although it's not easy to remember to do this, you should remove any blossom that trees planted in winter make in their first spring as soon as it emerges. This will encourage them to put all their energy into creating strong roots, giving you much better crops in the future.

449. Our plums are two colours. Could there be a problem?

It doesn't sound like anything is wrong with your plum tree. It is probably a simple explanation such as perhaps the plums on your tree are not quite ripe and when they are fully ripen they will be all the same colour. The parts that are lighter are probably the sides that receive the most sunshine. Also, some varieties of plum naturally have interesting variation in their shades, often being pink, greenish and yellow when ripe and ready to eat. It's a good idea to wait and see how they mature – you'll have clues that they're ready when they smell sweet and start dropping off the tree. Taste is the best way to tell if they are ripe. Once they are ripe, you can pick a couple and take them along to a local nursery for identification.

450. My cherry trees are so productive we can't eat all the fruit. Do I need to rake them off the lawn?

Cleaning up the fallen fruit is really important, so it's well worth raking them up every day or two. If you allow the fallen fruit to remain, it can be a nesting ground for insect and disease problems that can affect the cherries in subsequent years. One trick you can try to make this task easier is to lay a fine-mesh net under the tree to collect the fallen fruit. Pull it up every day or two and discard the cherries, then lay it back in place. You might want to ask around for a little help too – you may well have lots of friends and neighbours who would love to help you pick those extra cherries, and local charities might be very grateful for the opportunity to make them into pies and preserves.

Once cherry trees are established you may well find that you have more fruit than you can possibly eat. Fortunately, there are likely to be lots of people who can help with your harvest.

451. My 'dwarf' peach tree is becoming enormous. What can I do?

Most dwarf peach trees grow to 1.5–1.8 m (5–6 ft) tall – ask your supplier what the average size of the variety you purchased is supposed to be. Peach trees usually start bearing when they are three to four years old. However, the tree puts out more fruit than it can support, so fruit needs to be thinned to reach adequate size. When the fruits are about 2.5 cm (1 in) or so in size, pick off the excess. There should be about 25 cm (10 in) between the remaining fruits. This will allow them to become large and juicy.

452. How can I encourage my greengage tree to fruit?

Greengage trees are known as 'self-fertile' or 'self-fruitful', so having only one tree should not affect fruit production. What will cause poor fruiting includes immaturity (some trees just have to grow older before they're able to set fruit), lack of sufficient sunshine, poor pruning practices (accidentally cutting off fruiting branches), too much nitrogen fertiliser, a late cold snap, or water stress. If your tree is not flowering at all, it could be due to weather, age or poor pruning. If it is flowering but not setting fruit, it could be due to a cold snap or poor pollination (lack of insect activity). You'll need to decide which of the above might apply to your tree in order to correct the problem. Experiment and see what works.

If you only have a small space, the greengage is a good choice of fruit tree as you don't need another one to cross-pollinate it. The just-picked fruits are delicious.

453. Why do I never get any figs on my potted fig tree?

The tree is probably rootbound. Figs are very aggressive growers and rootbound figs are more likely to suffer from a lack of water. All it takes is one dry period in the pot and the fruit will drop. You can encourage figs grown in containers to bear fruit by ensuring that they are root-pruned annually. The best time to do this is early in spring before growth resumes. Remove the tree from the container and prune all the roots back by a third. Repot the fig in the same container and add fresh soilless mix and one cup each of bonemeal and lime. These amendments will add phosphorus and calcium, which figs crave. When placing the fig outside for summer, try planting it, pot and all, into the ground. The plant will grow lush and you'll probably have mature fruit by September. Then, dig up the container, prune off the roots that have grown out of the container and bring it in for winter.

454. How can you tell when apples are ripe and ready for picking?

Even if you haven't grown apples before, there are clues that can help you to tell when the fruit is ripe. It should come away easily if you twist it, and the pips will be brown.

Apples may begin to fall from the tree when they're ripe. Depending upon the variety, late summer marks the start of the apple season, but some can be harvested right up to just before winter. You can try to pick an apple to see if it comes off easily. Grasp the apple, twist and push up. If it comes off easily, it's probably ripe. To check, cut it open; if the seeds are dark brown, the apple's ripe. If not wait a week or two and try again.

Seasonal Crops

If you plan your fruit-growing carefully it is possible to eat fresh, homegrown crops for many months of the year. All you need is the space for a few trees, and you can be well on your way to self-sufficiency. First you'll need to draw up a list of the different fruits you enjoy and their respective harvesting seasons — for example, you can enjoy cherries in June and July, peaches, plums and greengages in August and September, then in October and November you can harvest your apples and pears. The secret is to choose some varieties that are best eaten right away, and others that are suitable for storage. Lots of eating pears will store until January and some apples can be kept in a cool place until mid-February and even March. What's more, they still taste delicious.

It's worth growing *Aronia* for the spectacular foliage alone, but the black berries are also very tasty when cooked with sugar and they can be used in pies and preserves.

Easy Pickings

People often think of fruit as being more tricky to grow than vegetables, but there are some options you can practically plant and then forget about until it's time to pick your crops every year. What's more, many varieties are so attractive that you'd be tempted to grow them even if they didn't fruit. *Aronia* or chokeberries are very easy to grow and extremely decorative. You can use them just as you would sloes to make a very tasty gin. The berries are quite small but they are produced in such abundance that it doesn't take long to harvest a good bowlful. Crab apples are another decorative tree that has lovely blossom in summer and pretty fruit in autumn. The tiny apples can be used in jellies and sauces. Try making a healthy, vitamin-rich tonic.

455. How do I take care of my *Aronia*?

The black chokeberry is quite hardy. It will grow to a height of 1.2 m (4 ft) with a spread of 1.5 m (5 ft). Expect this deciduous shrub to have a rounded form and grow less than 30 cm (12 in) per year. The flowers are white and the fruits will be dark purple to black. They are very high in vitamin C and ideal for making jams and puddings. *Aronia* is a suckering, thicket-forming shrub or small tree that adapts to wet or dry sites. The glossy foliage turns red in the autumn and is offset beautifully by the purplish-black fruit. The plant can be used in naturalistic plantings in sun or shade. No maintenance other than regular watering during the growing season is necessary. Because of its slow growth habit, annual pruning is usually not necessary.

456. Can I grow any other fruit trees near my walnut?

Walnut tree leaves contain a substance that inhibits the growth of other plants. It's best not to use the fresh leaves as mulch material, as some plants are very sensitive to the chemical. Walnut trees also provide dense shade and have feeder roots that are close to the surface. The roots will compete with other plants for moisture and nutrients. Try to plant at least as far away from the trunk as the spread of the canopy of the tree. Also walnut trees have a reputation for harbouring aphids, so watch your plants carefully and hose off any insects as soon as they appear. The honeydew they excrete can cause problems on plant leaves.

457. Is it true that pruning fruit is different from pruning other trees?

Fruit trees are pruned to encourage fruit, which differs from pruning for shape in ornamental trees. The 'modified leader' method is probably the best route for a home grown apple tree. It starts out with one leader, but as that central trunk becomes stronger it is allowed to form several tops. This helps the tree sustain the weight of the fruit. Eventually, you'll want to shorten the tree a bit, which will make it easier to pick the apples as well as allow sunlight and air to get into the central part of the tree. As to when you should prune, I would suggest waiting until the very coldest part of the winter is behind you, but the weather is not warm yet. It's a time you're anxious to get into the garden and there are many pleasant days when it's fun to do this. The tree will still be dormant with no leaves, so it's a good time to be able to stand back and make a good judgement about just what needs to go or stay. When you prune, the first thing you do is remove damaged, broken and diseased branches. Next, remove any branches that rub or touch each other. When that is done, stand back and study from all angles. Then carry out the suggestions above for the 'modified leader' method. If you do a fair amount of pruning, it will produce a big flush of growth in the spring; be on the lookout for suckers and water sprouts (vigorous vertical shoots) and take them out when they appear. When you cut, cut quite close

> Cut quite close to the nearest branch or trunk leaving just barely a 'neck'. Do not leave stumps as they will be a weak point on the tree and will invite disease and insects.

to the nearest branch or trunk, leaving just barely a 'neck'. Do not leave stumps as they will be a weak point on the tree and will invite disease and insects. Remember that pruning off too much at any given time will probably stress your tree.

A regular annual trim of your fruit trees will keep them in tip-top condition and can lead to bigger harvests and healthier trees which means less work for you in the long run.

Rather than having lots of small peaches, it's worth thinning your crop. You'll get fewer fruits but each one will be bigger and juicier.

458. Should I thin the fruits on my peach tree?

Peach trees have a helpful habit of thinning themselves in June by dropping excess fruit. However, on young trees that are getting established, it can be helpful to thin them out. Wait until natural fruit drop occurs and then hand-thin peaches in mid- to late June to an average spacing of one peach to every 15–20 cm (6–8 in) of fruiting wood.

459. My old apple tree bears lots of tasty fruit but they're tiny. What can I do?

The best way to improve the quality of your apples is to thin them out in late June. Reduce the number of apples by removing the smallest apples in each cluster, leaving only one or two of the largest fruits. As you are thinning, look out for any that look damaged or marked and remove these too. This will allow your tree to direct its energy into maturing only about half of the number of fruits it is capable of producing, resulting in larger, more delicious apples.

460. Any tips on starting an orchard?

Growing fruit trees is a rewarding enterprise, although the rewards are not always monetary. Differences in soil, water, tree variety selection, planting and care mix in with good fortune to influence the success rate. Weather often can be your best friend or worst enemy. The single best

> Weather often can be your best friend or worst enemy. The single best thing you can do is get expert local advice. Their experience in fruit growing in your area is a valuable guide in your early fact finding process.

thing you can do is get expert local advice. Their experience in fruit growing in your area is a valuable guide in your early fact finding process. You need to research the potential for various fruit species in your area and the 'how-tos' of their proper culture. There is nothing that can replace this early investigating and study. It is the single best investment you will make. Learn all you can so you can do your best to do things right the first time. Resist the urge to cut corners and do things halfway. It is better to start with a very small planting and to expand as you get the hang of it than to start too large and end up with more than you can handle.

While lemon trees are hardier than you might think, they can still take some time to recover from the adverse effects of a very cold winter.

461. I left my lemon tree out in the frost last year and it died down to the main trunk. Will it ever produce fruit?

If the branches got frozen but the trunk is still alive, the trunk should produce new branches. When those branches are a couple of years old, they should produce flowers and fruit. If you see no flowers, you will not get fruit. You can either wait a few years for the branches to develop and mature enough to flower, or you can simply replace the tree with a healthy new specimen. If you're keen to enjoy some home-grown lemons this year then it may be better to replace the tree. While it may someday produce fruit, the setback from the hard freeze can add a few extra years to your waiting for fruit, and you need to care for your tree in the meantime.

If you have room for a mulberry tree, they are well worth considering as the delicious berries are ideal for making jams and jellies and the trees are attractive all year round.

462. Is a weeping mulberry suitable for a small garden?

The weeping white mulberry (*Morus alba* 'Pendula') produces pendulous branches and gnarled, twisted growth. It bears tasty fruit and it's even interesting in the winter landscape when the branches can be easily seen. This cultivar of weeping mulberry grows 4.5–6 m (15–20 ft) high with an equal spread, so it's better suited to medium to large plots. Mulberry trees do take well to hard pruning, but you may be fighting the tree for years to come if you want to keep it significantly smaller than its natural size. Also, when a tree is stressed it's more likely to develop insect or disease problems.

463. Why do some leaves on my otherwise healthy apple tree have small brown spots?

It could be that you have some minor scab damage but if it is just the occasional leaf that has spots, and your plants are growing strongly, I wouldn't worry. There are other diseases, such as cedar-apple rust, that can also cause leaf spotting. Again, if it's just a few here and there, I wouldn't worry. To be on the safe side, clear away fallen leaves.

The Mulberry Tree

Have you got a large patch of grass in your garden that could be enhanced by planting a specimen tree? If so, a mulberry is a great choice. These trees take up lots of space but they're very undemanding and, once established, will reward you with pounds of sweet, juicy fruits that you're unlikely to find in the local shop. The berries are delicious and you'll get such a huge crop that you'll probably want to make some into jams and jellies. What's more, they ripen over a long period so you can pick them fresh for weeks. However, the purple fruits are extremely juicy – and the mess they make will give you away if you succumb to the temptation to eat a handful of berries every time you walk past the tree.

464. How can I encourage little figs to ripen on my tree?

In cooler areas, late frosts can affect fruit production. In some years the fruits will not have enough time to ripen; in other years you'll have a huge harvest. It's just the nature of this heat-loving tree. Fortunately, they look decorative and are worth having even without the fruit, and when you do get a crop, you enjoy it all the more if it's a rarity! In good years, when the fruits are swelling, cover the tree with netting to protect your figs from birds.

465. I'm planning a 12 m² cottage garden with fruit trees, vegetables, herbs and flowers. Any tips?

This is an ideal space for a productive garden, but 12 m² (40 sq ft) is a large area to tackle all at once. You might want to start at one end and work your way out over a few seasons so you're not overwhelmed. You might want to include a small fruit tree such as apple, crab apple, cherry or pear, and small fruit bushes such as redcurrants. You could grow blackberries or tayberries up a fence. In the kitchen garden area, it's traditional to mix the herbs and greens with classic 'cottage garden' flowers such as hollyhocks, lavender, black-eyed Susan, cosmos, primrose, zinnia, salvia, foxgloves, aquilegia and Canterbury Bells. These will help to confuse pests and attract beneficial insects, which can increase your yields of fruit and veggies.

You can harvest a lot of produce from a relatively small space by mixing fruit trees, fruit bushes, flowers, herbs and vegetables. If you plan it well, this space can also be very decorative.

466. When should I prune my walnut trees?

Walnut trees usually only need pruning to remove dead wood or correct the shape. Young trees should be trained to make a central leading shoot and begin branching high enough to allow foot traffic under the branches. Wait until late winter or early spring to prune. Pruning encourages new growth. If you prune before winter, any new buds or shoots will be susceptible to cold weather damage.

467. What should I do with the nuts from my almond tree when they look ripe?

Most people will harvest the nuts and store them in their shells at cool room temperature if they plan to use them fairly soon. If not, to conserve space you could always shell them first before packing and storing them in the freezer or refrigerator. Most recipes use raw nuts, but some call for lightly toasted nuts to enhance the flavour. To toast them, simply place the shelled nuts on a baking tray and roast gently in the oven. Your cookbook will usually tell you the time and temperature for the recipe you are using. If not, toast a few at a low heat and start testing them every few minutes and see when you like the taste. It shouldn't take too long.

468. How do I remove the outer coating of my chestnuts?

First, it's important to be aware that only American and Chinese chestnuts are edible; the horse chestnut is not. Confirm the identity of the tree before sampling its nuts! To harvest, collect the fallen chestnuts and spread them out to dry in a warm, dry area. Air drying usually takes a week or two. The outer husks will split open and the nuts will drop out.

Growing almonds is surprisingly easy. The trees produce very pretty blooms, and the nuts can simply be eaten straight from the tree or toasted and added to dessert recipes.

469. I've just moved to a house with an apple and pear tree. How do I look after them?

Take a while to look closely at both trees and think about what you'd like to prune off and how the size and shape of the trees affects the rest of your garden. In late winter you can get to work on pruning your fruit trees back. Remove any obviously dead branches as well as any crossing, rubbing or broken branches. Then remove misplaced branches. You should be able to rehabilitate your trees. Some apple trees are still productive at 100 years of age. If your trees are very overgrown it might take two to three years to get them back into shape.

470. We moved to a home with some very old, neglected fruit trees. Can they be saved?

Old, neglected trees can be difficult to rejuvenate, but it can be well worth the effort, depending on how far gone they are, of course. To judge the health of your trees, you can look at the growth they make in a single year. If new branches grow

If you've moved house and inherited a fruit tree, wait until late winter to prune it. Not only is this healthier for the tree, it gives you a chance to assess what work needs to be done.

productive, that's a very good sign too. It's a good habit to thin the fruit on your trees so that more energy is focused on fewer fruit, which increases size and quality. As you've seen first hand, apples and pears can be susceptible to many diseases and insect pests, but they can also be extremely resilient and bounce back with a little regular pruning. Given that it takes a lot of hard work to remove old trees and plant new ones, it's well worth giving these old ones a chance first to see what you can achieve. Who knows, they may even be heritage varieties that have some exceptional qualities!

> Apples and pears can be susceptible to many diseases and insect pests, but they can also be extremely resilient and bounce back with a little regular pruning.

30–40 cm (12–16 in). in a season, it's probably worth the effort, especially if the trees have other attributes you value, such as their inherent beauty and place in the landscape. If the trees are

Ripe plums are so tasty they can attract the attention of wild birds from far and wide. Small trees can be protected with netting, or you can pick slightly under-ripe fruit and cook it.

ripen on the tree, but as you have seen, that can be problematic. Some gardeners choose to cover their trees with netting to protect the fruit but that isn't easy on a big tree. If you pick them a little bit early, you can bring them indoors to ripen at room temperature, out of direct sun. Another option is to use a scarecrow to deter birds – this can be effective as a short-term solution.

472. Why do my fruit trees flower every year but not set fruit?

Fruit set is dependent upon pollination and on decent weather when the flowers are open. In order to pollinate one another most cherries, plums, apples and pears need two varieties in close proximity for good cross-pollination and good fruit set. Find out what varieties your fruit trees are and look for some suitable varieties that you can buy to cross-pollinate them – you should soon be having bumper harvests. You can get together with your neighbours and choose trees that will help to pollinate one another, or look out for 'self-fertile' options that don't need another tree of the same variety to bear crops.

471. My plum tree is fruiting well, but the birds get the ripe fruits before me. Any tips?

If you are going to use the plums for cooking or preserving, you can pick them when they are still slightly under ripe and the fruits are still a bit tart. When fully ripe, the plums will start to fall from the tree. Plums taste best when allowed to

473. What is the best and easiest way to harvest walnuts?

When the nuts are ripe they will simply fall to the ground. If the tree is small you can expedite the process by spreading tarps or old sheets under the tree and then shaking the trunk to dislodge the nuts. If the tree is too large to shake, you may have to wait for the nuts to drop on their own. In either case, gathering the nuts is easiest if you spread a tarp under the tree to catch them. Be aware that the soft outer casing of the nuts contains iodine, which can lead to brown stains on your clothing. The staining is usually only temporary, however.

474. Our apple tree was knocked down by a storm three years ago. It's still fruiting well, but it looks odd. What can we do?

Trees are amazing in their ability to adapt to situations such as this. However, there could be two possible problems with attempting to make your tree 'upright' again. Sawing off any substantial portion of it will create a huge opportunity for insects and disease to enter the trunk. But moving it further (by propping it up for example) may just break the last surviving critical roots that have kept it alive this far. It will also take years to reform the tree even if it is successful. Your best bet is probably to leave it in its wonky state. Having said that, if the tree is really unacceptable the way it is then trying to prop it up again is worth a try!

475. Do you have any advice on how I might start a mini orchard?

First think about the sort of fruit you enjoy eating and the space you have available. Draw up a plan of what you could include, taking into account the eventual height and spread of the different varieties. Look into pollination groups when working out a shortlist of what you'd like to include. Most fruit trees don't need much soil preparation (blueberry bushes are the exception to this rule as they grow best in acid soil). You can have your soil tested and amend it if the pH is unsuitable. Trees can be planted any time in the winter or spring when the ground is workable. They will need to be watered regularly in their first year, and ideally given a generous layer of mulch over the area covering the root ball, although not right up to the trunk as this can cause it to rot.

Maximising Space

There was a time when having a small garden meant that at best you could hope to grow one type of fruit tree. But the advent of cordon trees, created to be grown to around 2.1 m (7 ft) tall, means that anyone with a sunny patio can enjoy a selection of different varieties. You can plant them in large pots spaced around 0.9 m (3 ft) apart, and they can form a decorative feature in their own right or be used to screen a different area of the garden. Another advantage of growing smaller trees is that they are easy to protect from frosts and bad weather. They'll be portable so you can easily move them to a more sheltered spot.

Soft Fruits

When growing soft fruits, be prepared for the fact that many are so delicious they never make it into the kitchen before they're eaten. Snacking on fruit while you garden is a well-earned treat!

476. Can I plant raspberries in an area that was formerly laid to grass?

These vigorous plants should thrive in a site that was previously laid to grass. When planting the raspberries, it would be wise to set them a few centimetres deeper than they were growing at the nursery. Remember that, while growing (especially during flower and fruit production), your plants will need a regular water supply. To help keep the plants from drying out, a thick layer of mulch around the stems is beneficial. The mulch also helps keep weeds at bay. Plants should be top-dressed each year in early spring with a generous amount of organic material such as potting soil or rotted manure. You can also apply a fertiliser such as a 10–10–10 as a side-dressing at the same time.

Planting Raspberries

You can grow raspberries up a teepee of sturdy canes. Prepare the area that will be your raspberry bed by removing all perennial weeds and digging in lots of organic matter. Ensure you have the same number of supports as raspberry canes. Get the supports in place before you plant the canes – they'll need to be at least 15 cm (6 in) deep in the soil and around 40 cm (16 in) apart in a circle. Then bind the tops together with garden wire. Note the type of berry you have – this is important because it affects how you prune the plants. Dig individual holes for each raspberry cane, plant and water well. Finally, cut each cane down to around 30 cm (12 in) tall to encourage root growth.

477. How should I prune my raspberries?

There are two types of raspberry: summer-bearing and autumn-bearing. Each has its own pruning requirements. Autumn-bearing are the easiest to manage – just cut the canes all the way down after they've finished fruiting. New canes will grow in the spring and produce fruit in the autumn. If you have everbearing raspberries, cut back the fruiting part of the cane after harvesting in the autumn, but leave the rest of the cane. After harvesting the following summer, prune the rest of the cane all the way down to the ground. Summer-bearing raspberries bear fruit on two-year-old canes called 'floricanes'. Prune the bearing canes off at ground level immediately after harvesting. Canes that have not produced fruit should be cut back to 1–1.5 m (4–5 ft). These canes will develop fruiting wood the following spring. If the canes are crowded, thin them in early spring, before growth begins, to between two and four strong canes per 30 cm (1 ft).

478. Will fertiliser encourage my recently planted grapevine to bear fruit?

If the grapes were planted in the last couple of years, they won't produce a crop for at least another year, provided they're getting what they need. Hopefully the site is correct for them: full sun, rich, deep soil with a pH of 5.0–6.0. They also need to have good support and be properly pruned and trained. Grapes also need quite a lot of water to produce a good crop. Mulch the area heavily with wood chips or pea straw. Fertilise sparingly in late winter and early spring. Excess fertiliser can cause

It takes a fair amount of effort to get a heavy crop of grapes but the rewards are well worth it!

rampant vine growth at the expense of fruit, so use with care.

479. What is the best way to prepare ground for grapes?

Grapes do well in many soil types and with only average fertility, although a slightly acid pH is preferred. In selecting a site, keep in mind that grapes always require full sun, good air circulation and good soil drainage. Many grapes are planted on slopes because the drainage is improved and the airflow is also much better. Any soil preparation should be deep because grapes are extremely deep rooted.

Grapes do well in many soil types and with only average fertility, although a slightly acid pH is preferred.

480. Can several different varieties of strawberries be planted in close proximity?

There is no danger in planting these crops in close proximity. Cross-pollination is only a danger if you are trying to maintain pure seed strains – the seedlings of cross-pollinated varieties will have mixed genes. Fruit will be unaffected by close proximity unless there is overcrowding that leads to competition for resources, or encourages disease. Just follow planting and spacing instructions that come with the plants or are outlined in a gardening book.

481. How far away from my vegetable garden should I plant my raspberry patch?

Raspberry plants, if uncontrolled, can wander quite a distance. If you make a special bed for your raspberries, you can keep them in their places by annual pruning. Depending on whether you get one or two crops each year, prune them diligently and train the new canes so they stay within bounds. If your plants are autumn-bearing, cut the canes down to the ground after harvest. If they produce fruit in the spring and the autumn, cut back the flowering portion of the cane and wait until the rest of the cane flowers and fruits before cutting it down to the ground. New canes will sprout from the crown of the plant. If you can, aim to keep 1.2–2.1 m (5–7 ft) of separation between your veggie beds and the raspberry bed, so the canes won't reach out and grab you while you're weeding the veggies!

Although they are not quite as rampant as other fruit, raspberries can still send up new shoots a long way from the parent plant, so leave a wide path around your raspberry patch if you have room.

482. How can I tell if a kiwi plant is male or female?

Unless you have a self-fertile kiwi, you'll need both a male and a female plant to get fruit. Both male and female kiwi vines flower in the spring. When yours does, pick a flower and dissect it. Look for the female parts – a swollen ovary at the bottom of the flower, and a long thin stalk with a flattened receptacle at the top of the stalk. If you have a male flower, you will see long, thin anthers with pollen pads on the top, but no ovary at the bottom of the flower. Generally, the female flowers are larger than the male flowers. One male plant can help pollinate up to eight female plants.

One easy way to keep on top of pruning blackcurrant bushes is to cut off the whole fruiting branch, then you can sit down and remove the berries in comfort. Bushes fruit on new wood so you'll be helping to encourage new growth.

483. How can I get my three-year-old blackcurrant bush to produce fruit?

Currants are self-pollinating and generally produce their first crop within three years. Fruit is borne on new wood so if you haven't pruned your bush, you may need to cut back the old canes so new shoots will develop. In the early spring, cut back almost to ground level, leaving two to three buds on each stem. This will encourage new fruiting wood. You'll need to prune annually after harvest, cutting some of the old canes down to the ground and pruning one-third to half of the remaining canes to renew the plant and make it as productive as possible. It's well worth the effort!

Planting Blackcurrants

If you're planting blackcurrants, choose a sunny site and dig a deep hole – it's important that the old soil mark on the stem is 5 cm (2 in) below the surface of the earth, to encourage the plant to throw up more stems from below the ground. Blackcurrants aren't too fussy about the type of soil, but it's well worth ensuring that it's completely free from perennial weeds. Firm the plant down well, water and apply a generous layer of mulch. Cut each stem to just 5 cm above the soil level to encourage the plant to put down a really good root system in its first year. Blackcurrants are thirsty plants, especially when the fruits are forming, so water well in dry weather. Keep an eye on your crops; to protect fruits that are almost ripe from birds, net the bushes.

Strawberry plants start to lose their vigour after three or four years, so plan for new beds by pegging down runners to create new plants.

485. I have a two-year-old strawberry patch. Next year, should I let some of the runners establish new plants and remove the original plants?

There are differing opinions on how to treat your strawberry plants for best yields. Many people have good luck leaving 'mother' plants to produce for three to four years, all the while increasing the bed with the 'daughter' plants. Much depends on the conditions, too, as diseases and reduced soil fertility can take their toll on older plants and result in lower yields. The runners you set this spring and summer should produce a respectable crop next spring.

484. What fertiliser should I use for blueberries?

Blueberries should be fertilised just as the flower buds begin to open with an organic fertiliser. Apply 40 grams for each year the blueberry plant has been in the garden (to a maximum of 250 grams). Don't overfertilise or you'll end up with lots of foliage at the expense of fruits. You can mulch around the plants with pine needles or pine bark to help acidify the soil.

Don't overfertilise blueberries or you'll end up with lots of foliage at the expense of fruits.

Cultivating Blueberries and Cranberries

Blueberries and cranberries need an acid (also known as ericaceous or lime-free) soil to do well. As long as you prepare their planting site thoroughly, they will romp away and, once established, they are very productive and long-lived. Most people have neutral soil, but if you're unsure about the pH balance of your plot you can buy a soil-testing kit. If you don't have acid soil, it's not a problem as you can plant bushes in containers or a raised bed filled with the right growing medium. All of these bushes are very thirsty plants and will grow happily in bogs in the wild, so water them very well, especially when the fruits are forming. A thick mulch of organic matter such as chipped bark or pine needles spread around the soil will help to retain moisture.

486. Can I plant alpine strawberries under my blueberries?

Strawberries make a fine ground cover beneath a blueberry plant and, provided you take a little care when planting them, they shouldn't create any problems for your blueberries. If you're planting small strawberry plants among the roots of established blueberry plants, that should be fine. If you're planting strawberry plants near newly planted blueberry plants then you need to tread more carefully. Make sure you don't dig into the roots of the blueberries and you won't have a problem.

487. What is the best way of telling when a melon is ripe and ready to be picked?

It's not easy to tell when a melon is perfectly ripe, but when it's almost ready to harvest you'll begin to notice small cracks along the stem where the melon is attached to the vine. When the stem starts to shrivel a bit, pick the melon up and give it a twist. If it slips easily, it's ready to harvest. If not, leave it alone for a few days and try again.

Keep an eye on your melons – if you lift and twist them they should come away from the stem quite easily when they are ready for harvest.

488. How can I stop the birds from eating all my ripe blueberries?

You can use commonly available bird netting over your blueberry bushes to protect the fruit. If you secure the ends of the netting by anchoring them to the ground, birds should not be able to get inside the netting and become trapped. If your plants are small, you can make cylinders out of chicken wire to encircle the bushes. Then place a circle of the same material over the opening in the top. Either way, your blueberries will be safe from the birds and the birds won't get stuck inside the enclosure.

489. Can I grow raspberries and blackberries in garden beds next to each other?

You can grow different berries together in a single garden bed and they will all form fruit true to their genetic make up. Plants can only cross-pollinate their offspring, they don't mutate by being grown near to a similar variety, so this is only an issue if you're collecting seeds.

490. My watermelons grow well until they reach 10–15 centimetres long, but then just start turning black. Any idea what's wrong?

What you describe sounds like blossom-end rot. This is a physiological condition caused by a lack of calcium at the growing tip of the fruit. While your soil may have adequate calcium, fluctuations in soil moisture content from dry to wet really increase the incidence of blossom-end rot. It is especially bad on the early fruit each summer and in sandy soils. The damage occurs as cells die at the tip of the fruit. In time (and as the fruit grows) the spots enlarge and turn black. So, by the time you see it, the damage actually has already occurred some time back. Remedies include adding organic matter to a sandy soil to increase its moisture holding capacity and keeping plants evenly moist, especially during the development of the first fruits (mulch helps maintain soil moisture).

Birds find juicy blueberries as tempting as we do, but fortunately it is quite simple to secure a net over the bushes to protect your harvest.

491. The leaves on my gooseberries have dried up this summer. Will they survive?

Many plants shed their leaves early in drought conditions, so your plants may well still be alive, but all you can do is wait and see. Once they do start leafing out, any dead tips or branches should be pruned out. Meanwhile, if you did not prune them last year, you might consider pruning out some of the inner branches to open up the plants to more light and good air circulation. To keep them healthy, especially if you have another dry year, apply 8–10 cm (3–4 in) of organic mulch in spring. This will regulate the soil moisture.

492. Is there a way to contain the roots of blackberries to keep them under control?

To control brambles in a bed you need to create an underground barrier. You could dig down 0.5–1 m (2–3 ft) and put in a wood or metal barrier so the roots can't spread. Also, watch out for them jumping the barrier during the summer. Short of that, you could mow the new sprouts down with a lawnmower to keep them in line.

Once fruit bushes are established, they can usually withstand a period of drought, although it can affect crops the following year. For best results mulch them with a thick layer of bark in spring to help retain moisture.

The Benefits of Thinning Fruit Trees

There are a few different fruits that need to be thinned in order for the remaining fruitlets to grow to their full potential. This task is a treat when it comes to gooseberries, as the thinnings can be collected and cooked into a delicious crumble or fruit fool. As a general rule, aim to remove every other young fruit and the ones you leave will develop well, especially if you grow a dessert variety. Keep an eye out for gooseberry sawfly larvae too. The eggs are laid on buds at the tips of branches, so the tiny green caterpillars are most likely to be on the new growth. Pick off any that you see and pop them on your bird table. Do this for a few days and the problem will soon be under control.

Cranberries need moist soil in order to fruit well, but if you can provide them with the right conditions you should get good crops for many years.

493. What can I do to encourage my cranberry bush to bear fruit?

If your bush is flowering but not producing berries, either the soil is not wet enough or the soil's pH is too high. The growing medium should have a low pH of between 4.5 and 5.5. Partial shade is acceptable, although for good fruit production, full sun is best. Bushes will usually begin to produce fruit in the third year and will continue producing for many years.

494. What are the differences between blackberries and boysenberries?

The boysenberry is a blackberry cultivar, like the tayberry. The fruits ripen over a two-month period. The berries are large (3 cm [1¼ in] long and 2.5 cm [1 in] thick), reddish and soft. They are often chosen as a dessert berry to be eaten raw, perhaps with sugar and cream. They can also be used as an ingredient in pies and preserves.

Cultivating Tayberries

A cross between a blackberry and a raspberry, tayberries are one of the most productive fruits you can grow, and they are delicious either raw or cooked. The plants are very vigorous, so it's important to keep on top of tying in new growth to ensure that the ripening fruits get all the light and air they need to develop properly. Wearing thick gloves, tie stems in to wires attached to stout posts at regular intervals. Aim to harvest the berries regularly, as they will ripen for a few weeks along any one branch. Once you've picked all the berries, you can simply cut the whole stem down to ground level, as fruit is only produced on each year's new wood.

495. How can I prepare a wooden barrel for planting strawberries?

Everbearing strawberries are the best for a strawberry barrel, as they offer a consistent crop. Before planting, get a piece of PVC pipe about 5 cm (2 in) in diameter and cut it to be about 2.5 cm (1 in) taller than the soil line of your pot and drill small holes in it all along the length (perhaps 12 to 15 in total). Place this in the centre of the pot before you plant, being sure you have a lip sticking out of the soil at about 2 cm in height. Fill the tube with gravel. This creates a very efficient watering tube that ensures all the plants get ample water – you simply pour water down the tube. Add a little soil in the barrel, put a plant or two in the holes and then move up to the next layer until you have filled the whole barrel before finally planting the top of the pot. To keep soil from sifting out of the holes, you can pack moss gently around the plants. Use potting soil mixed with compost. Keep the soil moist, but not saturated, and fertilise the plants with a mild plant food (such as seaweed-based liquid fertiliser) in the spring and during the fruiting period. Place the pot in full sun, and protect the plants from frost. As the young plants are getting established, pick off their first round of buds to help them put energy into rooting. Keep an eye out for birds because they adore strawberries!

496. Are there any tips for growing bumper crops of rhubarb?

To perform best, rhubarb needs a long, cool spring and rich soil. You can begin harvesting stalks as soon as the leaves start to unfold to a flat surface. Leave at least two large stalks per plant to restore energy to the root system for next year. Rhubarb benefits from a mid-summer side dressing of potting soil or aged manure. You can repeat the application in the autumn. Using organic material will supply nutrients to the roots of the plants in small doses, giving the plants a constant supply of food, resulting in slow, even growth.

The thick stems of rhubarb are delicious cooked with sugar. They can be harvested from spring onwards, but it's important to leave some stems on the plant so it can build up reserves for the following year.

497. Is is feasible to move an old currant bush to another part of the garden?

It may prove to be easier to start with a new currant bush – once they've grown large, they're hard to transplant. Generally, a plant's root system matches the size of the crown, so it may be more trouble than it's worth! Whether you have old or new bushes, though they aren't heavy feeders, all currants do appreciate an annual addition of organic matter such as compost or aged manure. You can also mulch around the bases of the bushes with home-made leaf mould.

Once fruit bushes are a few years old they will have developed quite a large root system, so it can be quite hard work to move them.

498. Can I encourage my juniper bush to produce berries?

For fruit production, you'll need both male and female shrubs. If you're going to start a new planting, there are ways you can improve the harvest of berries. Junipers need a light, sandy, well-drained soil and full sun. Ideally, plant them in early spring or fall, though you can plant them any time the ground's not frozen. They'll need plenty of water in the first year, but once the roots are well established, they'll be pretty carefree. If you need to remove crowded, damaged or diseased branches, it's best to do so in early spring while they're dormant. Prune them off where the branch meets the trunk.

499. What's the best time of year to plant grapes to help them get established?

Grapevines are usually sold as dormant, bare-root plants and should be planted in late winter or early spring. The plants will remain dormant until both the soil and the air temperatures are warm enough to wake them up from their winter's slumber. The advantage of planting at this time is that when they begin growing roots, the roots will become established before the top growth begins. Grapes grow best in full sunshine, in well-draining soils. Newly planted vines will need to be watered regularly in their first year and during any dry weather after that.

500. What advice can you give on caring for my kiwi vine?

Kiwi plants grow strongly once they're established, and they fruit on one year old wood, so you'll need to have a regular pruning routine in early spring.

Winter pruning should take place towards the end of the season. Kiwis form fruit on one-year-old wood just like grapes. Prune yours back to three to four buds on each lateral stem. You can thin the plant out if you have an abundance of stems emerging from the main stem of your kiwi plant. Because kiwis grow so rapidly, summer maintenance pruning after flowering is also necessary. Some kiwis are self-fertile and some kiwi plants need a male kiwi in the general vicinity in order to produce fruit, so make sure you have either a self-fertile variety or both a male and a female plant. Kiwi plants typically do not need to be fertilised. If you decide you'd like to fertilise yours, choose a fertiliser low in nitrogen (which encourages lush, green growth) but high in phosphorous and potassium (the last two numbers in the fertiliser formula). A 5–10–10 general-purpose fertiliser sprinkled beneath your kiwi should be just fine. Apply in amounts as recommended on the fertiliser label.

> Kiwi plants typically do not need to be fertilised but if you do decide you'd like to fertilise yours, choose a fertiliser low in nitrogen . . . but high in phosphorous and potassium.

Index

Credits

© Paul Wagland 6, 29, 31, 38, 60, 63, 67, 69, 70, 71, 73, 74 left, 74 centre, 77, 78, 79, 80, 81, 88, 90, 93, 95, 96, 99, 101, 102, 115, 122, 127, 128, 129, 134, 136 left, 139, 142, 143, 144, 148, 149, 157, 159, 161, 163, 164, 166, 174, 177, 186, 191, 195, 196 left, 199, 200, 202, 203, 206, 207, 211, 212, 221, 223, 225, 229

© VJ Matthew 85, 103, 118 , 119, 167

© D Austin 169, 170, 173, 178, 179, 181

8 left	© Vaclav Volrab
8 centre	© simon@naffarts.co.uk
8 right	© Chris Price
9	© Yuriy Chertok
11	© Lindsay Douglas
12, 64	© Fotokostic
13	© 1000 words
14	© Sever 180
15	© Pixbox 77
16	© Arteretum
17	© Lucy Wright
18	© Irin-K
20	© Sunny S
21	© Igor Brodin
22	© Grandpa
24	© Knin
25	© Rene Ammundsen
27	© Julija Sapic
28	© Wutthichia
32	© Forestpath
34	© Kellis
35	© Mashe
36	© Susan McKenzie
39	© Magdalena Bujak
40	© Sarajo
41	© Ermess
43	© Sharom Day
44	© Perov Stanislov
45	© Kokhanchikov
47	© PozitivStudija
48	© Jerome Whittington
49	© Alekcey
51, 234	© Videowokart
52	© Sharon Kingston
54	© Oxbeast1210
55	© Stephen Rudolf
56	© Jeff Gynane
59	© Anna Bogush
61	SSAA Photos
65	© Tan4ikk
68	© Simon Andrew
72	© A Petelin
74 right, 117	© Dmitrijs Dmitrijevs
75, 83, 130	© Elena Elisseeva
82	© Luckypic
84	© Baldovina
86	© Jill Lang
89	© AA Photograph
91	© Deborah McCague
92	© Natalia Van D
94	© Electra
97	© Gabriel Scott
98	© Jason Vandehey
105	© Andreas Attenburger
107	© Hannah Mariah
108	© Mitzy
109	© Konstantin L
110	© Laura Stone
111	© Lijuan Guo
112	© Todd Boland
113	© Ingrid Balabanova
114	© Evgenya Moroz
116	© Alana Miv
121	© Christina Richards
123	© Snehit
125	© Bocharev Photography
126	© Chris Lo Photorgaphy
131	© Susan Fox
132	© RS Ryan
133	© Bonnie Watson
135	© Pattie Steib
136 centre, 160	© Charlene Bayerie
136 right, 180	© Malvern Hills
137, 185	© Firelia
140 & 151	© Tom Curtis
141	© Valentin Agapov
145	© Artem & Olga Sagepin
146	© Valerie Potova
147	© Irina Fischer
150, 193	© Mark Mirror
152	© Liane M
154	© Buccaneer | Dreamstime
155	© Avel Cheiko
156	© A Petrunovskyi
158	© Madlen
162	© Hartmut Morgenthal
165	© Jet Kat
172	© Jane McIlroy
183	© Otmar Smi
184	© Aleksandra Duda
187	© Vasily Vishnevsiy
188	© Margo Harrison
189	© Sally Wallis
190	© Chiyacat
192	© 2009Fotofriends
194	© Toriru
196 centre, 215	© Olga Selyutina
196 right, 237	© Colette
197, 250	© MaxPhoto
204	© Michael Flippo
208	© Craig Barhost
210	© Norma Cornes
213, 249	© Stefan Fierros
216, 220, 222	© Jacglad
217	© Dhoxax
218	© H Brauer
219	© Canoneer
224	© Ervin Moon
227	© Yuris
228	© Basphoto
230	© Aleksandr N
231	© Laine M
232	© Yuri Tuchkov
233	© Inacio Peres
235	© Richard Semik
236	© Varga Levente
238	© Tomas Pavelka
241	© Brandon Bourdages
242	© BestPhoto
243	© Pavalena
244	© ER_09
245	© Valery Kraynov
246	© Jeff Strickler
247	© Denis/Yulia Pogostins
248	© Antermoite
251	© Nikolay Petkov